Legal Form

A century after the publication of Evgeny Pashukanis' pivotal book *General Theory of Law and Marxism*, this collection presents a comprehensive account and analysis of his key concept of legal form.

Evgeny Pashukanis' *General Theory*, born amidst the fervour of the first socialist revolution, remains still a crucial reference point in Marxist theories of the law and critical legal theory. Its theoretical depth paved the way for new understandings of the relationship between Marxism and the law. Its crucial virtue continues to be, even after a century, the ability to articulate epochal concerns in the context of a socialist revolution that turned hitherto theoretical problems into dilemmas of practice. This book returns to Pashukanis' main concept: 'legal form'. Through this jurisprudential category Pashukanis aimed to grasp the dependence of the law on the economy, and at the same time, to enquire into the degree to which the law preserves its autonomy from economic relations. In other words, the legal form as a concept conveys both the law's dependence on the economic sphere of exchange and its greatest inherent specificity: the way it translates economic relations into its proper language and set of legal/ideological constructs. The contributions to this volume provide a range of perspectives on how the concept of legal form has been developed and reinterpreted.

Including the first English translation of Pashukanis' essay, 'Hegel, State and Law', this collection will be of considerable interest to scholars and students of legal and political theory.

Cosmin Cercel is Professor of Legal History at Ghent University, Belgium.

Gian-Giacomo Fusco is Lecturer in Law at Kent Law School, University of Kent, UK.

Przemysław Tacik is Assistant Professor at the Institute of European Studies at the Jagiellonian University of Kraków, Poland.

Part of the Nomos Studies in Law, Culture and Power Series

Legal Form
Pashukanis and the Marxist Critique of Law
Edited by Cosmin Cercel, Gian-Giacomo Fusco and Przemysław Tacik

Legal Form and the End of Law
Pashukanis's Legacy
Edited by Cosmin Cercel, Gian-Giacomo Fusco and Przemysław Tacik

A GlassHouse book

For more information about this series, please visit: https://www.routledge.com/

Legal Form

Pashukanis and the Marxist Critique of Law

Edited by
Cosmin Cercel, Gian-Giacomo Fusco and Przemysław Tacik

Routledge
Taylor & Francis Group
a GlassHouse Book

First published 2025
by Routledge
4 Park Square, Milton Park, Abingdon, Oxon OX14 4RN

and by Routledge
605 Third Avenue, New York, NY 10158

Routledge is an imprint of the Taylor & Francis Group, an informa business

A GlassHouse book

British Library Cataloguing-in-Publication Data
A catalogue record for this book is available from the British Library

Library of Congress Cataloging-in-Publication Data
Names: Fusco, Gian-Giacomo, editor. | Tacik, Przemysław, 1985– editor. | Cercel, Cosmin Sebastian, 1982– editor.
Title: Legal form : Pashukanis and the Marxist critique of law / edited by Gian-Giacomo Fusco, Przemyslaw Tacik, and Cosmin Cercel.
Description: Abingdon, Oxon [UK] ; New York, NY : Routledge, 2025. | Series: Nomos studies in law, culture and power | Includes bibliographical references and index.
Identifiers: LCCN 2024025776 (print) | LCCN 2024025777 (ebook) | ISBN 9781032724430 (hardback) | ISBN 9781032724553 (paperback) | ISBN 9781032724522 (ebook)
Subjects: LCSH: Law and socialism. | Law—Philosophy. | Law—Soviet Union—Philosophy—History. | Sociological jurisprudence. | Pashukanis, Evgeniĭ Bronislavovich, 1891–1937. Obshchaia teoriia prava i marksizm. English | Marx, Karl, 1818–1883. | Hegel, Georg Wilhelm Friedrich, 1770–1831.
Classification: LCC K357 .L43 2025 (print) | LCC K357 (ebook) | DDC 340/.1—dc23/eng/20240612
LC record available at https://lccn.loc.gov/2024025776
LC ebook record available at https://lccn.loc.gov/2024025777

ISBN: 978-1-032-72443-0 (hbk)
ISBN: 978-1-032-72455-3 (pbk)
ISBN: 978-1-032-72452-2 (ebk)

DOI: 10.4324/9781032724522

Typeset in Sabon
by Apex CoVantage, LLC

Contents

Contributors

Professor Bill Bowring teaches human rights and international law at Birkbeck College, University of London, since 2006. He entered academe in 1990, and taught at Polytechnic then University of East London, 1990–1996; University of Essex 1996–2000; University of North London/London Metropolitan University 2000–2006. A practising barrister since 1974, he has represented applicants at the European Court of Human Rights since 1992, especially against Turkey and Russia. He has acted as a consultant and expert for the United Nations, Council of Europe, Organisation for Security and Cooperation in Europe (OSCE), European Union and the UK Government. He founded in 2003 the European Human Rights Advocacy Centre (EHRAC). He has over 150 publications including monographs, edited collections, chapters and articles. His first monograph, *The Degradation of the International Legal Order: The Rehabilitation of Law and the Possibility of Politics* (2008), has been translated into Russian (2021). His second monograph is *Law, Rights and Ideology in Russia: Landmarks in the Destiny of a Great Power* (2013). In 2017 he was awarded a Fellowship of the Academy of Social Sciences (FAcSS) for his work on Russia.

Anna Lukina is a doctoral candidate at the University of Cambridge, having previously studied at the University of Oxford and Harvard Law School. Her research interests include jurisprudence, legal history (especially Soviet legal history) and public law. Anna's work has been published in the *Review of Central and East European Law*, *Jurisprudence*, *The Ideology and Politics Journal* and *Ratio Juris*. It has also appeared or is set to appear as part of edited collections on *Russian Discourses on International Law*, *Cultural Legalities of Video Games and Virtual Realities* and *Research Handbook on the Politics of Constitutional Law*.

Linda Lilith Obermayr has studied law and philosophy and obtained her doctorate in legal philosophy at the University of Vienna with a thesis on Marxist Legal Theory, which was published under the title *Die Kritik der marxistischen Rechtstheorie. Zu Paschukanis' Begriff der Rechtsform* (2022). She is currently researching and teaching at the Department of Legal Philosophy at the University of Vienna and has been a research scholar at the Committee on Social Thought at the University of Chicago in winter 2022/23. Her academic research focuses on materialistic legal theory and social philosophy, critical theory and classical German philosophy. Linda is co-founder and editor of the *Jahrbuch für marxistische Gesellschaftstheorie* (2022), in which Marxian thought is taken as the starting point for a reflection on present social reality as well as academic developments in the scientific community. Together with Alexander Somek she has recently co-edited a book on Hegel's Philosophy of Right (*Hegel in Wien. Eine Ringvorlesung zu Hegels Rechtsphilosophie am Wiener Juridicum*, 2023) and, together with René Bohnstingl and Karl Reitter, has written a book on the social impacts of the coronavirus pandemic (*Corona als gesellschaftliches Verhältnis. Brüche und Umwälzungen im kapitalistischen Herrschaftssystem*, [will be published in spring 2023]). In her latest research, she is tracing Hegel's interpretation of Pyrrhonian Skepticism as a specific negativistic ideology critique.

Gian-Giacomo Fusco is a lecturer in law at Kent Law School (University of Kent—Canterbury). He obtained his doctoral degree in Law at the University of Kent. His research interests include jurisprudence, critical theory, history of ideas and urban studies. His more recent monograph *Form of Life: Agamben and the Destitution of Rules* (2022), engaged with and developed further Agamben's concept of destituent potential as a critique of the law.

Daniel McLoughlin is a senior lecturer in the faculty of law at the University of New South Wales. He has published widely on theories of sovereignty, government and political crises, with a particular emphasis on the work of Giorgio Agamben and Carl Schmitt. His other research interests include Marxist state theory, the politics and theory of human rights, public law theory and the impact of neo-liberalism on the state. He is the editor of *Agamben and Radical Politics* (2016) and the co-editor of *The Politics of Legality in a Neoliberal Age* (2017).

Cosmin Cercel is Professor of Legal History at Ghent University. His research focuses on genealogies of law and politics with specific reference to twentieth-century continental legal history. He is the author of *Towards a Jurisprudence of State-Communism: Law and the Failure of Revolution* (2018) and has co-edited *States of Exception: Law, History, Theory* (2020). His recent publications include: 'Mapping the State of Siege: Law, Crisis and the Antinomies of Liberal Legality' (2022) 12(2) *Romanian Journal of Comparative Law* 193; 'Law, Politics, and the Military: Towards a Theory of Authoritarian Adjudication' (2021) 22 *German Law Journal* 192. He is the recipient of a Consolidator Grant from the European Research Council (ERC) to research the history of emergency legislation during the last century in Europe with a view to offering a legal historical explanation of how the experience of emergency has shaped constitutional and political cultures across Europe in the past century.

Dr Eric Loefflad is an interdisciplinary scholar specialising in the history and theory of public international law, broadly understood. He received his doctorate from Kent Law School in 2019 and also holds a bachelor's in political science from the Pennsylvania State University, a juris doctor from the Gonzaga University School of Law and an LLM from the School of Oriental and African Studies, University of London. Eric has been admitted as an attorney before both the Supreme Court of the Commonwealth of Pennsylvania and the Tribal Court of the Kalispel Nation.

Przemysław Tacik is Assistant Professor at the Institute of European Studies of the Jagiellonian University of Kraków, Poland, and Director of the Nomos: Centre for International Research on Law, Culture and Power. A philosopher, lawyer and sociologist by education, he holds doctorates in philosophy (2014) and international law (2016). He has been a visiting scholar at several universities (i.e. Columbia University, SUNY at Buffalo, Université Paris-1, Heidelberg Universität). In his academic work he combines both philosophical and legal perspectives, attempting to approach them from an interdisciplinary angle. His main fields of interest are: in philosophy—contemporary philosophy, Jewish philosophy and animal studies; in law—critical legal studies, international law, and human rights law. He has authored five books, as well as over 50 articles and one translation of a poetry volume (from French to Polish). His recent monographs include *The Freedom of Lights: Edmond Jabès and Jewish Philosophy of Modernity* (2019), *A New Philosophy of Modernity and Sovereignty: Towards Radical Historicization* (2021) and *Deconstructing the Right to Self-Determination in International Law: Sovereignty, Exception, Politics* (2023).

Rafał Mańko is Research Affiliate at the Central European University Democracy Institute, Budapest (Hungary) where he is a member of the Rule of Law Working Group and legal researcher at the European Parliamentary Research Service, Brussels (Belgium), where he specialises in the rule of law and private law. Previously, he was a fellow at the Centre for the Study of European Contract Law (CSECL) (later renamed to Amsterdam Centre for Transformative Private Law, 'ACT') at the University of Amsterdam (the Netherlands). In his academic work as a critical legal theorist, Rafał blends legal philosophy, sociology of law and comparative legal history to study the multifaceted relationships between law, ideology and the political, with a particular focus on legal interpretation and adjudication, on the one hand, and the resilience of legal forms despite political transformations, on the other. Rafał received his master's degree in (Roman) law from the University of Warsaw, followed by a doctorate in law from the

University of Amsterdam and a habilitation in law (doctorate habilitation degree) from the University of Wrocław. He is the author of over 100 scholarly publications, including two monographs in Polish, *Private Law in the European Union: Perspectives for the Future* (2004) and *Towards a Critical Philosophy of Adjudication: The Political, Ethics and Legitimacy* (2018). He has co-edited three volumes, including *Law and Critique in Central Europe: Questioning the Past, Resisting the Present* (2016), *Law, Space and the Political: An East-West Perspective* (2019) and *Legal Scholarship and the Political: In Search of a New Paradigm* (2020), as well as contributed to edited collections. He has recently been a guest lecturer at the Academy of European Law in Trier and a visiting scholar at the Oñati International Institute for the Sociology of Law.

Introduction

Cosmin Cercel, Gian-Giacomo Fusco and Przemysław Tacik

Making the case for reading Pashukanis today, one hundred years after the publication of his major work, *The General Theory of Law and Marxism*,[1] is not a hard task. Perhaps as never before, the veil of seemingly neutral reverence that has trussed up the legal sphere for centuries has dissipated revealing the symbiotic relationship between the law, the construction of capital, and the entrenchment of inequality. The legal form and the entire body of abstract principles delimiting its perimeter are core elements of the inexorable expansion of capitalism: they provide a source of legitimacy for the total appropriation of reality and the transformation of every single aspect of nature and life into a site of valorisation.[2] The many catastrophes directly and indirectly connected with the logic of capital accumulation are further proof that the law has lost its supposed normative/regulative force: ultimately, all those economic activities fuelling human and environmental degradation are most often lawful exercises of individual abstract rights over resources. When rights start colliding with the foundations of human living, rethinking the law radically becomes urgent. By exposing the genetic link between the commodity form and the legal form, and therefore placing the law as a vital constituent in the architecture of capital, Pashukanis' theory remains relevant for a critique of the present.

The starting point of this collective work is the recognition that the theoretical underpinning of Pashukanis' theory of the legal form sharply captures the dialectical relationship between law, the structuring of social life and the constitution of capital, while at the same time challenging the comforting narrative that portrays the law's operation as essentially a neutral instrument. The law, for Pashukanis, is grounded on a specific modern mode of production—that of capitalism—and on a specific set of values—the

1 Evgeny Pashukanis, 'Общая Теория Права и Марксизм' в: *Избранные произведения по общей теории государства и права* (Наука 1980 [1924]). English translation: *The General Theory of Law and Marxism* (Barbara Einhorn tr, Transaction Publishers 2002).

2 On this point see: Katharina Pistor, *The Code of Capital: How the Law Creates Wealth and Inequality* (Princeton University 2019).

DOI: 10.4324/9781032724522-1

possessive individualism of the bourgeoisie. His theory appears, therefore, as opposing radically any form of compromise between capital domination and rights and as an explicit warning against all the attempts at adopting legal paths towards limiting the perverse effects of accumulation (and valorisation). From our perspective, Pashukanis is an effective antidote able to question the ideological hegemonic faith in the law's power in regulating/limiting the excesses of capital, and in neutralising conflicts into pacified frameworks. If anything, the concept of legal form has an inherent critical potency opposing the enchantment with which we usually relate to the law, and which impedes to considering lucidly that far from being a panacea, legal normativity might be a constitutive part of the catastrophe towards which we are heading.

The General Theory of Law and Marxism

Prepared in 1920–21 while Pashukanis stayed in Berlin, *General Theory* was published in 1924 in parallel with Stalin's taking command of Soviet Russia with his programme of 'socialism in one country'.[3] Although conceived not as an organic treaty but more as a 'sketch' and a 'draft' of a Marxist critique of law,[4] this text ended up constituting the source of both Pashukanis' fame and his tragic demise. His theoretical contribution is traversed and informed by the experience of the October Revolution and by the intense debate over the role and fate of the law in light of the Marxist predicament: the elaboration of a materialist general theory of the law is, indeed, functional to thinking about the place of the legal apparatus after the revolution, and in the transition to communism.

Pashukanis' main thesis (his *commodity-form theory* of law) hinges upon a clear-cut statement: the foundational link between the form of the law and the relation of exchange. From his perspective, the law is not much of a technique for the organisation of social relationships in the hands of the ruling class, but in its specific form is a fundamental part of capitalist exchange. Legal categories and principles in their abstract reality are expressions of concrete material relations between subjects involved in commodity exchange; and this means that the law emerges in strict relation with the economic, mystical, element of value. For Pashukanis legal relations are

3 For an analysis of the historical and political context in which Pashukanis wrote and published his *General Theory*, see Piers Beirne and Robert Sharlet, 'Editors' Introduction' in Evgeny Pashukanis, *Selected Writings on Marxism and Law*, Peter B Maggs (tr) (Academic Press 1980); Michael Head, 'The Rise and Fall of a Soviet Jurist: Evgeny Pashukanis and Stalinism' (2004) 17 *Canadian Journal of Law and Jurisprudence*; Id., *Evgeny Pashukanis. A Critical Reappraisal* (Routledge 2016); Bill Bowring, 'Yevgeniy Pashukanis, His Law and Marxism: A General Theory, and the 1922 Treaty of Rapallo between Soviet Russia and Germany' (2017) 19 *Journal of the History of International Law*.

4 Pashukanis, *The General Theory* (n 1) 36.

the formal/abstract dimension complementing exchange relations. Consequently, the law as we know it emerges with the full development of the capitalist economy and with the transition to communism cannot but wither away; in other words, a proletarian law is a contradiction in terms. Despite different attempts to revise his theory and reposition his theoretical stance, Pashukanis' commodity-form theory marked his destiny when, during Stalin's purges, he was accused of being part of a 'band of wreckers' and a 'Trotsky-Bukharin fascist agents' and executed in 1937 without a trial. In the agitated phase of the Stalinist consolidation of power and the building of the Soviet State over a specific idea of socialist legality, Pashukanis' overall theoretical stance on law turned up against him in the most tragic way.[5]

The tension between the attempt at devising a proper Marxian theory of the law, and the need to consider the logical-practical outcome of such a theoretical stance in the context of the overcoming of the bourgeoise economy and society, pervades the whole of Pashukanis' general theory. This aspect is of the utmost interest not only because it offers a substantiated theory of 'law and/in revolution', but also because it represents an ingenious insight into the historically determined relationship between law as an abstract form and the social fabric. Sustaining that the law is essentially a functional attribute of commodity exchange has a series of distinct theoretical implications (which constitute the originality of Pashukanis' general theory and source of criticism), which we summarise in three propositions:

a) The entanglement of commodity and legal determinations appears inevitable. In a capitalist society, production is part of exchange, and this implies that the conditions allowing for market relations must be established. As Marx claimed in an oft-cited passage, 'commodities cannot go to market and make exchange of their own', to make objects enter into a relation, that is to become commodities, 'their guardians must place themselves in relation to one another . . . and must behave in such a way that each does not appropriate the commodity of the other': in other words, they must recognise in each other the right of private proprietor.[6] And this of course is already a juridical relation, which determines and is determined by the material relation of exchange. 'Legal fetishism', Pashukanis writes, 'complements commodity fetishism'.[7] Indeed, exchange requires equality between commodities but also among their owner: the first is obtained by calculating exchange value, and the second is essentially a legal product. In the practice of exchange, the owners become abstract legal subjects: a formally equal, disembodied entity.

5 Philip E Mosely, 'Freedom of Artistic Expression and Scientific Inquiry in Russia' (1938) 200 *The Annals of the American Academy of Political and Social Science* 267–68.

6 Karl Marx, *Capital Volume 1* (London: Penguin 1976) 178.

7 Pashukanis, *The General Theory* (n 1) 117.

b) The development of the legal form, the emergence of the capitalist mode of production and the markets (and commodity exchange in general) are concurrent historical phenomena. When production remains for use and not for exchange, legal determinations are unnecessary. The establishment of the law as we know it is, for Pashukanis, something related to the full development of the capitalist economy, with the total commodification of the real. The law is therefore essentially a modern phenomenon. However, this does not imply (as some have argued) the denial of the existence of previous stages of law's formation. As Lon Fuller rightly sustained, what the commodity-form theory of the law exposes, is that 'the only law is bourgeois law. To be sure, legal institutions in embryo can be found in a feudal or slave society, where they are intertwined with religious and military elements', however, the 'full inner logic of the conception of law can assert itself only under capitalism'.[8] Pashukanis' general theory of the law, is, therefore, also an account of the historical formation of the legal form, which does not take the law as a transhistorical or natural datum, but locates it in relation to specific material conditions and chronological determinations.

c) By designating the moment of exchange between subjects as the foundational element for the construction of the legal form, Pashukanis placed private law at the base of his *General Theory*, marginalising or better relativising public law and the sphere of command and punishment. In some respects, the *General Theory* both aligns and places itself in contrast with the legal theories of his time and with the positivist jurisprudential tradition: on the one hand, its focus on the law as form, and on the conceptual development of the law itself is a preoccupation that Pashukanis shares with modern jurisprudence, but on the other hand, the relativisation and the lack of centrality of coercion, commands and the role of the state in the formation of the law, make it at odds with much of his contemporary legal theorists. From Pashukanis' perspective, the functions of the state and criminal law are directly linked to and informed by the legal form. The evolution of the bourgeois state, he writes, 'can be traced back to a single principle, according to which neither of two people exchanging in the market can regulate the exchange relation unilaterally', and this necessarily 'requires a third party who personifies the reciprocal guarantees which the owners of commodities mutually agree to as proprietors, and hence promulgates the regulations governing transactions between commodity owners'.[9] But while the regulation of commodity exchange is a defining characteristic of the state

8 Lon Fuller, 'Pashukanis and Vyshinsky: A Study in the Development of Marxian Legal Theory' (1949) *Michigan Law Review* 1161.
9 Pashukanis, *The General Theory* (n 1) 148, 149.

form, the whole governmental apparatus—as an instrument for fostering and structuring class oppression—cannot be reduced to its legal structures. As Pashukanis claims, the state while 'as a guarantor of market exchange not only employs the language of law, but also functions as law and law alone, that is, it becomes one with the abstract, objective norm' when instead operates as an 'organisation of class rule, and for waging external wars, neither needs nor admits of any legal interpretation'.[10] It follows, then, that 'every juridical theory of the state which attempts to encompass all state functions is nowadays inadequate. It cannot accurately reflect all the facts of state life, it gives a purely ideological, that is, a distorted reflection of reality'.[11] The sphere of command and criminal sanctions are in Pashukanis' *General Theory* established on the ground of the 'legal form'. But although public and criminal law do not play a determining role in the production of the legal form, they are nevertheless functional to its reproduction and sustenance.

Legal Form as a Jurisprudential Problem

Along with its more political motifs and its original materialist methodology, what has driven us to put together this volume is also the fact that Pashukanis' theorisation of the legal form addresses genuine jurisprudential and historical questions about the nature and evolution of the law. As we have seen previously, his proposition is rather easy but with several incisive implications: the legal form, that is, the basic juridical concepts developed around the abstraction of the legal subject, must be understood in strict analogy with the commodity form. It is the relations of exchange which constitute the ground for the development of both the commodity and the abstract image of a legal subject possessing rights and duties. To the extent that commodity exchange could not take place without a subject owner bringing products to the market, the legal subject (and the whole body of norms establishing the relations between the subject and the commodity and between the subjects) emerges in the very process of exchange. The phenomenon of law, therefore, develops in symbiosis with the category of value, and legal relations are the abstract forms in which commodity exchange can materialise. And with the notion of 'legal form' Pashukanis named the dialectical emergence of legal abstractions (legal subjectivity, norms, legal relations, etc.) out of the material/practical sphere of exchange. The formal and purely abstract equality of legal subjects in law mirrors the abstraction of objects reduced to their value in the relation of exchange.

10 ibid 137.
11 ibid.

Pashukanis' inquiry into the law aims at finding a materialist explanation of the juridical regulation of the real according to which the law is more than a system of norms abstractly related but expresses a specific set of social and economic relations. Such an approach opposes those forms of normativism—like Kelsen's—which by reducing the whole existence of the law to a pure form of normativity, excludes any considerations of the social dimensions of the legal form and legal validity. This general theorisation of the law, for Pashukanis, 'explains nothing, and turns its back from the outset on the facts of reality'[12] on social life and power relationships structuring the economic life under capitalism. But his general theory of the law poses itself in some contrast also to the hegemonic Marxist conception of legal phenomena, according to which the juridical sphere is a reflection of the interest of the dominant classes or a mere ideological product—the superstructural element of a determinate mode of production.[13] For Pashukanis the law has a consistent autonomy grounded in the social relationships that give reality and validity to the legal form itself: the law, therefore, is not simply a superstructure of bourgeoise society but it is part of the same structure without which it would not exist.

The concept of legal form addresses a specific legal/theoretical problem; that of the relationship between the abstract dimension of the law and the concrete reality of its manifestation. Pashukanis challenges this question by providing a formal definition of the law, as essentially a relation between abstract legal subjects. However, such an abstraction is not a purely phantasmagorical datum, an illusion, or a spurious product of ideology; on the contrary, it is 'as real as the social relations of production themselves'.[14] The abstract forms of the law are essentially formal elements of a specific concrete legal form established by the full development of commodity exchange and the capitalist mode of production. The abstract subject of the law, as the possessor of rights and centre of imputations, is the real owner of commodities with its guaranteed liberties. In his commodity exchange theory of the law, Pashukanis does not simplistically derive the legal form (and the whole juridical apparatus) from the economic structure: the superstructural elements of the law are in a symbiotic, dialectical, affiliation with the reality they are called to regulate (and therefore to determine). The law in its abstract dimension has, Pashukanis writes, a

12 ibid 52.

13 On this issue see the recent intervention by Carl Wilén, 'Why Pashukanis Was Right: Abstraction and Form in the General Theory of Law and Marxism' (2023) *Capital & Class* <https://doi.org/10.1177/03098168231215417>

14 Étienne Balibar, 'Hegel, Marx, Pashukanis and the Idea of Abstract Right as a Bourgeois Form' in C Francis and D Gottlieb (eds), *Institution: Critical Histories of Law* (CRMEP Books 2023) 79.

> parallel in real history which unfolds not as a set of ideas, but as a specific set of relations which men enter into not by conscious choice, but because the relations of production compel them to do so Man becomes a legal subject by virtue of the same necessity which transforms the product of nature into a commodity complete with the enigmatic property of value.[15]

The law and its abstract forms seem to be embroiled in what Marx has named as the 'mute compulsion of economic relations', that form of 'impersonal, abstract, and anonymous form of power immediately embedded in the economic processes themselves rather than tacked onto them in an external manner' constituting a driving force for the capitalist dominion.[16] Law's abstractions, thus, are constitutive of the force with which economic power structures bourgeois society.

For Pashukanis, the legal form is essentially an abstract structure analogous to that of commodity fetishism. And to the extent value is not simply fictional, or the product of an ideological setting, but reflects a real relationship between commodities, the legal form too, is the abstract normative dimension of a specific relationship of production. This is the reason why he portrayed the juridical sphere as independent from state norm production. The relationship between equal subjects that Pashukanis placed at the centre of his image of the law, although essentially abstract represents an operational device, which allows for the reproduction of class rule. Indeed, the legal form in both its abstractness and concrete existence does not emerge as a neutralised element, on the contrary, its genetic link with commodity exchange makes it an embodiment of value and exploitation of one class over another. The constitution of legal subjectivity, as an entity abstracted (that is separated) from the real existence of humans, is in this sense the fetishisation of a concrete economic relationship based on exploitation: a relationship that is structurally reproduced by the legal form itself.

The Withering Away of Law

The thesis that the law (and the state apparatus) will eventually wither away is the logical outcome of Pashukanis' theory of the legal form. If the law is in fact genetically linked to the commodity exchange, and the specific mode of production of capitalism, once such material conditions are radically transformed the law would lose its function and disappear. Such an idea is not

15 Pashukanis, *The General Theory* (n 1) 68.

16 Søren Mau, *Mute Compulsion: A Marxist Theory of the Economic Power of Capital* (Verso 2023) 3, 4. The expression 'mute compulsion of economic relation' [*stumme Zwang*] that Mau makes as the title of his book is included in Karl Marx's first volume of *Capital*. The English translation renders it as 'silent compulsion', see Karl Marx, *Capital: A Critique of Political Economy* (Penguin 1978) 899.

a new one in the Marxian landscape, and indeed it has been elaborated by Marx and Engels and subsequently by Lenin.[17] Although the triad developed it with different variations, at the core of the hypothesis of the withering away of the law and the state is the conviction that with the transition from capitalism to communism, when new relations of production are established on the basis of the abolition of the exploitation abstract labour and of the private property of the means of production, the instruments of the reproduction of capitalism—state and law—will become obsolete, will 'die out'.[18] In line with such a hypothesis, Pashukanis, right in the introduction to his *General Theory*, writes that with the moving to a communist society,

> [t]he withering away of certain categories of bourgeois law (the categories as such, not this or that precept) in no way implies their replacement by new categories of proletarian law, just as the withering away of the categories of value, capital, profit and so forth in the transition to fully-developed socialism will not mean the emergence of new proletarian categories of value, capital and so on. The withering away of the categories of bourgeois law will, under these conditions, mean the withering away of law altogether, that is to say the disappearance of the juridical factor from social relations.[19]

The law, as already mentioned above, is functional to commodity exchange and the capitalist mode of production, and it exists as long as society remains organised by capital economic forces. With the transition to a communist society, what is left of the legal form is not another form of the law, since there is not another form of law that is not capitalist/bourgeois. To argue for the continuity of the law into a proletarian law is to proclaim the 'immortality of the legal form'.[20] From this perspective, to consider the law as a transhistorical datum, as an unspecified form that could be filled with whatever content, would be tantamount to falling back into an idealist position, contradicting the necessary historicisation that a materialist approach to the law requires. Pashukanis' political vision is radically anti-juridical,[21] it denies

17 Of course the reference here is to Karl Marx, 'Critique of the Gotha Programme' in Karl Marx and Friedrich Engels (eds), *Collected Works: Volume 24* (London: Lawrence and Wishart 2010); then Friedrich Engels, 'Anti-Duhring' in Karl Marx and Friedrich Engels (eds), *Collected Works: Volume 25* (London: Lawrence and Wishart 2010); and Vladimir I Lenin, 'The State and Revolution' in Vladimir I Lenin (ed), *Collected Works: Volume 25* (Moscow: Progress Publishers 1976).

18 Friedrich Engels, 'Anti-Duhring' in Karl Marx and Friedrich Engels (eds), *Collected Works: Volume 25* (Lawrence and Wishart 2010) 268.

19 Pashukanis, *The General Theory* (n 1) 61.

20 ibid.

21 Giso Amendola, 'The Abolition of Law or Law of the Common(s)? Pashukanis and the Revolution' (1 October 2017) 116(4) *South Atlantic Quarterly* 707–25.

the law's supposed instrumental neutrality, precluding in this way any form of redemption for the legal form.

In Pashukanis' version of the 'withering away of law' thesis, the *pars destruens* is stronger than the *pars construens*. And indeed, when it comes to describing what might replace the waning law in communist society, his proposal is not very clearly formed. When the material base for the legal form is transcended, and the preconditions for the necessity of the law's operation are deactivated, society will be organised through 'technical regulation'. While the opposition of private interest is the necessary condition for a rule to assume a juridical character, the precondition of technical norms is the 'unity of purpose'. Pashukanis provides as examples the rules governing railways and the relationship between patient and doctor; it is worth looking at them at length:

> The legal norms governing the railways' liability are predicated on private claims, private, differentiated interests, while the technical norms of rail traffic presuppose the common aim of, say, maximum efficiency of the enterprise. To take another example: healing a sick person presupposes a set of rules, for the patient as well as for the medical personnel. In so far as these rules have been prescribed for the express purpose of rehabilitating the sick person, they are technical in nature. The enforcement of these rules can be associated with some degree of constraint on the sick person. So long as this constraint is viewed from the standpoint of a goal which is the same for the person exercising the coercion as it is for the person coerced, it is a technically expedient act and no more. The content of the regulations is specified within these limits by medical science and undergoes change as medical science progresses. The lawyer has no place here. His role begins at the point where we are forced to leave this realm of unity of purpose and to take up another standpoint, that of mutually opposed separate subjects, each of whom represents his own private interests. Doctor and patient are thereby transformed into subjects with rights and duties, and the regulations which govern them are transformed into legal norms. Simultaneously with this, coercion is no longer considered under the rubric of expediency, but from the point of view of formal, that is of legal, admissibility.[22]

It is clear from this passage that what makes a norm a legal norm is its being the rule of opposing parties/interests. Once class antagonism is overcome, legal norms will wither away leaving room for technical administration of society, based on a generalised unity of interest. In this picture, Pashukanis

22 Pashukanis, *The General Theory* (n 1) 81.

acknowledges that a certain form of coercion will be necessary, but it would be a 'technical expedient' to reach a common goal.

If this proposal is somehow consistent, what is not clear is the political aspect of it, that is the 'how' the law will wither away. As Giso Amendola claims, in Pashukanis' theory the extinction of law can be interpreted in two ways. The first is 'where abolition is conceived as a progressive erosion of the legal form that gradually withers away to open up space for the economic technological management of society'. Such an interpretation would be in line with the optimism of the early Soviet revolution in the possibility of the development of the productive capacity through planning. The second instead 'is where the abolition of law is the arena of class struggle. Class struggle abolishes law by precluding the mystified synthesis of both the capitalist state and the proletarian state'.[23] In both cases, the strategy is that of overcoming the legal form and bourgeoise state; but while in the first it is a matter of producing communism by following and adjusting a certain social/historical tendency, in the second in question is the class disruption of the superstructural elements that sustain the reproduction of capitalism: the law and the state. Indeed, Amendola suggests, the horizon of class struggle is a constant presence in Pashukanis commodity form theory of law. And in this horizon, the political task, more than planning, would be to 'destroy the dispositifs of free appropriation of surplus value that lies behind the egalitarian logic of law and exchange', and institute a regime of inappropriation.[24] Alongside the somehow dystopian idea of a technical administration of the living, then, the withering away of law (and the state) involves also the thought of a creative way of rethinking the opening up of a space for a non-capitalist (communist) form of life. In any way, what seems at stake in Pashukanis' vision of law after capitalism is the possibility of thinking of a non-antagonistic normativity that has cut the ties with the organised unsanctionable violence that sustains the bourgeois society.

The idea of the eventual extinction of the law as the outcome of a radical change in the socio-economic structure of society is not an accessory element of a broad political vision but follows logically from the premise of Pashukanis' general theory of the law and gives it a particular characterisation. In contrast to the traditional approach in jurisprudence, tendentially oriented to the justification/legitimisation of law through utilitarian reasoning or by appealing to an alleged inclination of humans to regulate social life through normative means, Pashukanis materialist strategy reconceptualises radically the very nature of law. With an unquestionable utopian tone, his explorations into legal theory have consistently highlighted the necessity of law for the functioning of capitalism and bourgeois society

23 Amendola (n 21) 720.
24 ibid 721.

and at the same time its innate precarity. The historicisation of legal normativity, for Pashukanis, is meant to open up a space for thinking about a dimension exterior to any legal determination, in which the tradition of law could be abandoned and left in disuse. But this, however, implies that Pashukanis' legal philosophy should be better understood as a form of anti-jurisprudence.

Structure of the Book

The book comprises eight chapters along with an appendix. Overall, the contributions provide diverse viewpoints on Pashukanis' work, with a particular emphasis on Marxist critique and theory. The first three chapters offer a contextualisation of Pashukanis' *General Theory of Law and Marxism*, with a dedicated focus on the influences, cultural backgrounds and the circumstances surrounding its composition. The volume opens with Bill Bowring's 'What was Pashukanis Seeking to Do with his Concept of 'Legal Form', and Does it Have Continuing Relevance', which addresses the political situation in which the *General Theory* was written, looking at the meaning of the concept of legal form and its eventual relevance for a critique of law. This contribution explores the question of whether there has been a debate over the concept of legal form, before Pashukanis' theorisation, and by engaging with Spinoza's distinction between natural laws and human laws, it is argued that such a concept is essentially an original creation of the soviet lawyer since neither Marx nor Engels referred to or analysed the 'legal form' or any cognate concept, nor did they feel they needed to do so, or indeed could do so.

In the second chapter, 'Legal Form in the Soviet Dictatorship: Evgeny Pashukanis and His Interlocutors', Anna Lukina presents a systematic reconstruction of the theory of the legal form, comparing it with the propositions on law and state advanced by his various interlocutors, past and contemporary, namely Karl Marx and Friedrich Engels, Vladimir Lenin, Petr Stuchka and Andrey Vyshinsky. By analysing the similarities and differences between the theories of these authors, this text provides an interpretation of Pashukanis' downfall, pointing out that his theory was fundamentally unsuitable to the project of Soviet state-building, which explains why viewing law and state from the lens of the legal form was contested and eventually abandoned.

Next, in Chapter 3, Eric Loefllad's 'On the Lithuanian Question: Contextualising Pashukanis' Critique of the Legal Form', connects the position of the theory of the legal form to the cultural/material ground of Pashukanis' formative background. Toward this end, this chapter focuses on Pashukanis' Lithuanian heritage in relation to how the 'Lithuanian Question' of his day invoked deep histories that spoke to numerous contemporary questions concerning law, rights and identity. To uncover these histories, this contribution engages in the type of historical sociological inquiry into 'the juridical' that Pashukanis advocated in his General Theory of Law and Marxism. On this point, approaching Pashukanis through his background provides immense insights into his theoretical disagreement with his fellow Soviet jurist Pēteris Stučka, the leader of the short-lived Latvian Soviet Socialist Republic, on the nature of law. While Stučka disagreed with Pashukanis that 'law' was reducible to the commodity-exchange facilitating bourgeois legal form, the chapter argues that diverging historical sociological consciousnesses as a result of their differing Latvian versus Lithuanian backgrounds can, at least partially, explain their jurisprudential disagreement.

In turn, Chapters 4, 5 and 6 confront specific (critical) aspects of Pashukanis' *General Theory*. Rafał Mańko's 'Pašukanis on Ideology and the Juridical (A Note on the *General Theory of Law and Marxism*)' reconstructs the relationship between the concepts of law and ideology by examining Pashukanis views on the social ontology of law. The chapter identifies three strands of a critique of ideology: (1) the critique of the ideology of juridical form, that is, the fundamental and most general ideological presuppositions and implications of juridical form as such; (2) the critique of legal ideology, that is, the ideological presuppositions and implications of a concrete system of positive law (on the example of bourgeois legal form); (3) the critique of juristic ideology, that is, the professional (guild) ideology of the community of lawyers and jurists, including legal philosophers and theorists.

In Chapter 5, 'Fetishes of Criminal Law: Reading Pashukanis with Hegel and de Lagasnerie', Linda Lilith Obermayr proposes an original reading of the way criminal law has been theorised in the *General Theory*. A recurrent critique suggests that within Pashukanis' theory of the legal form, all law is reduced to the legal mediation of commodity exchange. To the extent that legal relations are identified with the exchange relation of two commodity owners, Pashukanis' theory would, hence, lack an understanding and proper reflection of public law. By critically engaging with Hegel and de Lagasnerie, this chapter aims to develop Pashukanis' theory of criminal law further showing how it remains a fundamental proposition to expose the class character of bourgeois fetish of criminal law without reducing it to a mere instrument of the ruling class, that is without relinquishing the theoretical claim of his theory of the legal form.

Gian-Giacomo Fusco's 'Legal Subjectivity and Abstractions: Tracing the Past of the Legal Form', tackles a fundamental problem of Pashukanis' *General Theory*, that is, that it seems to deny the existence of pre-capitalist legal forms. While his theory rests on the conviction that the [modern] legal form emerged with the bourgeois-capitalist society, Pashukanis does acknowledge at the same time that rudimental forms of law emerged in previous epochs, especially in Roman law. By taking the cue from this observation, this chapter will interrogate the past of the legal form, by tracing in a genealogical fashion the emergence of some embryonic elements of its modern fully developed version. To undertake this endeavour this chapter takes into consideration the nature of the legal form, that is the actual formation of the abstract (the fact that the relationship between people in the market becomes a relationship between abstract owners devoid of specific characteristics except being possessors of rights) out of the practice of exchange, for then exposing how the embryos of such abstraction can be traced back to the tradition of Roman law.

This is followed by two chapters approaching some of the weaknesses and problematic aspects of Pashukanis' theory of the legal form. In his 'Exchange or Production? Poulantzas on the Legal Form and Pashukanis', Daniel McLoughlin makes two essential contributions to debates on the legal form. First, this chapter argues that Poulantzas' account of the legal form provides us with an important alternative to the commodity exchange theory, one that avoids the problems commonly associated with Pashukanis' work. It should, therefore, be taken seriously by Marxists interested in the nature of legal relations. Second, while the critique of Pashukanis' economism, and his focus on exchange, have long been common in the critical literature, these points are rarely developed in a great deal of detail, and several important defences of Pashukanis have emerged in recent years. Poulantzas presents us with one of the most theoretically sophisticated versions of these criticisms, and this chapter both explains them in some detail and considers their implications for some of the recent defences of Pashukanis.

In Chapter 8, 'Impossible Objects of Marxist Legal Theory of Law: The Limits of the Legal Form', Cosmin Cercel argues that the ways in which Pashukanis builds his concept of legal form are characteristic of a strand of legal theory that could be called modernist. This strategy has important epistemological and political implications, some of which are entangled with his tragic end at the hands of Stalinist repression, as well as with the further politico-legal developments in the Soviet that ended up in a generalisation of repression, compulsion and emergency turning into a darker legacy of law. By making use of psychoanalysis in engaging with the concept of legal form, this contribution aims to show how Pashukanis clings to an embellished concept of the law, that disregards its collusion to violence, repression, and its necessary reliance on 'naked force'. Pivotal to his analysis is a specific forgetting of the figure of the principle of expediency and a problematisation of the concept of dictatorship, that pushes legal repression and legal violence at its margins. In doing so, this chapter intends to inquire into the ethical and political lessons that we can draw from his work, especially within the current context of critical jurisprudence.

The book ends with the translation by Anna Lukina and Bill Bowring of Pashukanis' article 'Hegel State and Law (On the Centenary of his Death)' [Гегель. Государство и право (К столетию со дня смерти)].[25] Originally

25 This article has been published in EB Pashukanis, *Soviet State and the Revolution of Law* [Советское государство и революция права], n. 8 (August) (1931), and then included in the

composed and published in 1931, as the title suggests, on the occasion of the centenary of Hegel's death, this essay develops a short but incisive analysis of the Hegelian philosophy, highlighting its role in laying the foundation of dialectical materialism. Against the reactionary/fascist interpretation that makes use of Hegel to justify a politics of conquest and imperialist violence, Pashukanis asserts that the core element of the Hegelian philosophy is dialectic, which expresses the movement of the historical process, giving sense and orientation to otherwise different facts. Although he acknowledges that the Hegelian philosophy must be observed as it is, that is the product of a specific time and place and bears the signs of the backwardness of the socio-political situation of 19th century Germany, he nevertheless identifies in Hegel (much in line with the Leninist positioning of dialectical materialism), as kind of 'algebra for revolution'. Once more, here, Pashukanis leads us to consider the role of theory and philosophy in serving and orienting the political praxis of radical change.

* * *

This volume, together with a twin book titled *Legal Form and the End of Law. Pashukanis' Legacy*, is the outcome of two workshops hosted by Nomos: Centre for International Research in Law, Culture and Power (Jagiellonian University—Krakow), in association with the Centre for Critical Thought (University of Kent), which took place respectively on the 18th June 2022 in Canterbury (United Kingdom) and on 14th–15th April 2023. We would like to thank all the participants in the workshops, the University of Kent and Jagiellonian University for their support in making all this possible. The research and publication have been supported by a grant from the Faculty of International and Political Studies under the Strategic Programme Excellence Initiative at Jagiellonian University.

collection of articles by different authors titled *Hegel and Dialectical Materialism. Collection of Articles for the 100th Anniversary of Hegel's Death* [Гегель и диалектический материализм. Сборник статей к 100-летию со дня смерти Гегеля] (Moscow: Party Publishing House 1932). The text can be found also in: EB Pashukanis, *Selected Works on the General Theory of Law and State* [Избранные произведения по общей теории права и государства] (Nauka 1980) 195–215. For a critical overview of this essay and its theoretical implications, see: Carlo di Mascio, *Note su 'Hegel. Stato e diritto' di Evgeny Pashukanis* (Phasar Edizioni, 2020).

Chapter 1

What was Pashukanis Seeking to Do With his Concept of 'Legal Form', and Does It Have Continuing Relevance?

Bill Bowring

Introduction

In this chapter, I start with Yevgeny Pashukanis himself. I engage with the history of his General Theory of Law and Marxism, and the context in which it was written, identifying startling problems with the translations into English. Second, I ask the question what was his intention in concentrating on 'legal form', and why does it continue to exert such a powerful influence today? Third, I ask whether there had in fact been a serious debate as to 'legal form' prior to the work in 1920–1924 of Yevgeny Pashukanis. Fourth, I distinguish between 'natural laws' and 'human laws' as analysed by Baruch Spinoza. This distinction was maintained by his disciples Karl Marx and Friedrich Engels. For them, a key natural law was the 'law of value', which, like the law of gravity, determines the activity of capitalists whether they like it or not. Fifth, I maintain that 'legal form' refers to human laws only, and that neither Marx nor Engels referred to or analysed the 'legal form' or any cognate concept, nor did they feel they needed to. While Marx intended a volume on The State he did not propose to write on The Law.

What did Pashukanis Want to Achieve? His Intellectual History

Pashukanis was born in 1891. In 1909 he started to study law in Petersburg but left Russia for Germany in 1910. He continued his studies at the Ludwig-Maximilians-Universität in Munich, where he specialised in the contemporary philosophy of law and political economy. His doctoral dissertation was entitled *Statistik der Gesetzwidrigkeit im Arbeitsschutz* (Statistics of legal infractions in labour protection). This was not at all, therefore, a work of legal theory, but an indication of his interest in the workers' movement in Germany.[1] At some point during World War I, he returned to Russia.

1 Andreas Diers, '*Opfer des 'Grossen Terrors': Eine biographische Werknotiz zum 75. Todestag von Eugen Paschukanis*' (Victim of the 'Great Terror': A Biographical Note for the 75th

DOI: 10.4324/9781032724522-2

In October 1917, following the Bolshevik seizure of power, Pashukanis worked in the Sushchevsko-Mariynskiy Military Revolutionary Committee in Moscow and was later elected a member of the Cassation (Appeal) Tribunal attached to the All-Russian Central Executive Committee (VTsIK),[2] acting as a revolutionary judge.[3] Even during the bitter and bloody Russian Civil War, 7 November 1917–16 June 1923, there was a need for at any rate the forms of socialist legality.

From 1920 to 1923 Pashukanis served in the People's Commissariat for Foreign Affairs as the deputy head of the Economic Law Department. As a legal adviser, he was involved in one of the first and most important actions of the young Soviet Russia in the field of international law. During this time, he worked in the Soviet Russian representation in Berlin, where in due course he took part in preparing the Rappalo Treaty with Germany.[4]

It may well be that Pashukanis' experience as a responsible working diplomatic legal expert, engaged in international negotiation at the highest level, informed his later writing to at least the same extent as his German-centred theoretical scholarship.

However, as he disclosed rather late in 1930, it was while in Berlin in 1921–22, that Pashukanis prepared his *General Theory of Law and Marxism*, which was completed in 1923 and published in 1924. He also published his first scholarly article in 1921, while in Berlin.

The Selected Works of Pashukanis published in Russia in 1980[5] has a Bibliography[6] of the 'Fundamental Works of Pashukanis'; but one work is missing. This was Pashukanis' first published article, which appeared in 1921, and was entitled '*Burzhuazniy yurist o prirode gosudarstvo* (A bourgeois

Anniversary of the Death of Yevgeny Pasukanis) (3 September 2012) <https://www.rosalux.de/fileadmin/rls_uploads/pdfs/sonst_publikationen/Paschukanis_Sept_2012.pdf>; see also Andreas Harms, *Warenform und Rechtsform. Zur Rechtstheorie von Eugen Paschukanis* (Commodity Form and Legal Form. On the Legal Theory of Yevgeny Pashukanis) (*ça ira Verlag* 2009).

2 These courts were established by the Decree of November 22 (December 5) 1917 "On the Court": Decree of the Council of People's Commissars SU 1917–1918, No. 4, item 50. English translation in Zigurds L Zile (ed) *Ideas and Forces in Soviet Legal History: A Reader on the Soviet State and Law* (Oxford University Press 1992) 95, 96.

3 Yevgeniy Pashukanis, 'Pervye mesiatsy sushchestvovanii moskovskogo narodnogo suda (The First Months of the Existence of the Moscow People's Court)' (1922) Nos 44–45 *Yezhenedelnik Sovetskoi Iustitsii* (*Soviet Justice Weekly*) 15–16; see also Pyotr Stuchka, 'Stariy i noviy sud (The Old and New Court)' (1918), English translation at Zile, ibid 96–98.

4 This section draws from Bill Bowring, 'Yevgeniy Pashukanis, His Law and Marxism: A General Theory, and the 1922 Treaty of Rapallo between Soviet Russia and Germany' (2017) 19 *Journal of the History of International Law* 274–95.

5 Yevgeniy Pashukanis, *Izbranniye proizvedeniya po obshei teorii prava i gosudarstvo* (*Selected Works on the General Theory of Law and State)* ("Nauka" Publisher 1980)—Academy of Science, Institute of State and Law.

6 ibid 261–67.

jurist on the nature of the state)'.[7] It appeared in the literary journal *Krasnaya Nov (Red Virgin Soil)*, which was the first Soviet literary 'thick' journal and was published between 1921 and 1941. From 1921 to 1927 it was edited by Aleksandr Voronkov (1884–1937), who was close to Trotsky, agreed with Trotsky's 1923 *Literature and Revolution*, did much to encourage new literary talent, and in 1937 was executed for Trotskyism. However, there is no hint that Pashukanis ever referred to Trotsky's work or was, in any sense, a Trotskyist.

The subject of the article was the scholarship of Professor Maurice Hauriou of the University of Toulouse (1856–1929);[8] whose textbook on *Principles of Public Law* was published in 1910. Pashukanis did not refer in his 4,000-word article to any other literature. Not least in this regard, the article contrasts strongly with the *General Theory*, which has many references, particularly to several German authors. He referred to Marx, but without indicating his source. Most of the article consisted of often sarcastic references to Hauriou's positivist doctrine. Pashukanis' concluding paragraph was as follows:[9]

> In one of his speeches Cde Lenin remarked that sincere defenders of capitalism may now be found only among our SRs (Social Revolutionaries) and Mensheviks. In the West they have become extinct. We can see the cause of this. Russia underwent an accelerated course of capitalism and therefore our intelligentsia may *bona fide* come out in defence of the sublime beginning of democracy and freedom, without sensing that it has been crucified by capitalism. But in order to be a sincere defender of capitalism in the West, where social relations have been able to mature and over-mature, one must sincerely, like Hauriou, assert that the principles of freedom, democracy, individual rights and so on, conceal behind themselves quite simply *faire valoir de la propriété*![10] And such courage is not given to everyone.

There is, in fact, a connection between Pashukanis' sole publication before the *General Theory*, his 1921 article, and the 1924 *General Theory* itself, although Pashukanis did not refer directly to his earlier work. Notably, Maurice Hauriou was cited three times[11] in the *General Theory*, but this time

7 Yevgeniy Pashukanis, 'Burzhuazniy yurist o prirode gosudarstvo (A Bourgeois Jurist on the Nature of the State)'(1921) 3 *Krasnaya Nov* (*Red Virgin Soil*) 223–32 <http://www.ruthenia.ru/sovlit/j/106.html>

8 For biography see http://www.universalis.fr/encyclopedie/maurice-hauriou/ He was a positivist, influenced by Aquinas, Comte and Bergson.

9 Pashukanis, *Bourgeois Jurist* (n 7) 231–32.

10 Enforce property!

11 Pashukanis, *General Theory* 1983 (n 1) 122, 123, 134.

with approbation and twice with the epithet 'astute' as in 'one of the most astute bourgeois theorists'[12] and 'an astute jurist like Hauriou'.[13] And there were many references to the German legal scholars whom Pashukanis read in Munich and during his time in Berlin.

However, Pashukanis' paramount reason for writing the *General Theory* was not to renew or explain his critical relationship with Hauriou, but to identify 'law in its general definition, law as a form'.[14] That is, to tackle the question of the nature of law as a materially grounded abstraction. Pashukanis is now best known for his 'commodity-form' theory of law, more recently extended by his contemporary followers to a 'commodity-form theory of international law'.[15]

In the first of several recantations of his work in 1921, published in 1930, Pashukanis wrote the following about the genesis of the *General Theory*:

> It is clear that much which was written in the first years of NEP[16] deserves criticism and suffers from obvious anachronisms and now and then simply mistakes . . . But the question is not only that of particular formulations. The question concerns some defects of a general character. This was the overestimation of the role and significance of market relations which was without doubt characteristic of my first work. It is impermissible to hide from view the fact that this book was written at a time when the collective of Marxist legal scholars had not come together. It was written when I was alone, and it could not be exposed to the process of critical re-working. It was written finally, before the publication of Lenin's notebooks on dialectics and on the works of Marx which were published in the 'Archive'. It appeared before the discussions with the 'mechanists', before the discussions in the fields of political economy, literature etc. Therefore it was completely natural, that the book, which was written in 1923, and prepared still earlier in 1920–1921, displays defects, when we look at it from our higher present-day theoretical and methodological point of view.[17]

12 ibid 123.

13 ibid 134.

14 ibid 68.

15 For a recent exposition and defence of this theory, see China Miéville, 'The Commodity-Form Theory of International Law: An Introduction"' (2004) 17(2) Leiden Journal of International Law 271–302, and China Miéville, *Between Equal Rights: A Marxist Theory of International Law* (Brill Academic Publishers 2005)

16 The New Economic Policy, a partial restoration of capitalist market relations, under state control, was introduced by Lenin in 1921. Despite Lenin's death in 1924 the success of the policy meant that it continued until sharply reversed by Stalin in 1928.

17 Yevgeniy Pashukanis, 'Polozheniye na teoreticheskom pravovom fronte (The Situation on the Theoretical Legal Front)' (1930) 11–12 Sovetskoye gosudartsvo i revolutsiya prava (*Soviet State and Revolution of Law*) 16–49, 26.

This concerned Pashukanis' theoretical work from 1920 to 1923; in particular his work on the *General Theory* while he was in Berlin.

Pashukanis became in the next ten years a staunch loyalist of the regime—in my opinion, by conviction rather than as the result of any sort of pressure.

In 1931, following the dramatic recantation of his previous views previously noted, Pashukanis became the Director of the Institute of Soviet Construction and Law of the Communist Academy. He was effectively the USSR's director of legal research and legal education. The American scholar John Hazard,[18] who studied in Moscow under Pashukanis from 1934 to 1937, summarised his effect on legal education, as follows:[19]

> Believing that the state was slowly withering away as socialism came nearer to achievement, Pashukanis advocated the cessation of courses in civil law. He understood civil law to be the regulation of the relations of men under the trading conditions of capitalism, and, as such, no longer of importance, as the remnants of capitalism disappeared.
>
> His influence was so marked that the courses in civil law in the law school were abolished, and to replace them there appeared a course called economic-administrative law, concerning itself with regulation of the relations between state enterprises.[20]

Following Pashukanis' fall in 1937, courses on (Soviet) civil law were reintroduced to the syllabus.

By 1932, Pashukanis, who had become editor-in-chief of the official law journal *Soviet State*, was able to write a 'hallelujah' in response to Stalin's letter 'Some questions on the history of Bolshevism'.[21] Pashukanis' major work on international law, *Essays in International Law*, appeared in 1935.[22] These did not refer to his 'commodity form theory', and were straightforward expositions of orthodox Soviet legal theory.

On 16 November 1936 Pashukanis reached the high point of his career: the Presidium of the Central Executive Committee of the USSR appointed

18 1909–1955.

19 John Hazard, 'Housecleaning in Soviet Law' (1938) 1 *American Quarterly on the Soviet Union* 5–16 <http://www.unz.org/Pub/AmQSovietUnion-1938apr-00005?View=PDF>; and John Hazard, 'Cleansing Soviet International Law of Anti-Marxist Theories' (1938) 32(2) *American Journal of International Law* 244–52.

20 Hazard, 'Housecleaning' (n 19) 13.

21 Ye Pashukanis 'Pismo tov. Stalina i zadachi teoreticheskovo fronta gosudarstvo i pravo (The Letter of Comrade Stalin and the Tasks of the Theoretical Front of State and Law)' (1932) 1 Sovetskoe gosudarstvo (*Soviet State*) 4–48, cited in EA Skripilev, 'Nashemy zhurnalu—70 let (Our Journal Is 70 Years Old)' (1987) (2) Sovetskoye Gosudarstvo i Pravo (*Soviet State and Law*) 17.

22 Ye Pashukanis, *Ocherki po Mezhdunarodnomu Pravu (Essays in International Law)* (Soviet Legislation 1935).

him Deputy Peoples Commissar for Justice of the USSR. In the same year, he was deputy chairman of the Drafting Committee for the 1936 'Stalin Constitution',[23] and the Institute of State and Law proposed him as a candidate for membership of the Academy of Science of the USSR. Also in 1936, he became the chairman of the Academic Council attached to the Peoples Commissariat of Justice of the USSR.

But within a year he was dead, following *Pravda*'s announcement on 20 January 1937 that he had been found to be an enemy of the people—just two months after he had been named by the regime to supervise the revision of the whole system of Soviet codes of law. On the same day, he was arrested. On 4 September 1937, a Military Collegium sentenced him to death. He was condemned as a member of a 'band of wreckers' and 'Trotsky-Bukharin fascist agents'. He was posthumously rehabilitated in 1956.

What did Pashukanis Want to Achieve? The General Theory

As noted above, Pashukanis wrote his General Theory while working as the Soviet Russian government legal adviser in Berlin, in 1921–2.

It is clear to me that he wished to prove that with the proletarian revolution law would cease to exist and would be replaced by technical administration. That was why he worked out in detail his thesis that developed capitalism required and generated a 'legal form', unique to developed capitalism. While he did not specify a homology between the 'commodity form' and the 'legal form', as advocated by Balbus (see further down), his conception of the 'legal form' was not a possibility before Marx's work in the 18th century.

Furthermore, as Pashukanis himself made clear in 1930, he was working in Berlin until 1923 and was not familiar with the theoretical debates and developments within Bolshevism. For this reason, very little Soviet Russian scholarship is cited in the General Theory.

Instead, even in the 3rd Edition, published in 1929, there are voluminous footnotes, most of which do not appear in the first translation to be commented upon by English language scholars, for example, Chris Arthur, by Barbara Einhorn (she worked from a German translation from Russian), or the later Maggs translations into English. Indeed, the great majority of citations are to German scholars, no fewer than 19 footnotes, mostly to German language sources, mostly from the late 19th and early 20th century,[24] many

23 John Hazard, 'Memories of Pashukanis' Foreword to *Evgeny Pashukanis, Selected Writings on Marxism and Law* (Academic Press 1980) 273–301 <http://www.marxists.org/archive/pashukanis/biog/memoir.htm>

24 Some of the authors concerned are См. Карнер, 'Социальные функции права', русск. пер., 1923, стр. 11; Wundt, 'Ethik', S. 1; Сравн. Simmel, 'Einleitung in die Moralwissenschaft'; J Offner, 'Das soziale Rechtsdenken', 1923, стр. 54; A Ferneck, 'Die Rechtswidrigkei', 1903,

of them textbooks, the most recent reference being to Kelsen's 1922 *Der soziologische und der juristische Staatsbegriff* (The sociological and legal concept of the state).[25]

The English language reception of Pashukanis in the 1970s and 80s was, therefore, based on incomplete translations.

As is noted in the online publication of the Maggs translation,[26] 'The complete footnotes to the General Theory have been translated in J Hazard (ed.), *Soviet Legal Philosophy* (1951), Harvard University Press, Cambridge, translated by H Babb, pp. 111–225. [ed.]'.

With some difficulty, I obtained a copy of this book, with its translation[27] of the *General Theory* by Hugh W Babb.[28] The book also contains a

стр. 11; H Kelsen, 'Der soziologische und der juristische Staatsbegriff', 1922, стр. 96; Bierling, 'Juristische Prinzipienlehr', т. I, стр. 145; Jellinek, 'System der subjektiven öffentlichen Rechte', стр. 13); Fichte, 'Rechtslehre' vom 1812, Leipzig, стр. 10; O. Gierke, 'Geschichte des deutschen Körperschaftsbegriff', Berlin 1873, стр. 30; Гирке, цит. соч., стр. 648; Пухта, 'Курс римского гражданского права', русск. перев. 1874 г; Гумплович, 'Rechtsstaat und Sozialismus'; Гумпловича (см. его Rechtsstaat u. Sozialismus и Geschichte der Staatstheorien); Мэн, 'Древнее право', Русск. пер. 1873 г., стр. 40 и 47; Binder, 'Rechtsnorm und Rechtspflicht', 1912; ГС Мен, Древнее право, перев. Н. Белозерской, 1872, стр. 283. Э Ферри, Уголовная социология, том II, пер. с пред. Дриля, стр. 37; Иеринг, 'Дух римского права', I, стр. 118, 'русск. перев'. ГС Мен, 'Древнее право', 1873 г., стр. 269; Иеринг, 'Дух римского права', I, стр. 259 и след., русск. пер., 1875; Wilda, 'Strafrecht der Germanen', 1842, стр. 219, Спенсер, 'Принципы социологии', 1883, стр. 659; F v Listz, 'Lehrbuch d. deut. Strafrechts', 1905, § 15; Kraepelin, Die Abschaffung des Strafmasses (Stuttgart 1880), стр. 13; Aschaffenburg, 'Das Verbrechen und seine Bekämpfung', 1905 г., стр. 200.

English translation from German. Some German sources were translated into Russian:

См. Карнер, 'Социальные функции права' русск. per., 1923, str. 11th; Wundt—"Ethik", p. 1; Сравн. Simmel, 'Introduction to Moral Science'; J Offner, 'Social Legal Thinking', 1923, str. 54; A Ferneck, 'Unlawfulness', 1903, str. 11; H Kelsen, 'The Sociological and Legal Concept of the State' 1922, str. 96; Bierling, 'Legal Principles Teaching', т. I, str. 145th; Jellinek, 'System of Subjective Public Rights', str. 13); Fichte, 'Rechtslehre' from 1812, Leipzig, str. 10th; O Gierke, 'History of the German Concept of Corporate Body' (Berlin 1873), str. 30th; Гирке, цит. соч., стр. 648; Пухта, 'Курс римского гражданского права', русск. perev. 1874 g; Гумплович, 'The Rule of Law and Socialism'; Гумпловича (см. его rule of law and socialism и history of state theories); Man, 'Drevnee Pravo'. Русск. per. 1873 g., str. 40 and 47; Binder, 'Legal Norm and Legal Obligation', 1912; GC Мен, Древнее право, перев. N. Belozerskoye, 1872, str. 283. E Ферри, Уголовная социология, том II, пер. с пред. Дриля, стр. 37; Иеринг, 'Duh rimskogo prava', I, str. 118, russian. перев'. ГС Мен, 'Древнее право', 1873 g., str. 269th; Иеринг, 'Дух римского права', I, str. 259 and след., русск. per., 1875; Wilda, 'Criminal Law of the Germans', 1842, str. 219, Спенсер, 'Principal Sociology', 1883, str. 659; f v Listz, 'Textbook d. German Criminal Law', 1905, § 15; Kraepelin, 'The Abolition of Punishment' (Stuttgart 1880), str. 13; Aschaffenburg, 'Crime and Its Fight', 1905 г., стр. 200th.

25 Kelsen, 'Der soziologische und der juristische Staatsbegriff' (n 20) стр. 96.

26 https://www.marxists.org/archive/pashukanis/1924/law/.

27 I have scanned the translation of the *General Theory* and will send this to anyone interested.

28 Professor Hugh Babb received a law degree from Harvard in 1916 and served in a private law firm before joining the Boston faculty four years later. He left Harvard in 1958 and taught for five years at the University of Maine law school. He died on 2 January 1971.

translation of Pashukanis' painful 1930 recantation to which I already referred, an article entitled 'The Situation on the Legal Theory Front (Some Results of the Debate)'.[29]

Pashukanis' tragedy was that in 1921, while he was still in Berlin, Lenin, conscious of the impossibility of constructing socialism in one beleaguered country, launched the New Economic Policy (NEP), which required laws, in particular civil laws, and courts. Pashukanis maintained his position as to the necessary disappearance of law, the 'legal form' of developed capitalism, for as long as he could. Contrary to Pashukanis' expectations, at the fourth session of the ninth Congress of the All Russian Central Executive Committee of the Soviets, held in October 1922, a Civil Code was enacted, to take effect on 1 January 1923.[30] This closely followed the Russian Empire's Civil Code of 1853, which itself followed the German model, as noted, in his 1923 article, by Jacob Kantorovitch. He wrote:[31]

> The very fact of the adoption of a code of laws intended to uphold and regulate private property relations in Soviet Russia is a striking indication of the departure of the governing party from the communistic experiment which had been carried on by it during the first three and a half years of its rule . . .
>
> The communistic departures of the Soviet Code from the capitalistic code relate only to two divisions of the law of property: real property and inheritance. In all the rest, the communist theory has found no objection at all.

Stalin brought the NEP to an end with his Great Break a few years after Lenin's death on 21 January 1924. The new Soviet system of Socialism in One Country required more laws than ever before. In his 2014 masterpiece *Law and the Making of the Soviet World. The Red Demiurge*,[32] Scott Newton argued that the Soviet order was a work of law. He drew on Russian-language Soviet statutes and regulations, jurisprudence, legal theory and English-language 'legal Kremlinology'. On this basis, he analysed the central significance of law in the design and operation of Soviet economic, political and social institutions. He, therefore, concluded that the USSR was an exemplary, rather than aberrant, case of the uses to which law was put in twentieth-century industrialised societies.

29 Pashukanis, *Sovetskoe Gosudartsvo i Revolutsiya Prava* (Soviet State and the Revolution in Law) (Institute of Soviet Construction and Law, The Communist Academy 1930) No. 11–12, pp. 16–49.

30 Jacob Kantorovitch, 'The Civil Code of Soviet Russia' (1923) 32(8) *The Yale Law Journal* 779–89.

31 ibid 779, 781–82.

32 See https://www.routledge.com/Law-and-the-Making-of-the-Soviet-World-The-Red-Demiurge/Newton/p/book/9781138211247#.

No wonder Pashukanis was shot, despite his best efforts at conforming to Stalin's regime. The continuing relevance of his work in 1921–22 is that it is the only thoroughly serious attempt to formulate a socialist theory of the law, or the 'legal form', despite Marx and Engels having insisted that no such thing was possible or desirable.

Legal Form Apart from Pashukanis—And with Him?

I already referred to the history of publication of Pashukanis' *General* Theory in English, and the missing footnotes.

These appearances of Pashukanis in English, after so many years, elicited serious reviews, in 1980, from Roger Cotterrell, of the Maggs translation;[33] and in 1981 by Ronnie Warrington[34] of the Einhorn translation, with a reply by Alan Norrie in 1982.[35] The most recent serious exposition of Pashukanis' theory, by Matthew Dimick, appeared in the 2021 *Research Handbook on Law and Marxism.*[36]

Neither Kant nor Hegel investigated something akin to the 'legal form'. However, in 1977 Chicago professor Isaac Balbus published 'Commodity Form and Legal Form: An Essay on the "Relative Autonomy" of the Law'.[37] He argued that 'the logic of the legal form and the logic commodity form are one and the same'.

> [T]he relative autonomy of the legal form from the will of social actors entails at the same time an essential identity or homology between the legal form and the very 'cell' of capitalist society, the commodity form.
>
> The legal form . . . defines distinctions of interest and origin out of political existence, just as the commodity form defines distinctions of use and labor out of economic existence. And, just as the commodity form 'replaces' use-value and concrete labor with the abstractions of exchange-value and undifferentiated labor-power, the legal form 'replaces' the multiplicity of concrete needs and interests with the abstractions of 'will' and 'rights,' and the socially differentiated individual with the abstraction of the juridical subject or the legal person

33 Cotterrell, 'Review of *Pashukanis: Selected Writings on Marxism and Law*, by P. Beirne, R. Sharlet, & P. B. Maggs' (Winter 1980) 7(2) *British Journal of Law and Society* 317–21.

34 Warrington, 'Pashukanis and the Commodity Form Theory' (1981) 9 *International Journal of the Sociology of Law* 1–22.

35 Norrie, 'Pashukanis and the "Commodity Form Theory": A Reply to Warrington' (1982) 10 *International Journal of the Sociology of Law* 419–37.

36 Matthew Dimick, 'Pashukanis' Commodity-form Theory of Law' in Paul O'Connell and Umut Özsu (eds), *Research Handbook on Law and Marxism* (Edward Elgar 2021) 115–38.

37 Isaac D Balbus, 'Commodity Form and Legal Form: An Essay on the "Relative Autonomy" of the Law' (Winter 1977) 11(3) *Law and Society Review* 571–88.

And in a footnote

> Only after 'working out' the homology between the commodity form and the legal form did I discover that Pashukanis had developed essentially the same analysis roughly fifty years ago! Almost all subsequent Marxist work on the law is, unfortunately, a regression from the standard established by Pashukanis' pioneering efforts.

But analysis of the 'legal form' is not only to be found in the scholarship inspired by Pashukanis' appearance in English. In 2005 Cornell scholar Robert B Summers published 'On Giving Legal Form Its Due. A Study in Legal Theory'[38]—without mentioning Pashukanis, let alone Marx. His position?

> Here, I use the word 'form' to mean the purposive systematic arrangement of the parts and the whole of a legal phenomenon. I use the phrase 'legal phenomenon' to mean any type or sub-type of functional legal unit in a system of law, including an institution such as a legislature or court, a species of law such as a rule, principle, contract or property interest, a methodology such as one for the interpretation of statutes or for the application of case law, and a sanction or a remedy such as imprisonment, or money damages . . .
>
> Few legal theorists have taken interest in developing a general theory that gives legal form its due in a frontal and systematic fashion. Such a theory must, among other things, differentiate types of legal phenomena, and must differentiate between the formal and the non-formal in legal phenomena.[39]

His main source was the German realist scholar Rudolf von Jhering, who had a profound influence on the American Legal Realist School, especially Karl Llewellyn (1893–1962), and thus on American critical legal studies.[40] Duncan Kennedy, in an article on Lon Fuller, published in 2000 in the *Columbia*

38 Summers, 'On Giving Legal Form Its Due. A Study in Legal Theory' (June 2005) 18(2) *Ratio Juris* 129–43.

39 ibid 129–30.

40 von Jhering Rudolf, *Geist des Römischen Rechts: Auf den Verschiedenen Stufen Seiner Entwicklung* (The Spirit of Roman Law: At the Different Stages of its Development) (Scientia (1915/1997) 1933). Jhering is best known in English for *The Struggle for Law* (JJ Lalor tr, Lawbook Exchange reprint), and see Roger Cotterrell, 'The Struggle for Law: Some Dilemmas of Cultural Legality' (2008) 4(4) *International Journal of Law in Context* 373–84.n and Bill Bowring 'The reception or the lack of it, of the concepts of Rudolf von Jhering in the English speaking world' https://bbowring.com/2021/03/20/the-reception-or-the-lack-of-it-of-the-concepts-of-rudolf-von-jhering-in-the-english-speaking-world/.

Law Review,[41] places Fuller's analysis of contract questions in the context of the critique of the 19th century will theory of contracts, and the rise of sociological jurisprudence and legal realism, wrote, in a footnote

> Between 1972 and 1975, I read Rudolf von Ihering's *The Spirit of Roman Law* (in French translation) because Fuller had cited it. Ihering's seemed to me a much better, indeed an unutterably brilliant, take on the issues Fuller discussed, and this greatly reduced my admiration for Fuller. My article downgrades him for this reason.

So in conclusion, a discussion concerning 'legal form' without reference to Pashukanis seems to have taken place.

Natural Laws and Human Laws: Marx on Natural Laws[42]

Marx referred many times to 'the law of value', and as has been pointed out, practically never to a 'labour theory of value'. What kind of a law is the 'law of value'? In Volume 3 of *Capital* Marx wrote explicitly that:

> Since these latter [individual capitalists] confront one another only as commodity-owners, and everyone seeks to sell his commodity as dearly as possible (apparently even guided in the regulation of production itself solely by his own free will), the inner law enforces itself only through their competition, their mutual pressure upon each other, whereby the deviations are mutually cancelled. Only as an inner law, vis-à-vis the individual agents, as a blind law of Nature, does the law of value exert its influence here and maintain the social equilibrium of production against its accidental fluctuations.[43]

That is for Marx, the law of value is an 'inner law', a law of nature. Individual capitalists believe that they are acting of their own free will, but, in reality, their activity is subject to the Law of Value, as inexorable and impossible to avoid as the law of gravity or the laws of motion. The Law of Value expresses the innermost laws of motion of Capital, as what is new and unprecedented in human history. This is one of the points at which Marx demonstrates

41 Duncan Kennedy, 'From the Will Theory to the Principle of Private Autonomy: Lon Fuller's "Consideration and Form"' (2000) 100(1) *Columbia Law Review* 94.

42 This section draws on my contribution to the Research Handbook on Political Economy and Law, Bill Bowring, 'The Law of Value and the Law' in Ugo Mattei and John Haskell (eds), *Research Handbook on Political Economy and Law* (Edward Elgar 2015) 158–76.

43 Karl Marx, *Capital: A Critique of Political Economy* (first published 1867, Lawrence and Wishart 1984) 880.

his debt to Spinoza. Yirmiyahu Yovel, in his *Spinoza and Other Heretics*,[44] asserted that

> Marx used Spinoza's thought far more than he admitted. Spinoza was above all a counterbalance and corrective to Hegel, restoring the concept of nature and man as a concrete, natural being from what seemed to Marx his immersion in the lofty and semireligious heights of the Hegelian *Geist*. . . . Marx's new philosophy of immanence, though strongly influenced by Hegel and his milieu, goes back to Spinoza in more ways than one. Indeed, Spinoza is almost always present in Marx's thought. But, we may add, the actual presence of Spinoza in Marx far surpasses his direct mention by name.

Indeed, one of the passages Marx transcribed from Spinoza in 1841, from Chapter IV of the *Theological-Political Treatise* (TTP), 'Of the Divine Law', was as follows:

> The word law (*lex*) in an absolute sense signifies that, in accordance with which, each individual thing, or all things, or all things of the same kind, behave in one and the same fixed and determinate way, depending upon either [*vel*] natural necessity or [*vel*] a human decision.[45]

This paragraph continues (though the continuation was not transcribed by Marx) and explains the first sentence:

> A law that depends upon natural necessity is one that necessarily follows from the very nature or definition of a thing. A law that depends on a human decision, which is more properly called a decree (*jus*), is one that men prescribe to themselves and to others in order to achieve a better and safer life, or for other reasons.

Does this mean that a law of nature, an expression of natural necessity, is equivalent, for Spinoza, to a human decree? Not at all. Marx next transcribed the following passage, two paragraphs lower on the page:

> Firstly, in so far as man is a part of nature, he is also part of nature's power. Hence whatever follows from the necessity of human nature (that is, from nature itself in so far as we understand it to be expressly determined by

44 Yirmiyahu Yovel, *Spinoza and other Heretics: The Adventures of Immanence*, vol 2 (Princeton UP 1992) 78–103, 78–79.

45 Karl Marx and Friedrich Engels, *Marx-Engels Gesamtausgabe MEGA IV I* (Dietz Verlag 1976) 248; Benedict de Spinoza, *Theological-Political Treatise* (Michael Silverthorne tr, Jonathan Israel ed, CUP 2007) 57.

> human nature) results also, albeit necessarily, from the capacity of men. Hence the decreeing of these laws may quite correctly be said to follow from human will, because this depends especially on the power of the human mind in the sense that our mind, so far as it perceives what is true or false, can very clearly be conceived without those decrees, but not without the necessary law of nature as we have just defined it.[46]

That is, a human decree, and the enforcement of it, are themselves the expression of the power of nature, and subject to the same iron necessity as everything else in nature. In pronouncing a decree and enforcing it, humans may believe that they are acting of their own free will, but in fact are, as humans, expressing determined and inevitable natural forces.

In *Spinoza's Revolution in Natural Law*, Andre Santos Campos[47] explains that

> The fact remains that natural laws for Spinoza are neither mere descriptions of what a thing is in itself nor propositional inferences referring to *a priori* given data. They are mostly that which is so distinctive to each individual thing that it allows the thing to posit itself as a real individual being.[48]

Campos continues that

> The laws of nature of each individual thing are hence the inscription of a thing's essence and of everything that follows from it because the thing *is*. They are the inscription of the thing's power—and that is the very nature of law (*jus*), that is, the thing's natural 'right-law'.[49]

Thus Spinoza's (and, I argue, Marx's) laws of nature are not explained by any kind of normatively moral natural law theory, but rather a necessitarian deterministic natural law theory. Moreover, these laws cannot be confused with the laws of natural science, which are descriptive of actions and experiences. Campos explains that Spinoza's laws are *inscriptive* rather than *descriptive*.

> [I]nscriptive natural laws are the intrinsically original characteristics that an individual has—and the actions he performs as a follow-up to those characteristics—in order to express self-productive immanent Nature.[50]

46 cf Marx and Engels (n 56) 248; Spinoza (n 56) 57.
47 Andre Santos Campos, *Spinoza's Revolution in Natural Law* (Palgrave MacMillan 2012)
48 ibid.
49 ibid 75.
50 ibid.

The Law of Value for Marx had, I propose, precisely these characteristics of a Spinozan natural law. It is possible to trace the development but also the consistency of Marx's understanding of the operation of this Law over the years. In 1859 in the *Critique of Political Economy* Marx wrote:

> David Ricardo, unlike Adam Smith, neatly sets forth the determination of the value of commodities by labour-time, and demonstrates that this law governs even those bourgeois relations of production which apparently contradict it most decisively. Ricardo's investigations are concerned exclusively with the magnitude of value, and regarding this he is at least aware that the operation of the law depends on definite historical pre-conditions. He says that the determination of value by labour-time applies to 'such commodities only as can be increased in quantity by the exertion of human industry, and on the production of which competition operates without restraint'.[51]
>
> This in fact means that the full development of the law of value presupposes a society in which large-scale industrial production and free competition obtain, in other words, modern bourgeois society. For the rest, the bourgeois form of labour is regarded by Ricardo as the eternal natural form of social labour.[52]

Thus, the Law of Value, which finds expression in the whole of human recorded history most certainly since the agricultural revolution 10,000 years ago, only finds its full development under the rule of Capital. In his 1867 Preface to the first German edition of *Capital* Volume I, Marx wrote of the 'value-form, whose fully developed shape is the money-form'. He also wrote of the 'natural laws of capitalist production . . . these tendencies working with iron necessity towards inevitable results'.[53] In 1867, in Chapter 1 of *Capital*, 'The Commodity', Marx wrote that:

> The general value-form, in which all the products of labour are presented as mere congealed quantities of undifferentiated human labour, shows by its very structure that it is the social expression of the world of commodities. In this way it is made plain that within this world the general human character of labour forms its specific social character.[54]. . . in the midst of

51 David Ricardo, *On the Principles of Political Economy, and Taxation* (3rd edn, John Murray 1821) 3.

52 Karl Marx, 'Historical Notes on the Analysis of Commodities' (Marx Engels Archive) <https://www.marxists.org/archive/marx/works/1859/critique-pol-economy/ch01a.htm> accessed 1 January 2015.

53 Karl Marx, '1867 Preface to the First German Edition' in *Capital Vol. I* (Marxist Archive) <http://www.marxists.org/archive/marx/works/1867-c1/p1.htm> accessed 1 January 2015.

54 Karl Marx, *Capital: A Critic of Political Economy*, vol 1 (Ben Fowkes tr, Penguin Books 1976) 160.

> the accidental and ever-fluctuating exchange relations between the products, the labour-time socially necessary to produce them asserts itself as a regulative law of nature.[55]

In Chapter 11 of *Capital*, 'The Rate and Mass of Surplus-Value', Marx refers to three laws, all of which are necessary consequences of the Law of Value. First, there is the law that 'the supply of labour exploitable by capital is independent of the supply of workers', to which he added in a footnote:

> This elementary law appears to be unknown to the vulgar economist, who imagines, like an inverted Archimedes, that in the determination of the market price of labour by supply and demand he has found the fulcrum by means of which he cannot so much move the world, as bring it to a standstill.[56]

The second law is,

> The absolute limit of the average working day—this being by nature always less than 24 hours—sets an absolute limit to the compensation for a reduction of variable capital by a higher rate of surplus-value, or for the decrease of the number of workers exploited by a higher degree of exploitation of labour-power.[57]

The third law is as follows:

> the masses of value and of surplus-value produced by different capitals—the value of labour-power being given and its degree of exploitation being equal—vary directly as the amounts of the variable components of these capitals, i.e. the parts which have been turned into living labour-power.[58]

Marx continues that

> This law clearly contradicts all experience based on immediate appearances. . . . Classical economics holds instinctively to this law, although it has never formulated it, because it is a necessary consequence of the law of value.[59]

55 ibid 168.
56 ibid 419.
57 ibid 420.
58 ibid.
59 ibid.

I repeat that this Law, which is at the heart of the operation of Capital, is a thoroughly Spinozist law, the result of which is that humans, believing that they are acting of their own free will, are, in fact, expressing a determinate necessity.

Marx on Human Laws

Marx had very little to say about law constructed by humans as such.[60] His attitude to (man-made) law remained consistent throughout his life. In the 1857 *Introduction* to the *Grundrisse*, he wrote:

> Quite apart from this crude tearing-apart of production and distribution and of their real relationship, it must be apparent from the outset that, no matter how differently distribution may have been arranged in different stages of social development, it must be possible here also, just as with production, to single out common characteristics, and just as possible to confound or to extinguish all historic differences under *general human* laws. For example, the slave, the serf and the wage labourer all receive a quantity of food which makes it possible for them to exist as slaves, as serfs, as wage labourers. The conqueror who lives from tribute, or the official who lives from taxes . . . all receive a quota of social production, which is determined by other laws than that of the slave's, etc.
>
> The two main points which all economists cite under this rubric are: (1) property; (2) its protection by courts, police, etc. To this a very short answer may be given:
>
> to 2. Protection of acquisitions etc. When these trivialities are reduced to their real content, they tell more than their preachers know. Namely that every form of production creates its own legal relations, form of government, etc. . . . All the bourgeois economists are aware of is that production can be carried on better under the modern police than e.g. on the principle of might makes right. They forget only that this principle is also a legal relation, and that the right of the stronger prevails in their 'constitutional republics' as well, only in another form.[61]

In the Preface to his *A Contribution to the Critique of Political Economy* (*Zur Kritik der Politischen Oekonomie*), published in Berlin in 1859, the text in which his ideas concerning Capital achieved their explicit shape, Marx wrote;

> My inquiry led me to the conclusion that neither legal relations nor political forms could be comprehended whether by themselves or on the

60 For a characteristic Soviet presentation of Marx's 'theory of law' see LS Mamut, 'Theory of Law' *Sovetskoye Gosudarstvo i Pravo* (1967) in Csaba Varga (ed), *Marxian Legal Theory* (New York UP 1993) 3–10.

61 Karl Marx, *Grundrisse* (first publish 1800, Martin Nicolaus ed, Penguin Books 1993) 87–88.

> basis of a so-called general development of the human mind, but that on the contrary they originate in the material conditions of life, the totality of which Hegel, following the example of English and French thinkers of the eighteenth century, embraces within the term 'civil society'; that the anatomy of this civil society, however, has to be sought in political economy.[62]

Much later, in his 1875 *Critique of the Gotha Programme*, Marx elaborated on this, writing:

> Do not the bourgeois assert that the present-day distribution is 'fair'? And is it not, in fact, the only 'fair' distribution on the basis of the present-day mode of production? Are economic relations regulated by legal conceptions, or do not, on the contrary, legal relations arise out of economic ones? Have not also the socialist sectarians the most varied notions about 'fair' distribution?[63]

This approach to the question of human law is very much in line with the attitude of Marx and Engels to the possibility or desirability of 'socialist law' or a 'socialist theory of law' while insisting on the need for workers to make legal demands, to which I turn next.

Are 'Socialist Law' or 'Socialist Legal Theory' Desirable or Even Possible?

In their 1887 polemic *Juridical Socialism*[64] (the German title, *Juristen-Socialismus*, would be better translated as 'Lawyers' Socialism') Friedrich Engels and Karl Kautsky[65] explained—and Marx, who died four years earlier, would not have disagreed—how the main battle cry of the bourgeoisie became 'equality before the law', because their struggle had to be based around legalistic demands. 'This solidified a world view based on legal

62 Marx, 'Preface to the Critique of Political Economy' (n 29) 262.

63 Karl Marx, 'Critique of the Gotha Programme' The Marxist Archive available at <http://www.marxists.org/archive/marx/works/1875/gotha/ch01.htm> accessed 29 October 2013.

64 Friedrich Engels and Karl Kautsky, 'Juridical Socialism' (1977) 7(2) *Politics and Society* 203–20; 'Juristen-Socialismus' (1887) (2) Die Neue Zeit (Stuttgart), translated by Piers Byrne.

65 The translator, Piers Byrne, explained that this was one of a series of articles confronting reformist tendencies in German Social Democracy, in this case, the legalistic demands for social reform made by the Austrian jurist Anton Menger. The original manuscript was prepared by Engels in October 1886, but when he became ill, he suggested that the article be completed by the editor of *Die Neue Zeit*, Karl Kautsky. See Piers Beirne, 'Introduction to "Juridical Socialism"' (1977) 7(2) *Politics and Society* 199–201.

rights . . . at first the proletariat had embraced the world view of legal rights, and sought weapons in it for use against the bourgeoisie'.[66]

Engels and Kautsky insisted that:

> Marx . . . presents no legalistic demands at all in his theoretical work. . . . Legal rights, which always reflect the economic conditions of a specific society, are treated only in a very secondary manner in Marx's theoretical studies, as opposed to the primary historical topic of situating particular circumstances, means of acquisition, and social classes in specific periods.[67]

But they also insisted that socialists would not fail to present certain legalistic demands:

> Every struggling class must therefore formulate its demands as legalistic demands within a program . . . however, no existing socialist party has thought of making a new legal philosophy of its program, and this will not happen in the future.

Peter Schöttler explained their position as follows:

> there is indeed *no* proletarian or socialist legal ideology (just as there can be no *socialist philosophy of law*), but there are proletarian, or socialist, *legal demands*, and these are necessary, nay indispensable, if the proletariat wishes to articulate its interests *politically* in opposition to the bourgeoisie and the bourgeois state. The political class struggle includes making legal demands.[68]

In precisely the same sense, Marx and Engels would have had no difficulty in associating themselves with 20th- and 21st-century demands framed within the international law right of people to self-determination.[69]

66 ibid 204.

67 ibid 212.

68 Peter Schöttler, 'Friedrich Engels and Karl Kautsky as Critics of "Legal Socialism"' in Csaba Varga (ed), *Marxian Legal Theory* (New York UP 1993) 11–42, at 28–29.

69 See also Bill Bowring, 'The Soviets and the Right to Self-Determination of the Colonized: Contradictions of Soviet Diplomacy and Foreign Policy in the Era of Decolonization' in Jochen von Bernstorff and Philipp Dann (eds), *The Battle for International Law: South-North Perspectives on the Decolonization Era* (Oxford University Press 2019) 404–25; Bill Bowring, 'Marx, Engels, and Lenin on the Right of Nations (Peoples) to Self-Determination, and Its Impact on International Law' in Paul O'Connell and Umut Özsu (eds), *Elgar Handbook on Law and Marxism* (Edward Elgar 2021); and Bill Bowring, 'Marxist International Law Methodology?' in Rossana Deplano and Nicholas Tsagourias (eds), *Research Methods in International Law: A Handbook* (Edward Elgar 2021) 162–80.

Chapter 10 of Volume 1 of *Capital* was devoted to 'The Working Day'.[70] Three of its seven sections start with the phrase 'the Struggle for a Normal Working Day'. Marx is clear that

> these highly detailed specifications [in the additional Factory Act of 7 June 1844], which regulate, with military uniformity, the times, the limits and the pauses of work by the stroke of the clock, were by no means a product of the fantasy of Members of parliament. They developed gradually out of circumstances as natural laws of the modern mode of production. Their formulation, official recognition and proclamation by the state were the result of a long class struggle.[71]

The Chapter concludes as follows:

> For 'protection' against the serpent of their agonies, the workers have to put their heads together and, as a class, compel the passing of a law, and all-powerful social barrier by which they can be prevented from setting themselves and their families into slavery and death by voluntary contract with capital. In the pace of the pompous catalogue of the 'inalienable rights of man' there steps the modest Magna Carta of the legally limited working day, which at last makes it clear 'when the time which the worker sells is ended, and when his own begins. *Quantum mutatus ab illo!*'[72]

Marx is not writing about 'legal form', but about the class struggle, in which workers take up legal demands.

Law and legislation reappear in Part Eight, 'So-Called Primitive Accumulation', Chapter 27 'The Expropriation of the Agricultural Population from the Land'.[73] Marx describes how between the fifteenth and the sixteenth centuries, 'the English working class was precipitated without any transitional stages from its golden age to its iron age'.[74]

And after the restoration of the monarchy in 1660

> the landed proprietors carried out, by legal means, an act of usurpation which was effected everywhere on the Continent without any legal formality. They abolished the feudal tenure of land, i.e. they got rid of all its obligations to the state, 'indemnified' the state by imposing taxes on the peasantry and the rest of the people, established for themselves the rights

70 Karl Marx Chapter 10 in *Capital. A Critique of Political Economy. Volume 1* (Ben Fowkes tr, Penguin Classics 1990) 340–416.

71 ibid 394–95.

72 ibid 416.

73 ibid 877.

74 ibid 879.

> of modern private property in estates to which they had only a feudal title, and finally, passed those laws of settlement which had the same effect on the English labourer, *mutatis mutandis*, as the edict of the Tartar Boris Godunov had on the Russian peasantry.[75]

So, Marx explains, the 'legal means', or what might now be called 'the legal form', was what distinguished the English usurpation of the peasantry which elsewhere was carried out without such niceties, by force.

Marx was nowhere arguing for the existence of the 'legal form' as a 'materially grounded abstraction' as Pashukanis wanted to assert (see above). The 'legal means' were just the kind of laws against which the English workers had to struggle in the 19th century, and to fight for their reform.

Conclusion

In this chapter I have hoped to show that while working as a Soviet-Russian government legal adviser in Berlin, Pashukanis wrote a completely serious and compelling, even heroic, attempt to do the impossible, namely to propose a Marxist theory of law. A theory of law, according to which, after the October Revolution in Russia civil law would disappear, to be replaced by the law of administration. His recantation in 1930 was painful in the extreme, and, having recanted, he rose to the highest positions in the Soviet legal system, only to be arrested and shot for crimes he could not possibly have committed. His *General Theory* is still the centre of scholarly and political attention, for good reasons. His work repays repeated visits.

In order to make good my own (respectful) interpretation and critique of Pashukanis, by whom I continue to be fascinated, I explored the question of whether there had been a serious debate as to 'legal form' prior to his work primarily in Berlin, in which he referred to German rather than Soviet authors. In order to elucidate my own position, I adopted the distinction between 'natural laws' and 'human laws' upon which Baruch Spinoza insisted. I asserted that this distinction was maintained by his disciples Karl Marx and Friedrich Engels. For them, a key 'natural law' was the 'law of value', which, under capitalism, like the law of gravity in everyday life, governs the activity of capitalists whether they like it or not. My argument was that 'legal form' refers to human laws only, and that neither Marx nor Engels referred to or analysed the 'legal form' or any cognate concept, nor did they feel they needed to do so, or indeed could do so.

75 ibid 883–84. The reference is to the Edict of 1597, by which peasants who had fled from their lords could be pursued for five years and forcibly returned to them when caught.

Chapter 2

Legal Form in the Soviet Dictatorship

Evgeny Pashukanis and his Interlocutors

Anna Lukina[1]

Introduction

Evgeny Pashukanis, the founding father of the theory of the legal form, is, without exaggeration, one of, if not the most, famous Soviet legal theorists in the Western world. This is quite paradoxical since, once celebrated as the foremost legal theorist within the Soviet Union in the mid-1920—early 1930s, in the 1930s he found his position marginalised and himself sentenced to death as an 'enemy of the people'. In this chapter, I attempt to show that Pashukanis' theory was just as unique as his life story, signifying a major break from both his intellectual forefathers and contemporaneous interlocutors. I ultimately turn to the fact that Pashukanis' rapid downfall cannot be reduced to mere chance or political scheming of his rivals, the real reason being that is that his theory presented a significant challenge to the Stalinist political project.

My goal is thus to introduce and critically examine Pashukanis' theory, as well as his place in the Soviet intellectual canon. I shall begin with a short outline of Pashukanis' life. Then, I will proceed with outlining his theory of law as a commodity form, expressed primarily in his seminal work *General Theory of Law and Marxism*[2], which I argue can be deconstructed in the following three theses: the (i) Commodity Form

1 I am indebted to the editors of this volume, Dr Cosmin Cercel, Dr Gian-Giacomo Fusco, and Dr Przemysław Tacik, for their invitation to take part in the project and their editorial work, including the organisation of the Legal Form Workshop (2023) where I discussed an earlier draft of this Chapter, I also thank the audience at the ASEEES (Association for Slavic, East European, and Eurasian Studies) 55th Annual Convention (2023), where I presented this chapter, and Dr Immo Rebitschek in particular for his comments as a discussant. Finally, I am grateful to Dr Alex Green, Professor Kathryn Hendley, and Dr James Ryan for their help in refining the paper. All mistakes remain my own.

2 Evgeny Pashukanis, 'Общая Теория Права и Марксизм' *Избранные произведения по общей теории государства и права* (Наука 1980 [1924]). Translated as Evgenii Pashukanis, 'The General Theory of Law and Marxism' in Peter B Maggs (ed), *Pashukanis: Selected Writings on Marxism and Law* (Academic Press 1980 [1924]).

DOI: 10.4324/9781032724522-3

Thesis (that all law could be read as a regulation of commodity exchange), the (ii) Bourgeois Law Thesis (that all law is bourgeois in nature) and the (iii) Withering Away Thesis (that all law would wither away under communism). Next, I will attempt to put his theory in context by testing the three theses against the theories of Pashukanis' different interlocutors throughout history: Karl Marx and Friedrich Engels, Vladimir Lenin, Petr Stuchka and Andrey Vyshinsky. Reflecting on these differences, I will draw a conclusion about the uniqueness of Pashukanis' approach and indications as to why it was relegated to the sidelines.

Pashukanis Introduced: A Short Biographical Sketch

Early Years

Pashukanis was born in 1891 in a doctor's family.[3] His political views were formed from an early age as his mother was a member of the Bolshevik party since 1903, and his uncle—a famous Bolshevik Martyn Liadov.[4] Pashukanis, following their footsteps, actively took part in all sorts of revolutionary activity,[5] even though early on he aligned himself with the Mensheviks.[6] Upon starting a law degree at the Saint Petersburg University in 1909, he became targeted by the secret police (*okhranka*) and, threatened with exile, had to flee Russia.[7] He continued his legal studies at the University of Munich, where he completed a doctoral dissertation entitled *Statistics of Legal Infractions in Labour Protections* ('*Statistik der Gesetzwidrigkeit im Arbeitsschutz*') in 1914.[8] Later, during World War I, he returned to Russia and found himself in Moscow in the middle of the October Revolution.[9] Shortly afterwards, he took part in the Sushchevsko-Maryinskyi Military Revolutionary Committee and became a member of the Cassation (Appeal) Tribunal of VTSiK, acting as a revolutionary judge.[10] In 1918, Pashukanis joined the Bolshevik party.[11] He spearheaded his academic career by becoming a member of the Socialist

3 Leonid Ratner, 'Жизненный Путь Евгения Брониславовича Пашуканиса' in Evgeny Pashukanis, *Избранные произведения по общей теории государства и права* (Наука 1980) 237.

4 ibid.

5 ibid.

6 Michael Head, 'The Rise and Fall of a Soviet Jurist: Evgeny Pashukanis and Stalinism' (2004) 17 *Canadian Journal of Law and Jurisprudence* 6, 269.

7 Ratner (n 3) 237. Piers Beirne and Robert Sharlet, 'Editors' Introduction' in Evgeny Pashukanis, *Selected Writings on Marxism and Law* (Peter B Maggs tr, Academic Press 1980) 1.

8 Bill Bowring, 'Yevgeniy Pashukanis, His Law and Marxism: A General Theory, and the 1922 Treaty of Rapallo between Soviet Russia and Germany' (2017) 19 *Journal of the History of International Law* 274, 278. Also, Ratner (n 3) 237.

9 Bowring, 'Yevgeniy Pashukanis, His Law and Marxism' (n 8) 278. Head (n 6) 6. Ratner (n 3) 238.

10 ibid.

11 Head (n 6) 6. Ratner (n 3) 238.

(from 1924—Communist) Academy of Social Sciences.[12] He combined his academic work with a career as a civil servant, working in the People's Commissariat for Foreign Affairs in 1920–1923, during which he took part in the preparation of the Rapallo Treaty with Germany[13]

Prominence in the Mid-1920s—Early 1930s

Pashukanis found prominence as a scholar in around 1922, when he and Peteris Stuchka, another famous Soviet jurist and statesman, established a Section of the General Theory of Law and State in the aforementioned Socialist Academy. In 1924, he, in the words of Beirne and Sharlet, 'emerge[d] from relative obscurity'[14] by publishing his most famous work, *General Theory of Law and Marxism* (*'Общая теория права и марксизма'*). As a result of the growing popularity of his work, he gained tremendous influence up to becoming, in 1931, the Director of the Institute of Soviet Construction and Law of the Communist Academy.[15] In the meantime, together with Stuchka and Vladimir Adoratsky, he published the first Soviet Encyclopedia of Law and State during the years 1935–1937.[16] In 1936, Pashukanis took a role in drafting a new 'Stalin's', Constitution of the USSR.[17] The same year, he became the Deputy People's Commissar of Justice.[18]

Downfall

However, just within months of this high point in his career, Pashukanis suffered a rapid downfall. Put under pressure by newly emerging faces of Stalinist jurisprudence, such as the infamous Andrey Vyshinsky, he had already published a number of 'self-criticisms' in 1930, 1934 and 1936 denouncing his previously expressed ideas,[19] culminating in *State and Law Under Socialism* (*'Государство и право при социализме'*) in 1936 where he repudiated central tenets of his theory.[20] But these efforts did not save him. In 1937,

12 Ratner (n 3) 238.

13 Bowring, 'Yevgeniy Pashukanis, His Law and Marxism' (n 8) 278–79. Head (n 6) 6. Ratner (n 3) 238.

14 Beirne and Sharlet (n 7) 2.

15 Bowring, 'Yevgeniy Pashukanis, His Law and Marxism' (n 8) 291. Head (n 6) 6–7.

16 Head (n 6) 7. Ratner (n 3) 238.

17 Bowring, 'Yevgeniy Pashukanis, His Law and Marxism' (n 8) 294. Head (n 6) 7.

18 ibid. Also Ratner (n 3) 239.

19 Head (n 6) 5. Introductory Note at Evgenii Pashukanis, 'State and Law Under Socialism' in *Pashukanis: Selected Writings on Marxism and Law* (Peter B Maggs tr, Academic Press 1980 [1936]) 347.

20 Evgenii Pashukanis, 'State and Law Under Socialism' in Peter B Maggs (ed), *Pashukanis: Selected Writings on Marxism and Law* (Academic Press 1980). See an Introductory Note at ibid 346.

Pashukanis was arrested and later sentenced to death for alleged participation in a 'band of wreckers' and 'Trotsky-Bukharin fascist agents'.[21] On 4 September 1937, Pashukanis was executed.[22] In 1956, in the aftermath of Khruschev's secret speech at the 20th Party Congress that spearheaded the de-Stalinisation, he was posthumously rehabilitated by the Military Collegium of the USSR Supreme Court.[23]

Outline of Pashukanis' Theory of Law

Introductory Remarks: The Three Theses

After examining Pashukanis' life and death, I shall turn to his legacy. I start by giving an overview of Pashukanis' theory of law as a commodity form, primarily explored in his magnum opus, *General Theory of Law and Marxism*. On the most abstract level, Pashukanis' theory of the legal form can be summarised in three theses, which I name the (i) Commodity Form Thesis, the (ii) Bourgeois Law Thesis, and the (iii) Withering Away Thesis. These constitutive parts of Pashukanis' theory will be considered in turn.

Commodity Form Thesis

Law as a Commodity Form

According to Pashukanis' (i) Commodity Form Thesis, law cannot be reduced to mere regulation of social relationships, this regulation 'must assume a legal character'.[24] There is something that should distinguish law from other systems of rules regulating relationships between 'bees and ants',[25] life in 'primitive tribes'[26] and 'technical rules' such as 'train schedules'[27] and rules for 'curing a sick person'.[28] To Pashukanis, the law regulated a distinct kind of social relationship—'the relationship of possessors of commodities',[29] or the commodity exchange. By commodities, Pashukanis referred to 'objects whose concrete multiplicity of useful qualities becomes merely a simple physical covering of the abstract quality of value, and which appears as the

21 Bowring, 'Yevgeniy Pashukanis, His Law and Marxism' (n 8) 294. Head (n 6) 7.
22 Bowring, 'Yevgeniy Pashukanis, His Law and Marxism' (n 8) 294.
23 ibid. Head (n 6) 7. Beirne and Sharlet (n 7) 5. DA Loeber, 'The Rehabilitation of Pashukanis' (1979) 6 The Soviet and Post-Soviet Review 212.
24 Pashukanis, 'The General Theory of Law and Marxism' (n 2) 58.
25 ibid.
26 ibid.
27 ibid 58–59.
28 ibid 60.
29 ibid 61.

ability to be exchanged for other commodities in a definite ratio'.[30] The legal form exists to protect these commodities from appropriation and, therefore, facilitate the commodity exchange by realising the relationship between individuals as 'subjects "whose will rules objects"'.[31] As a result, 'simultaneously with the product of labour assuming the quality of a commodity and becoming the bearer of value, man assumes the quality of a legal subject and becomes the bearer of a legal right'.[32]

Criminal Law as Commodity Exchange

Pashukanis' theory sits most naturally with private law (such as contract and tort law), which is most easily understood as a site of commodity relations. However, the existence of other areas of law—namely criminal law and public law (such as constitutional and administrative law)—is challenging for his theory. Nevertheless, Pashukanis worked hard to integrate these counterexamples into his conceptual schema, notably using two different tactics. With criminal law, he tried to recast the legal rules in question as analogous to the commodity exchange. He located the origins of criminal law in the blood feud. The principle underlying this proto-criminal law, *lex talionis*, involved a literal exchange of 'an eye for an eye and a tooth for a tooth'.[33] Pashukanis wrote that '[this] notion of equivalence, this first purely juridic idea, always has its source in the form of a commodity'.[34] As criminal law developed, self-help was replaced with legally enforced sanctions but the commodity form remains, as 'punishment proportionate to guilt chiefly represents the same form as revenge related to damage'.[35] Therefore, even though as a society we have moved on from retaliation, criminal law, bearing its scars, still assumes a character of commodity exchange.

Public Law as raison d'état

Pashukanis chose a different tactic in relation to public law, where, as he admitted, his 'philosophy faces the greatest difficulties'.[36] To him, public law was built on a different type of interest than the one central to civil law (and, as explained above, criminal law)—'general impersonal state interest' as opposed to 'distinct private interest'.[37] Still, he stuck to his theory of law

30 ibid 75.
31 ibid 75–76.
32 ibid 76.
33 ibid 111.
34 ibid.
35 ibid 120.
36 ibid 73.
37 ibid.

by claiming that '[p]ublic law can exist only as the reflection of the form of private law in the sphere of political organization, or else it ceases to be law'.[38] Pashukanis seemed to favour the latter conclusion, writing that.

> The state as an organization of class domination, and as an organization for the conduct of external wars, does not require legal interpretation and in essence does not allow it. This is where so-called *raison d'etat* (the principle of naked expediency) rules.[39]

As a result, to Pashukanis, 'most of the concepts of private law' have a 'transient and artificial nature',[40] which he addressed precipitating this discussion earlier. Therefore, one can provisionally conclude that Pashukanis, similarly to criminal law, saw public law as law only insofar as it could be reducible to the commodity exchange, therefore, flattening the public/private law divide.[41] In the event that this reinterpretation of public law norms as private law norms could not be done, he denied the former their legal character altogether.

Bourgeois Law Thesis

Consequently, Pashukanis adopted a (ii) Bourgeois Law Thesis—he believed that all law was bourgeois in nature, distinguished from how it appeared in the past before capitalism and would appear in the future under communism. As for the past, he wrote about how early law of 'primitive peoples' and 'even in medieval Europe' was 'underdeveloped', or, as Fuller called them, 'embryonic'[42]– as a result, '[o]nly bourgeois-capitalist society creates all the conditions necessary for the legal element in social relationships to achieve its full realization'.[43] Only in bourgeois society, Pashukanis claimed, were there characteristic distinctions between 'law as an objective norm and law as a power', 'public and private law' and 'man as a private person and man as a member of the political union'.[44] However, perhaps this interpretation of Pashukanis is too strict—in the Preface to the Second Russian Edition of the same work he wrote that, despite the foregoing conclusions, 'a developed and consummate form does not of course exclude undeveloped and rudimentary

38 ibid.
39 ibid 92.
40 ibid 45.
41 As highlighted by Beirne and Sharlet in Beirne and Sharlet (n 7) 10.
42 Lon L Fuller, 'Pashukanis and Vyshinsky: A Study in the Development of Marxian Legal Theory' (1949) 47 *Michigan Law Review* 1157, 1161.
43 Pashukanis, 'The General Theory of Law and Marxism' (n 2) 44.
44 ibid 44–45.

forms, rather to the contrary, it presupposes them'.[45] What is less ambiguous and more interesting for the purpose of this chapter is that Pashukanis made a similar statement about the law's future after capitalism or under communism. Specifically, he contested the idea that the tasks of the Marxist theory of law should be searching for 'other generalising concepts' of 'proletarian law'.[46] He claimed that just like the categories of 'value, capital, profit, etc.' could not be rendered into 'proletarian categories', the 'bourgeois law' could not be transformed into 'proletarian law'.[47] 'Proletarian law' is therefore an oxymoron.

Withering Away Thesis

To continue with the 'future' theme, the above is connected with Pashukanis' (iii) Withering Away Thesis—a belief that the law and state would 'wither away' under communism. This suggests that 'proletarian', 'communist' or 'Soviet' law would exist 'to proclaim the immortality of the legal form since it tries to wrench this form away from those definite historical conditions which enable its full fruition, and to declare it capable of constant renewal'.[48] Instead, Pashukanis claimed that the 'withering away' of the categories of bourgeois law would, under these conditions, signify the withering away of law in general, that is, the gradual disappearance of the juridic element in human relationships.[49] He admitted that some of the aforementioned 'technical rules' would exist under communism.[50] However, these would not be law under Pashukanis' very idiosyncratic definition thereof.

Pashukanis and his Interlocutors

Marx and Engels

Building on and frequently referring to Marx's and Engels's work was critical to every Soviet legal scholar—Pashukanis was not an exception. Tracing Pashukanis' work to its ultimate intellectual origins is even more important considering his veneration as the true heir of Marxist legal philosophy,

45 ibid 44. The legal form in pre-capitalist societies—with emphasis on Roman law in particular—is explored in detail in Gian-Giacomo Fusco, 'Legal Subjectivity and Abstraction. Tracing the Past of the Legal Form' in Cosmin Cercel, Gian-Giacomo Fusco and Przemysław Tacik (eds), *Legal Form: Pashukanis and the Marxist Critique of the Law* (Routledge forthcoming).

46 Pashukanis, 'The General Theory of Law and Marxism' (n 2) 46.

47 ibid.

48 ibid.

49 ibid.

50 ibid 58 ff. As emphasised by me earlier in Anna Lukina, 'Between Exception and Normality: Schmittian Dictatorship and the Soviet Legal Order' (2022) 35 *Ratio Juris* 139, 147.

particularly in the West. I shall test the truth of this connection by looking at whether the three theses identified above match the original Marxist teachings.

As per the (i) Commodity Form Thesis, Pashukanis clearly seems to be influenced by the main tenet of classical Marxism—the distinction between the 'base' of relations and forces of production united in a mode of production and the 'superstructure' they determine and are sustained by, including philosophy, morality, religion and, most importantly for our purposes, law and state.[51] However, the fact that, in Pashukanis' terms, commodity exchange—the capitalist mode of production—determines the superstructure, does not necessarily mean that the superstructure, including law, necessarily needs to regulate this social relation and this social relation alone. As eloquently expressed by Hirst, there are two functions that law performs according to Marxism: the legal regulation of possession 'giv[ing] the existing relations of production in form the form of right' and the legal regulation of the class struggle that 'serves to contain and repress the antagonism of the exploited class within the forms of right legitimated by the order of the state'.[52] The former fits squarely into Pashukanis' definition of law as expressed in the Commodity Form Thesis, while the latter reaches beyond it. Thus, Marx and Engels, unlike Pashukanis, on this understanding, would accept criminal law (without turning it into another form of commodity exchange) and public law (altogether) as law.

Writing about his (ii) Bourgeois Law Thesis, Pashukanis stated that, to Marx, 'the transitional period [between capitalism and communism—addition mine] is characterized by the fact that human relationships will for a time involuntarily be limited by the "*narrow horizon of bourgeois law* [emphasis mine]"'.[53] To that effect, Pashukanis cited Marx's famous passage from the *Critique of the Gotha Programme* (1875).[54] However, despite Pashukanis' claims to the contrary, the actual passage appears more ambiguous. Marx

51 See, for example,

> [M]en enter into definite relations that are indispensable and independent of their will, relations of production which correspond to a definite stage of development of their material productive forces . . . the sum total of these relations constitutes . . . the real foundation on which rises a legal and political superstructure and to which correspond definite forms of social consciousness.

Karl Marx, 'Preface to a Contribution to the Critique of Political Economy' in *Karl Marx and Frederick Engels: Selected Works (I)* (Progress Publishers 1969 [1859]) 503. As mentioned in Maureen E Cain and Alan Hunt, *Marx and Engels on Law* (Academic Press 1979) 52

52 Paul Q Hirst, *On Law and Ideology* (Macmillan 1979) 96.

53 Pashukanis, 'The General Theory of Law and Marxism' (n 2) 46.

54 Karl Marx, 'The Critique of the Gotha Programme' in *The Collected Works of Marx and Engels*, Volume XXIV (London: Lawrence and Wishart 1989 [1891]) 87.

referred not to bourgeois law in general, but to a specific 'bourgeois right'—that 'a given amount of labor in one form is exchanged for an equal amount of labor in another form'.[55] If we take Pashukanis' idiosyncratic view of law that defines law solely in terms of this exchange, these remarks will apply to law are large. However, if one adopts a broader perspective on the law, as per the previous passage, Marx and Engels did, then this 'right' would only represent some, and not all, law. Turning to more specific instances of 'law' that does not resemble the 'bourgeois right' in question, we find ourselves wondering what is 'bourgeois' about the principles underlining it. This is true of criminal law, even if we do not accept Pashukanis' interpretation of it in commodity exchange terms, let alone public law, that Marx and Engels, unlike Pashukanis, still found to be a 'true' example of the legal form.

Despite these conclusions, the final tenet of Pashukanis' thought, his (iii) Withering Away Thesis is, however, in congruence with classical Marxism. The very expression 'withering away' is originated from Engels's oft-quoted statement in *Anti-Dühring* (1878): to him, under communism proper, 'the state is not "abolished", it "withers away"'.[56] One should note, however, that Engels was talking about the *state* [emphasis mine], not *law* [emphasis not mine]. Perhaps then, some legal norms that can exist without the state could persist. To this effect, Johansen reiterates that Marx and Engels 'saw the need for both ordering in the form of administration and regulation . . . [t]hey were clear that some forms of authority in order to organise social life'.[57] These 'forms of authority' might possibly include Pashukanis' 'technical rules' such as the 'train schedules'.[58] It is unclear, however, whether Marx and Engels would refer to such rules as 'law'—the classical Marxist iteration of the Withering Away Thesis is therefore inconclusive and generally tracked in Pashukanis' moves.

Lenin

In October 1917, Bolsheviks aimed to put the agenda laid down by Marx and Engels into practice. This adaptation of classical Marxism to suit the practical needs of revolutionaries is best traced by looking at Vladimir Lenin's *The State and Revolution* (*'Государство и революция'*) (1917), written shortly before the October Revolution. As the title of his work suggests, Lenin was interested in extending Marxist ideas on the role in which the state—and, by extension, legal—machinery would play in transitioning to communism.

55 ibid 86.

56 Frederick Engels, 'Anti-Dühring' in *The Collected Works of Marx and Engels*, Volume XXV (London: Lawrence and Wishart 1987 [1877]) 268.

57 Tormod Jonahsen, 'Law Beyond the Legal Form', in Cosmin Cercel, Gian-Giacomo Fusco, Przemysław Tacik (eds) *Legal Form and the End of Law. Pashukanis' Legacy* (Routledge 2024).

58 Pashukanis, 'The General Theory of Law and Marxism' (n 2) 58–59.

Like with Marx and Engels, it is not clear whether Lenin supported the (i) Commodity Form Thesis, so conclusions have to be drawn from disparate remarks scattered across his works, similarly to Marx and Engels. Most notably, Lenin seems to recognise public law that was labelled as non-law by Pashukanis. Lenin wrote: '[o]f course, bourgeois law in regard to the distribution of consumer goods inevitably presupposes the existence of the bourgeois state, for law is nothing without an apparatus capable of enforcing the observance of the rules of law'.[59] Like Pashukanis, he emphasised the primary role of law as a 'distribution of consumer goods', but seemed to believe that rules that do not directly bear on it (most prominently, rules of the state or public law) are essential to commodity exchange.

Lenin's position on the (ii) Bourgeois Law Thesis remains as ambiguous as Marx's and Engels's. Lenin reinforced the Marxist concept of the 'dictatorship of the proletariat',[60] defining it as a 'special coercive force for the suppression of the bourgeoisie by the proletariat'.[61] Even though he supposedly claimed this dictatorship was 'unrestricted by law',[62] he nevertheless saw, as Beirne and Hunt note, the role of the legal machinery in eradicating the remnants of bourgeois power, suppressing dissent, educating people and fostering discipline, and acquiring control over capital.[63] In addition, Lenin considered law crucial in 'educating' the population by making observance of various social rules a habit.[64] This dovetailed with the advent of Lenin's concept of 'revolutionary legality' that underscored some importance of fidelity law for building a new socialist state, although the extent of this fidelity was a subject of vigorous debate by early Soviet lawyers and statesmen.[65] What is the character of the law in question? It seems to match Marx, Engels, and Pashukanis, as Lenin approvingly cites Marx's aforementioned *Critique*

59 Vladimir Lenin, 'The State and Revolution' in *Collected Works*, Volume XXV (London: Lawrence and Wishart 1974 [1917]) 471.

60 Originally appeared in Marx's *Class Struggles in France, 1848–1850* (1850) to describe the transitional period between capitalism and communism. Karl Marx, 'The Class Struggles in France, 1848–1850', *The Collected Works of Marx and Engels*, Volume X (London: Lawrence and Wishart 1978 [1850]) 127.

61 Lenin, 'The State and Revolution' (n 59) 397.

62 Attributed to Lenin by Stalin, but not contained verbatim in the text of *The State and Revolution* itself. Joseph Stalin, 'Foundations of Leninism ('The Dictatorship of the Proletariat')' in *J. V. Stalin: Works* (Foreign Languages Publishing House 1953 [1924]) 118.

63 Piers Beirne and Alan Hunt, 'Law and the Constitution of Soviet Society: The Case of Comrade Lenin' in Piers Beirne (ed), *Revolution in Law—Contributions to the Development of Soviet Legal Theory, 1917–1938* (Routledge 1990) 72–77.

64 Lenin, 'The State and Revolution' (n 59) 474. *See also* my analysis in Anna Lukina, 'Legal Nurturing: The Educational Function of Law in the Soviet Union' (2021) 2(18) *The Ideology and Politics Journal* 57, 62–63. More thoughts on this paradox can be found in my article on the topic. Lukina, 'Between Exception and Normality' (n 50) 144–45.

65 Vladimir Gsovski, *Soviet Civil Law: Comparative Survey* (University of Michigan Law School 1948) 160 ff.

of the Gotha Programme passage about the 'narrow horizon of *bourgeois* [emphasis mine] law',[66] adding that 'under communism there remains for a time not only bourgeois law, but even the bourgeois state'.[67]

As for the (iii) Withering Away Thesis; Lenin's stance was slightly different from Marx's and Engels's, as well as Pashukanis'. While Lenin envisioned the Communist society 'without any rules of law',[68] he nevertheless saw such a society operated by the 'rules of social intercourse' that would be followed without coercion imposed by the state, as some 'individual excesses' would be dealt with 'by the armed people themselves'.[69] It is hard to say whether these rules would be recognised as law by Pashukanis, however, one can see some indication of that in the example Lenin uses. Lenin wrote about the 'crowd of civilised people . . . interfer[ing] to put a stop to a scuffle or to prevent a woman from being assaulted'.[70] These are situations that appear to be regulated by criminal law, which Pashukanis recognised as law. Therefore, some laws will remain. Moreover, Lenin clearly did not see these rules as regulating commodity exchange, which is yet another significant difference from Pashukanis.

Stuchka

Once the October Revolution was over, it was the time to build a 'dictatorship of the proletariat' that Lenin sought. Enter Peteris (or Petr) Stuchka, Lenin's right hand in building state power in preparation for communism. Stuchka initially was one of the first Commissars (Ministers) of Justice, designing a range of laws for the new Soviet state. Later, he established himself as a theoretical authority on Soviet law, his most famous work on the subject being *The Revolutionary Role of Law and State* ('*Революционная роль права и государства*') (1921). It is particularly interesting that Stuchka, who would soon become Pashukanis' main interlocutor and critic, maintained a charitable and friendly demeanour towards his fellow jurist by encouraging his work and, according to Sharlet, Maggs and Beirne, 'helped raise Pashukanis from academic obscurity to the forefront of the "revolution of law"'.[71]

66 Lenin, 'The State and Revolution' (n 59) 471.
67 ibid.
68 Vladimir Lenin, 'The State' in *Soviet Legal Philosophy* (Hugh W Babb tr, Harvard UP 1951 [1919, 1929]) 15.
69 Lenin, 'The State and Revolution' (n 59) 464. '*See also* Vladimir Lenin, 'Report on Subbotniks Delivered to a Moscow City Conference of the R.C.P.(B.)' in *Lenin: Collected Works*, Volume XXX (Progress Publishers 1970 [1919]) 84. As noted by me in Lukina, 'Between Exception and Normality' (n 50) 175.
70 Lenin, 'The State and Revolution' (n 59) 464.
71 Robert Sharlet Peter B Maggs, and Piers Beirne, 'P.I. Stuchka and Soviet Law' in Piers Beirne (ed), *Revolution in Law—Contributions to the Development of Soviet Legal Theory, 1917–1938* (Routledge 1990) 52.

Let us proceed to the differences between Stuchka's and Pashukanis' theories. Stuchka, unlike his predecessors, gave a definite answer on whether the (i) Commodity Form Thesis is a valid one. He even went so far as to produce a definition of law as a 'system (or order) of social relationships which corresponds to the interests of the dominant class and is safeguarded by the organised force of this class'.[72] This is a broader notion of law than the one articulated by Pashukanis, and, on a certain reading Marx, Engels and Lenin, as it includes not only law regulating the commodity exchange, but 'social relationships' in general. This is confirmed by his recognition of two types of law—one stemming from the 'sectional, private interest' (similar to what Pashukanis conceived of as law proper) and one consisting of 'technical rules of purely administrative nature'[73] (what Pashukanis denied was law.)

Therefore, Stuchka was not bound to say that all law of the transitional period was bourgeois, as the leeway he gave himself in his definition and taxonomy of law allowed him to carve out a distinctive space for socialist law, rejecting the (ii) Bourgeois Law Thesis. As many scholars highlight, Stuchka saw a space for distinctively 'Soviet', or 'proletarian', law which was markedly different from bourgeois law.[74] However, this should not be overclaimed, as this idea appeared in Stuchka's writings only in an embryonic form. In fact, Stuchka mentioned 'Soviet law' in *The Revolutionary Role of Law and State* only in passing.[75] He further elaborated on this idea in his subsequent *Encyclopedia of State and Law* (1925–1927) entry on Soviet law which he defined as 'the law of the transitional period from capitalism to communism, from class society to classless society'[76] but his thoughts on such law's character appear inconclusive. On the one hand, he described the Soviet state as a '*new* [emphasis mine] type of state power'.[77] However, just a few paragraphs later, he appears to agree with Lenin's assessment of future Soviet law as being 'bourgeois law, but without bourgeoisie'.[78] Stuchka's position and its relation to those advanced by his predecessors and contemporaries is therefore more unclear than it might initially seem.

72 Petr Stuchka, 'The Revolutionary Part Played by Law and the State: A General Doctrine of Law' in *Soviet Legal Philosophy* (Hugh W Babb tr, Harvard University Press 1951 [1921]) 20.

73 ibid 51.

74 See, for example, Robert Sharlet, 'Stalinism and Soviet Legal Culture' in Robert C Tucker (ed), *Stalinism: Essays in Historical Interpretation* (Transaction Publishers 1999) 158–60. Sharlet, Maggs and Beirne (n 71) 50. I claimed it myself in Lukina, 'Between Exception and Normality' (n 50) 146.

75 Stuchka 'The Revolutionary Part Played by Law and the State' (n 73) 66–67. As cited in Sharlet, Maggs and Beirne (n 71) 50.

76 Petr Stuchka, 'Soviet Law' in Robert Sharlet, Peter B Maggs and Piers Beirne (trs), *Selected Writings on Soviet Law and Marxism* (Routledge 2015 [1925–1927]) 162.

77 ibid.

78 ibid 163. Citing Lenin, 'The State and Revolution' (n 59) 467, 671.

Finally, Stuchka still retained the Marxist fidelity to the (iii) Withering Away Thesis. He saw Soviet law as necessary for the transition from capitalism to communism, the endpoint of this transition still being in sight. This is proven by the fact that Stuchka repeatedly referred to Soviet law as the law of a transitional period in his *Encyclopedia* entry.[79] In that sense, his theory tracked the previous writings of Marx, Engels and Lenin, and was similar to the subsequent writings of Pashukanis.

Vyshinsky

Just as Lenin found his ally in the theoretical and practical development of the law in Stuchka, Stalin's rise to power brought a new name into the legal arena—Andrey Vyshinsky, commonly known as the prosecutor in the Moscow Show Trials[80]—to build socialism in one country. Vyshinsky was not only a reformer and legal practitioner, but also a highly influential legal scholar, and one of Pashukanis' contemporaneous opponents in the 1930s. Unlike Stuchka, Pashukanis' earlier interlocutor, Vyshinsky was hardly sympathetic to Pashukanis' stance on law and state, his interactions with the scholar bursting with invective characteristics of the Stalinist era. He was, also, as noted before, instrumental in Pashukanis' demise in 1937. While keeping this in mind, I however, argue that this personal animus should not affect our conclusion as to whether we ought to treat Vyshinsky's contributions seriously as part of the legal-theoretical canon. I posit that his theory should, likewise, be assessed on merit.

Let us thus examine the three theses in relation to Vyshinsky. As for the (i) Commodity Form Thesis, Vyshinsky rejected it by embracing a broader view similar to that of Stuchka. His famous definition of law, reproduced in *The Law of the Soviet State* (1948), read as follows:

> the totality (a) of the rules of conduct, expressing the will of the dominant class and established in legal order, and (b) of customs and rules of community life sanctioned by state authority—their application being guaranteed by the compulsive force of the state in order to guard, secure, and

79 Stuchka, 'Soviet Law' (n 76) 162 ff.

80 Vyshinsky played many roles in the Stalinist Soviet Union. In the 1924, he served as a Rector of Moscow University and later—as a judge in early show trials. Becoming a Procurator General of the RSFSR in 1931, he then assumed the offices of the First Deputy Procurator General of the USSR in 1933 and the Procurator General himself in 1935. In 1939, he became the Deputy Chairman of the Soviet People's Commissariat in 1939, and the Commissar (and then Minister) for Foreign Affairs in 1940–1953. Since then and before his death in 1954, he served as the Soviet Union's Permanent Representative to the United Nations. He was also the director of the Academy of Sciences of the Institute of State and Law in the USSR.

> develop social relationships and social orders advantageous and agreeable to the dominant class.[81]

This definition like Stuchka's, did not only include what Pashukanis deemed law proper and was capacious enough to include both 'outliers' to Pashukanis' theory—criminal and public law. This is also proven by Vyshinsky's earlier remarks in his *The Fundamental Tasks of the Science of Soviet Socialist Law* (*'Основные задачи науки советского социалистического права'*) (1938), a speech to the First Congress on Problems of the Sciences of Soviet State and Law, in which he laid down the agenda for the future of academic studies of law in the Soviet Union. Vyshinsky claimed that law could not be reduced to 'economics' (the reduction he attributed to Stuchka—although it works against Pashukanis' Commodity Form Theory as well) or 'politics' (which can be read against Pashukanis' description of public law as *raison d'etat*.[82])

Moreover, Vyshinsky continued Stuchka's project by recognising—and valorising—distinctive Soviet law, rejecting the (ii) Bourgeois Law Thesis. Most of his venom towards Pashukanis—whom he repeatedly mentioned by name alongside other scholars he deemed 'wreckers'—was directed at that Thesis. In *The Fundamental Tasks of the Science of Soviet Socialist Law*, Vyshinsky said, after recounting the (ii) Bourgeois Law Thesis under which the Soviet law is seen as bourgeois law, and law itself—a bourgeois category, that, to the contrary, 'law is elevated under socialism to the highest stage of its development'.[83] He stated, '[i]t is not the epoch of imperialism—it is the epoch of socialism—that is the epoch most favourable for the development—and for the triumph of socialist legality'.[84] Therefore, as Fuller remarked, Vyshinsky thought of Soviet law as being not only distinct from, but 'bigger, better, and purer'[85] than bourgeois law.

Vyshinsky, in line with the Marxist-Leninist tradition, could not abandon the (iii) Withering Away Thesis entirely, as he had to appeal to the authority of Marx, Engels and Lenin and minimise any potential friction. Therefore, like his predecessors, he talks about Soviet law as a temporary arrangement.[86] However, for him, that was a more far-fetched possibility.[87] Vyshinsky said that Soviet law would be obsolete not simply when the economic transformation occurs, but when capitalism is 'annihilated . . . in human consciousness'.[88]

81 Andrey Vyshinsky, *The Law of the Soviet State* (Hugh W Babb tr, Macmillan 1948) 50.
82 Andrey Vyshinsky, 'Fundamental Tasks of Soviet Law' in *Soviet Legal Philosophy* (Hugh W Babb tr, Harvard University Press 1951) 329.
83 ibid 328.
84 ibid.
85 Fuller (n 42) 1163.
86 Vyshinsky, *The Law of the Soviet State* (n 81) 52.
87 I write about it in Lukina, 'Between Exception and Normality' (n 50) 149–150. The following is a paraphrase of my conclusions there.
88 Vyshinsky, *The Law of the Soviet State* (n 81) 50.

As Fuller noted, by doing so Vyshinsky 'implies that this transformation of man's nature is a long way off; the withering will be a very slow process'.[89] Moreover, the incorporation of the (iii) Withering Away Thesis into Vyshinsky's thought is further complicated by the fact that, according to Fuller, unlike Pashukanis, he did not see morality disappearing under communism, but, on the contrary, moral conviction becoming so strong that legal coercion is not needed.[90] This makes his stance similar to Marx's and Engel's readiness to abandon the state—and not law—under communism and Lenin's admission that 'rules of social intercourse' would operate even in a post-transition society, both points underappreciated by Stuchka and especially Pashukanis. Like those rules, the moral precepts in question might be seen as law—just not the kind of law Pashukanis talks about. This reaffirms Johansen's insight that 'after the end of the legal form we will find the law'.[91]

Key Takeaways

Table 2.1 therefore summarises the results of the comparison between Pashukanis' theory of law and similar theories of his predecessors and contemporaries. As a result, one can draw the following conclusions. *Firstly*, the (i) Commodity Form Thesis is an idiosyncratic feature of Pashukanis' account, and cannot be found in Marx and Engels, whom Pashukanis appeals to, let alone Lenin and two Soviet jurists I survey—Pashukanis and Vyshisnky. Pashukanis' stance on the law as necessarily regulating commodity exchange is not authentically Marxist. Moreover, it was probably not shared by Pashukanis' interlocutors as, per Cercel, it presented a 'blind spot' in relation to public law in particular, since 'by reducing the experience of the legal form to its ability to code and support relations of production, Pashukanis obfuscate[d] the nexus between repression and ideological interpellation that is at the core of the operation of the law'.[92] Public law was an important part not just of understanding the bourgeois law, but law in general, including Soviet law which could not abandon it as a particularly important tool of state-building.

Secondly, the (ii) Bourgeois Law Thesis, while more in line with classical Marxism than the aforementioned (i) Commodity Form Thesis, was still contested. Both Stuchka and Vyshisnky seemed to reject it. I think that this fact can be attributed to historical reasons. Both Stuchka and Vyshinsky were reformers aiming to put the (respectively) Leninist and Stalinist visions of law

89 Fuller (n 42) 1163.

90 ibid.

91 Johansen, 'Law Beyond the Legal Form' (n 57).

92 Cosmin Cercel, 'Impossible Objects of Marxist Legal Theory of Law: The Limits of the Legal Form' in Cosmin Cercel, Gian-Giacomo Fusco and Przemysław Tacik (eds), *Legal Form: Pashukanis and the Marxist Critique of the Law* (Routledge 2024)?

Table 2.1 Pashukanis' Theory of Law in Comparison

	Marx and Engels	*Lenin*	*Stuchka*	*Pashukanis*	*Vyshinsky*
(i) Commodity Form Thesis	○	○	○	●	○
(ii) Bourgeois Law Thesis	◐	●	◐	●	○
(iii) Withering Away Thesis	●	◐	●	●	◐

in practice. Even though these visions were different, Vyshinsky and Stuchka both saw the necessity for law for establishing and governing a large-scale enterprise of the Soviet state, even though they recognised its ultimate point as accelerating the 'withering away' of the law and state (as per the (iii) Withering Away Thesis) altogether. This is particularly relevant when it comes to Vyshinsky, who built his theory on an explicit rejection of Pashukanis' writings in the service of Stalin's new 'socialism in one country' policy, as further elaborated in my previous work on the topic.[93] The Soviet state ultimately needed law—as per Berman:

> Without a legal system and a legal order—without Law with a capital L—the Stalinist regime could neither control the social relations of the people nor keep the economy going nor command the political forces in the country as a whole.[94]

Thirdly, the (iii) Withering Away Thesis itself was the least controversial pronouncement made by Pashukanis as all of the surveyed theorists, in some shape or form, recognised the ultimate 'withering away' of the state. However, as noted in the preceding paragraph, this 'withering away' gradually became a justification for not getting rid of the state, but for strengthening it, culminating in Vyshinsky's 're-fetishisation of law'. Therefore, even though Pashukanis was an enthusiastic supporter of the (iii) Withering Away Thesis, the same Thesis later led to his demise.

Concluding Remarks: Pashukanis and Law's Necessity

The preceding sections tried to introduce Pashukanis' theory of the legal form by providing an account of his life and work, breaking down his theory into three theses the (i) Commodity Form Thesis, the (ii) Bourgeois Law

93 Lukina, 'Between Exception and Normality' (n 50).

94 Harold J Berman, *Justice in the U.S.S.R.: An Interpretation of Soviet Law* (Harvard University Press 1963) 64.

Thesis and the (iii) Withering Away Thesis, and comparing his theory with the visions of law of both his predecessors and contemporaries—Marx and Engels, Lenin, Stuchka and Vyshinsky. I argued that Pashukanis' theory represented an innovation in, more broadly, Communist and, more specifically, Soviet legal thought as it defined law narrowly to mean only law that regulates commodity exchange (as per the (i) Commodity Exchange Thesis) and subsequently claimed that the law of the transitional period between capitalism and communism could only have a bourgeois character (as per the (ii) Bourgeois Law Thesis). Moreover, these two features of Pashukanis' account of law sit rather uneasily with the practical needs of a socialist state both in itself and as a transitional stage before communism (as per the (iii) Withering Away Thesis). In my view, the ultimate demise of Pashukanis' theory of law—and Pashukanis himself—was rooted in this inability to comprehend the necessity of law for a state, even a Communist one, to stay in power.

Chapter 3

On the Lithuanian Question

Contextualising Pashukanis' Critique of the Legal Form

Eric Loefflad

Where Does the Legal Form Theorist Write From?

When accounting for the 'legal form' and the links it forges between material and juridical realities, an understandable entry point is Karl Marx's 1843 text 'On the Jewish Question'.[1] Here, Marx famously exposed the false dichotomy that shaped contemporary debates on cultural autonomy versus 'emancipation' via liberal citizenship as the appropriate path for European Jews.[2] Regarding the latter option, despite celebratory affirmations to the contrary, promises of 'emancipation' were premised on an empty view of the individual as an abstract rights-holder—a consciousness limiting one's ability to comprehend the indispensable materialist foundations of social relations.[3] While this assertion has set the stage for much Marxian engagement with questions of law, rights, and the legal form,[4] others have focused on what this text means in relation to Jewish identity/destiny, antisemitism, Marx's own Jewish heritage, and the many connections between these matters.[5] The many embedded roles performed by ideas of Jewishness leave no shortage of interpretive possibilities.[6] Moreover, these issues, as they pertained to Marx's time, only became exponentially more complex by the subsequent

1 Karl Marx, 'On the Jewish Question' in Robert C Tucker (ed), *The Marx-Engels Reader* (2nd edn, Norton 1978) 26.
2 ibid 27.
3 ibid 43–45.
4 See for example, Andrew Vincent, 'Marx and Law' (1993) 20 *J Law and Soc'y* 371; Brad Roth, 'Marxian Insights for the Human Rights Project' in Susan Marks (ed), *International Law on the Left: Re-examining Marxist Legacies* (CUP 2008) 220.
5 Shlomo Avineri, 'Marx and Jewish Emancipation' (1964) 25 *J Hist of Ideas* 445; Joel Kovel, 'Marx on the Jewish Question' (1983) 8 Dialectical Anthropology 31; Michael Maidan, 'Marx on the Jewish Question: A Meta-Critical Analysis' (1987) 33 *Stud Soviet Thought* 27; Robert Fine, 'Rereading Marx on the "Jewish Question": Marx as a Critic of Antisemitism?' in Marcel Stoetzler (ed), *Antisemitism and the Constitution of Sociology* (University of Nebraska Press 2014) 137; Chad Alan Goldberg, 'The Two Marxes: From Jewish Domination to Supersession of the Jews' (2015) 15 *J Classical Sociology* 415.
6 Adam Sutcliffe, *What Are Jews For? History, Peoplehood, and Purpose* (Princeton UP 2020).

DOI: 10.4324/9781032724522-4

advent of the Holocaust, the rise of international human rights law, and the seemingly intractable Palestinian-Israeli Conflict.[7] In taking these matters seriously, what would it mean to theorise Marx's ideas, through Marx's own methods, in relation to how the material force of ethnic categorisation (Marx's and beyond) shapes the production of ideas that, in turn, justify material realities?

Posing this multi-layered question invites numerous subsequent questions on the many interplays between positionality, materiality, and temporality—especially as it challenges the Marxist quest to expose social contradictions in the name of achieving true human emancipation. Regardless of how grand one's formulation might be, the formulator always articulates ideas from a very specific place and time that are seamlessly embedded within the totality they seek to depict.[8] On this point, how is the scholar to consider truth-destabilising 'genealogical anxiety' and truth-affirming 'genealogical luck' as it relates to both the specifics of their subject of inquiry and how they might filter their knowledge of said subject through their own lens of genealogical inheritance?[9] This notion of particularity in relation to broader categories only becomes more complex when questions of law and legal form are brought to bear on this task. After all law, through its construction of 'personality', is an active component in the social process that animates the meaning of perceived human difference on a deep material level.[10] How then should this inquiry confront the way in which law's resilience, resurgence, and reproduction across varied spatial and temporal contexts requires a suitably appropriate method of historicisation.[11] This issue of juridical persistence is especially pertinent if the basis of 'law' is understood to be the 'legal form'.[12]

As a means of uncovering the varied manifestations of material context that might enable more thorough approaches to these questions, my focus in this chapter is on Evgeny Pashukanis and how his theory of the legal form

7 Tony Kushner, *The Holocaust and the Liberal Imagination: A Social and Cultural History* (Wiley-Blackwell 1994); Robert Meister, *After Evil: A Politics of Human Rights* (Columbia UP 2011); Stephen Friedman, *Good Jew, Bad Jew: Racism, Anti-Semitism and the Assault on Meaning* (Wits UP 2023).

8 Richard Drayton, 'Where Does the World Historian Write From? Objectivity, Moral Conscience and the Past and Present of Imperialism' (2011) 46 *J Contemp Hist* 671; Richard Drayton and David Motadel, 'Discussion: The Futures of Global History' (2018) 13 *J Global Hist* 1.

9 Amia Srinivasan, 'Genealogy, Epistemology and Worldmaking' (2019) 119 *Proc Aristotelian Soc'y* 127.

10 Colin Dayan, *The Law Is a White Dog: How Legal Rituals Make and Unmake Persons* (Princeton UP 2013).

11 Edward Cavanagh, 'Legal Thought and Empires: Analogies, Principles, and Authorities from the Ancients to the Moderns' (2019) 10 *Jurisprudence* 463.

12 Rafał Mańko, 'Legal Survivals and the Resilience of Juridical Form' (2023) *L Critq* 1.

might be interpreted through his Lithuanian heritage. While it certainly occupies a less prominent place than the 'Jewish Question' within present consciousness, the 'Lithuanian Question' nevertheless raised many interesting issues of history, identity, and rights emblematic of the greater late-nineteenth and early-twentieth century 'Age of Questions'.[13] Although there is minimal direct evidence of Pashukanis' thoughts on Lithuanian nationalism (a highly indeterminate designation in and of itself), it is reasonable to assume he would have been familiar with the many discourses on nationality that defined his contexts of engagement. Beyond his own discrete identity, Pashukanis' time was one of intensive debate within Marxist circles on whether independent statehood via the 'right of nations to self-determination' was or was not a demand of revolutionary praxis.[14] As these debates deeply implicated questions of legal form—whether individual, collective, or in relational conjunction—Pashukanis had much to consider. It is highly unlikely he was able to conclusively exclude the immanent reality of his own identity from this process. As such, Pashukanis' Lithuanian heritage, and the depths of its context in relation to his legal form theory, provide a profound opportunity for exploring how the materiality of the region deemed 'Eastern Europe' contributed to the production of grand (but under-theorised) jurisprudential innovations, an analysis made exceptionally fitting by Pashukanis' tireless commitment to materialist critique.

In this effort to theorise Pashukanis through Lithuania and Lithuania through Pashukanis, it is vital from the onset to realise that 'Lithuania' as it is currently understood is not what it was in Pashukanis' formative contexts of influence. Today Lithuania is typically conceptualised as a small nation of approximately two million inhabitants in northeastern Europe that, alongside Latvia and Estonia, is one of the three Baltic states. However, given the immense historical and cultural differences between these three nations, the term 'state' performs a tremendous degree of work in affirming the 'Baltic states' as a coherent unifying category. As Anatol Lieven noted in his seminal study of Lithuanian, Latvian, and Estonian independence through the broad historical and international contexts, there is nothing that can be called a common identity-based 'Baltic region'.[15] Lithuanian and Latvian are the only two remaining members of the Baltic branch of the Indo-European language family, while Estonian is a non-Indo-European Finno-Ugric language. Lithuania is predominantly Roman Catholic whereas Latvia and Estonia are

13 Holly Case, *The Age of Questions: Or, A First Attempt at an Aggregate History of the Eastern, Social, Woman, American, Jewish, Polish, Bullion, Tuberculosis, and Many Other Questions over the Nineteenth Century, and Beyond* (Princeton UP 2018).

14 Michael V Kryukov, 'Self-Determination from Marx to Mao' (1996) 19 *Ethnic and Racial Stud* 352.

15 Anatol Lieven, *The Baltic Revolution Estonia, Latvia, Lithuania, and the Path to Independence* (2nd edn, Yale UP 1994) xxxv.

predominantly Lutheran. The lands of present-day Latvia and Estonia were long the domains of German and Scandinavian lords whereas Lithuania was a part of the vast Polish-Lithuanian Commonwealth that, even when distinguished from the Polish Crownlands, was many times its current size.[16] Yet despite Lithuania's greater historical connections to present-day Belarus, Ukraine, and Poland,[17] the great unifying facet of Lithuania, Latvia, and Estonia as the three 'Baltic states' are shared issues relating to their international legal personality via independence in 1919, long-term Soviet occupation beginning in 1940, and restored statehood in 1990.[18] In this sense, the common grouping of Lithuania, Latvia, and Estonia despite their great differences is a testament to the substance-evading qualities of the very legal form theorised by Pashukanis.[19]

Part I of this chapter explores how Pashukanis' *General Theory* can be interpreted as a call for historical sociology-focused accounts of law. While there are many options for this undertaking, I argue that an especially productive exploration can be made regarding Pashukanis' Lithuanian background in relation to his efforts to materially theorise law at the level of form. Part II then explores this background through a high-altitude overview of the origins, functions, and legacies of the unique juridical entity deemed the Polish-Lithuanian Commonwealth that defined Pashukanis' formative context. From here, Part III turns to the debate on the nature of law between Pashukanis and his fellow Soviet jurist Pēteris Stučka and how this can be understood in relation to their respective Lithuanian and Latvian backgrounds—identities whose connections were increasingly forged by nationalist activists in the late-nineteenth and early-twentieth centuries. Finally, Part IV shows how, in light of Stučka's critique, Lithuanian history—especially as it was inseparably connected to Poland *and* fundamentally distinct from Latvia—might explain why Pashukanis was so dedicated to a totalising critique of law that defied Stučka's comprehension.

16 Darius Staliūnas, *Spatial Concepts of Lithuania in the Long Nineteenth Century* (Academic Studies Press 2016).

17 Timothy Snyder, *The Reconstruction of Nations: Poland, Ukraine, Lithuania, Belarus 1569–1999* (Yale UP 2003).

18 See Ineta Ziemele, *State Continuity and Nationality: The Baltic States and Russia—Past, Present and Future as Defined by International Law* (Brill 2005); Lauri Mälksoo, *Illegal Annexation and State Continuity: The Case of the Incorporation of the Baltic States by the USSR* (2nd edn, Brill 2022); Evgeny Tikhonravov, 'The International Community's Reaction to the Soviet Annexation of the Baltic Republics: The Recognition Dilemma' (2023) 70 *Neth Intl L Rev* 251.

19 While this chapter focuses on Lithuania and Latvia, this should not discount Estonia's incredibly rich tradition of legal thought, see Lauri Mälksoo, 'The Science of International Law and the Concept of Politics: The Arguments and Lives of the International Law Professors at the University of Dorpat/Iur'ev/Tartu 1855–1985' (2005) 76 *Brit Yb Intl L* 383.

What Does the *General Theory* Demand of Our Analysis?

In devising his theory of law as the 'legal form' that only arises through capitalism's dominance, Pashukanis lambasts the specific way in which the field of jurisprudence, unique amongst disciplines, cannot but abstract its analysis from its primary subject matter.[20] While he proffered the theory of legal form as the specific configuration of commodity-exchange enabling abstracted personality (and ideological acceptance thereof) as a means of transcending this distortion,[21] this led him to confront a secondary barrier in the form of the substantively empty 'state' that grants an illusory coherence to positivist jurisprudence.[22] Building on his observation that positivism represented an even greater coherence regression than the natural law it sought to supersede, the positivist jurist, '[f]or, so long as he remains a jurist, . . . starts from the concept of the state as an autonomous force, set apart from all other individual and social forces'.[23] When confronted with this problem of the abstracted autonomous state as the perpetual concealer of consciousness surrounding the legal form and its constitutive effect on material reality, Pashukanis' *General Theory* can be read as a call for extensive research on the historical sociology of law/the legal form and its constitutive effects on concrete social relations. This necessarily entails a materialist account of the abstracted state and how its multiplicity in the international realm is ordered according to a specific logic of sovereignty/sovereign equality that proclaims a general duty of substantive ignorance in the name of 'non-intervention'.[24] Through such an account, according to Pashukanis, the theorist can directly confront the ways in which legal positivism inevitably and perpetually reproduces '[a] certain discrepancy between legal truth and the truth to which historical and sociological research aspires'.[25]

However, despite the clarity of his overall theoretical thrust and numerous historical illustrations (particularly on the contrast between feudal authority and modern legality), using Pashukanis to craft a historical sociology of the legal form raises many questions of method. This is especially true when the application of Pashukanis is viewed in conjunction with efforts to merge Marxian historical sociologies of the transition to capitalism with insights from the fields of International Relations ('IR') and international

20 Evgeny Pashukanis, *Law and Marxism: A General Theory* (Barbara Einhorn tr, Chris Arthur, ed, Pluto Press 1989) 49.

21 ibid 59.

22 ibid 146–48.

23 ibid 147.

24 Anthony Carty, *The Decay of International Law: A Reappraisal of the Limits of Legal Imagination in International Affairs* (Manchester UP 2019) 137–40.

25 Pashukanis, *General Theory* (n 20) 147.

law.[26] While such endeavours are concerned with the origins of the modern state in relation to the origins of the modern states-system, Pashukanis' commodity-form theory of law has generated much controversy on this front. Famously, China Miéville applied Pashukanis' frame to international law to show how this regime's lack of centralised authority illustrates law's operation at the level of form in that sovereign states are akin the individual private law subjects—that is, formally equal units in a system defined by substantive inequality.[27] However, for Anthony Carty, reifying the absolute character of the sovereign state acts as a Hegelian path for reproducing the presumptions of nineteenth-century positivists and their exclusion of premodern and non-Western thought.[28] For Susan Marks, the commodity-form theory's all-encompassing logic does not sufficiently account for the 'public cultural dimensions' of base-level social change that ultimately manifests as international legality.[29] More recently, Maia Pal argued that the commodity-form theory 'fails to account for pre- and non-capitalist legal agency or for legal relations occurring during the process of transition as autonomous from or contesting the process of capitalist transition'.[30] Additionally, Robert Knox though a proponent of legal form analysis, claims that Mieville's framing does not adequately account for the constitutive relationship between racialisation and capital accumulation on a broad world-historical scale.[31]

Compounding these many debates on the present value of Pashukanis, there is also the way in which broader contested debates on the transition to capitalism can shape which histories and/or legal traditions one looks to when accounting for the origins of the legal form. If one adheres to Immanuel Wallerstein's location of capitalist origins in the increasing volume and scale of sixteenth-century commerce[32] then one is apt to study the Roman law traditions and its formative provision of juridical linkages that proved more than capable of surviving and adapting long after the fall of the Roman

26 Only recently have there been concerted efforts to merge Maxian IR theory with Marxian international legal theory, see Eric Loefflad, 'Unpartitionable: CH Alexandrowicz, Sovereign Divisibility, and the Longue Durée of the Polish-Lithuanian Commonwealth' (2023) 24 *German LJ* 912, 916–20.

27 China Mieville, *Between Equal Rights: A Marxist Theory of International Law* (Haymarket Books 2005) 117–51.

28 Anthony Carty, 'Marxist International Law Theory as Hegelianism' (2008) 10 *Intl Stud Rev* 122, 124.

29 Susan Marks, 'International Judicial Activism and the Commodity-Form Theory of International Law' (2007) 18 *EJIL* 199, 207.

30 Maia Pal, *Jurisdictional Accumulation: An Early Modern History of Law, Empires, and Capital* (CUP 2020) 81.

31 Robert Knox, 'Valuing Race? Stretched Marxism and the Logic of Imperialism' (2016) 4 *Lond Rev Intl L* 81, 100–1.

32 Immanuel Wallerstein, *The Modern World-System I: Capitalist Agriculture and the Origins of the European World-Economy in the Sixteenth Century* (University of California Press 2011).

Empire.[33] The power of Roman law as a widely recognised medium of commercial transaction unmoored from state authority was certainly not lost on Pashukanis.[34] Conversely, if one adheres to the narrative of 'Political Marxism' that capitalism resulted from contingent class configurations purely internal to England,[35] then the particularities of English Common Law and Constitutional history must be of indispensable importance.[36] Here, the view of Hobbesian absolutism as the grounding of universal rights—via its transcending of the substantive particularities of tradition-based medieval constitutionalism impeccably resonates with Pashukanis' view that the abstraction of the 'legal person' from their substantive material conditions is vital to enabling commodity-exchange via the legal form.[37] If one takes a more integrative approach, such as Alexander Anievas and Kerem Nişancıoğlu's application of 'uneven and combined development',[38] then world legal systems, and how their deep interactions paradoxically shaped their proclaimed particularities, must be of great importance.[39] This can easily bring matters of comparative law, and its many complications (especially from a critical perspective), into the analytical matrix.[40]

Given the risks of entropy in this outward radiation of analytical complexity, approaching these issues through Pashukanis' own material contexts in relation to his materialist theory provides something of an anchor in this vast sea of possibility. Fortunately, as a prelude to this exploration, recent scholarship enables an array of new insights into how the ideas of leading jurists might be understood through their meta-contexts. Rather providentially, Natasha Wheatley has masterfully performed this task in relation to

33 On Roman Law and the legal form, see the contribution of Fusco in this volume.

34 Evegeny Pashukanis, 'Appendix: Pashukanis on International Law' in Miéville (n 27) 321, 326.

35 Benno Teschke, *The Myth of 1648: Class, Geopolitics, and the Making of Modern International Relations* (Verso 2003); Ellen Wood, *The Pristine Culture of Capitalism: A Historical Essay on Old Regimes and Modern States* (Verso 2015); Spencer Dimmock, *Origins of Capitalism in England 1400–1600* (Haymarket Books 2015).

36 This is especially pertinent given Frederick Maitland's observation that the true constitutional law of England its land law. Anne Orford, *International Law and the Politics of History* (CUP 2021) 117; see Paskukanis, *General Theory* (n 20) 126–27

37 ibid 123–24; Kinch Hoekstra, 'Early Modern Absolutism and Constitutionalism' (2013) 34 Cardozo L Rev 1079. Importantly, Hobbes's grand abstractions were closely linked to his reading of the customs and traditions of his formative context, see Thomas Hobbes, *A Dialogue between a Philosopher and a Student of the Common Laws of England* (Jospeh Cropsey ed, University of Chicago Press 1997).

38 Alexander Anievas and Kerem Nişancıoğlu, *How the West Came to Rule: The Geopolitical Origins of Capitalism* (Pluto Press 2015).

39 Fernanda Pirie, *The Rule of Laws: How 4,000 Years of Law Shaped the World as We Know It* (Profile Books 2021).

40 Günter Frankenberg, *Comparative Law as Critique* (Edward Elgar 2019).

Pashukanis' central foil—Hans Kelsen.[41] Through his 'pure theory of law', Kelsen positivistically framed the task of the jurist to thoroughly detail the normative structure of an idealised legal configuration existing above and beyond material reality.[42] According to Pashukanis: '[u]nquestionably one must give Kelsen credit for one great service. As a result of his undaunted consistency, he reduced Neo-Kantian methodology, with its two categories, to absurdity. For it turns out that the 'pure' category of *Ought*, cleansed of all impurities from the *Is* . . . neither has nor possibly can have, any rational definition whatsoever'.[43]

However, as Wheatley's *The Life and Death of States* shows, an interpretation of Kelsen through the meta-contexts of his intellectual origins and influences reveals why he viewed his pure theory as anything but absurd. In centring the Habsburg Empire, Wheatley shows that Kelsen, as part of the Neo-Kantian revival of the philosophical tradition in an increasingly mechanised age, sought to bring order to a land whose juridical structure rendered it renown as an object of curiosity and ridicule.[44] From the time the Empire set out to reform its constitutional structure following the Revolution of 1848, there emerged much-defining debate between historically rooted custom versus ethnic/national identity as the supreme basis for rights.[45] However, in attempting to resolve such matters domestically, the Empire created a new legal controversy at the international level. This notably occurred through the 1867 *Ausgleich* where the Empire became the Dual-Monarchy of Austria-Hungary, an entity that generated ceaseless debate as to whether it was one or two sovereigns in relation to a prevailing international legal positivism that viewed the sovereign state as an indivisible entity.[46] Against these backdrops, Kelsen's pure theory can be read as an attempt to transcend contradictions by liberating law from its materiality through converting it into a quest for a gapless normative structure.[47] This is to say nothing of how Kelsen's particular relationship to his Jewish heritage cultivated fantasies of an 'assimilation through law' whereby 'scientific' identification of pure norms could alleviate the burdens of particularity in a context of embedded antisemitism.[48]

41 Natasha Wheatley, *The Life and Death of States: Central Europe and the Transformation of Modern Sovereignty* (Princeton UP 2023).
42 Hans Kelsen, *Pure Theory of Law* (Max Knight tr, Lawbook Exchange 2009).
43 Pashukanis, *General Theory* (n 20) 52.
44 Wheatley (n 41) 153–54.
45 ibid 107–10.
46 ibid 81.
47 ibid 168–72.
48 Eliav Lieblich, 'Assimilation through Law: Hans Kelsen and the Jewish Experience' in James Loeffler and Moira Paz (eds), *The Law of Strangers: Jewish Lawyers and International Law in the Twentieth Century* (CUP 2019) 51.

If such meta-contexts can provide insights into a jurist seeking to escape from the material contradictions spawned by multiple pressure points in a world of empires, then might a similar analysis also explain a very different jurist consciously dedicated to exposing those same material contradictions? To provide any such explanations is to make some broad statements on Pashukanis' lifepath, a task made even more difficult by the limited knowledge of his early life. While born of Lithuanian heritage in Russia (and to a Russian mother) in 1891, Pashukanis' Lithuanian identity was that of a minority at most.[49] As such, without a 'thick' communal environment to provide him with formative meaning, Pashukanis' relation to his own identity in this regard could easily have been a 'thin' matter of distanced observation as opposed to any all-encompassing sphere of meaning. Leaving Russia for Germany in 1909, Pashukanis developed as an intellectual at Munich's Ludwig Maximillian University before returning to Russia in the context of the Revolution in 1918 where he worked in a number of capacities, including the negotiation of friendly relations between the Soviet Union and Germany via the Treaty of Rapallo in 1922.[50] That same year, he joined forces with Pēteris Stučka to organise the law division of the Communist Academy, produced the *General Theory* in 1924, and was eventually executed during Stalin's Great Purge in 1937.[51] In light of the dearth of evidence regarding his connection to Lithuania, on what basis could it be said that his Lithuanian background had anything to do with any aspect of his work and/or life? In approaching this question through a materialist lens, we must examine the vast contexts of 'Lithuania' as a groundwork for theorising what it might have meant to Pashukanis.

Lithuania Between Medieval and Modern Empires

While today a small nation in northeastern Europe where the majority of the population are Roman Catholic speakers of the Baltic language of Lithuanian, 'Lithuania' in Pashukanis' time was something altogether different. Consciousness of this entails a basic knowledge of the life, death, and legacy of the early modern divided sovereignty form known as the Polish-Lithuanian Commonwealth. In 1775 it ceased to exist on the map of Europe. Between that moment and the end of the First World War, contestation over the ultimate fate of these lands arguably entrenched the right of nations to self-determination

49 Bjarne Melkevik, 'Pashukanis, Evgeny Bronislavovich' in Gianfrancesco Zanetti, Mortimer Sellers, and Stephan Kirste (eds), *Handbook of the History of the Philosophy of Law and Social Philosophy—Volume 3: From Ross to Dworkin and Beyond* (Springer 2023) 233.

50 Bill Bowring, 'Yevgeniy Pashukanis, His *Law and Marxism: A General Theory*, and the 1922 Treaty of Rapallo between Soviet Russia and Germany' (2017) 19 *J Hist Intl L* 274.

51 Melkevik (n 49) 235.

as a foundational pillar of international society.[52] According to Victor Kattan, the continued national assertions in these lands of the former Commonwealth against the partition perpetrating Russian, Prussian, and Austrian empires is the umbilicus of self-determination that connects the American and French Revolutions to the proclamations of Woodrow Wilson and Vladimir Lenin.[53] Within the two partitioning empires Pashukanis was most connected to, Russia and Prussia-spawned Germany, debates on the possible fates of the lands of the former Commonwealth were never far from consciousness—especially for those of Lithuanian heritage (itself a rather indeterminate concept).[54] Locating possible factors on how Pashukanis' identity might have influenced his juridical theory necessitates a deep delve into the broad histories that, especially in their resurrection for turn-of-the-century political projects, animated consciousness in Pashukanis' world.[55]

Home to Europe's last remaining Pagans, beginning in the twelfth century, the various Slavic, Baltic, and Finno-Ugric peoples of the Eastern Baltic found themselves on the receiving end of imposition from various Scandinavian and Germanic princes, as well as military religious—most infamously the knights of the Teutonic Order forged in the Middle Eastern Holy Land Crusades.[56] While a multitude of pagan peoples fell to the conquerors, the most powerful amongst them, the Lithuanians, not only mounted a successful resistance but organised as the Grand Duchy, established dominion over vast swaths of the Orthodox Christian lands to the east and south that had been devastated by the Mongol invasions.[57] Also involved was the Slavic Kingdom of Poland whose close ties to the Roman Catholic Church following conversion

52 Tadeusz Kamusella, 'Germanization, Polonization, and Russification in the Partitioned Lands of Poland-Lithuania' (2013) 41 *Nationalities Papers* 815.

53 Victor Kattan, 'To Consent or Revolt? European Public Law, the Three Partitions of Poland (1772, 1793, and 1795) and the Birth of National Self-Determination' (2015) 17 *J Hist Intl L* 247, 251.

54 Vytautas Petronis, *Constructing Lithuania: Ethnic Mapping in Tsarist Russia, Ca. 1800–1914* (Stockholm Universitet 2007).

55 Lithuanian identity was even expounded upon in the leading publication of the nascent field of 'International Relations', *Foreign Affairs*, or, as it was named at the time, the *Journal of Race Development*. Thomas Shamis, 'Lithuanians' (1918) 9 *J Race Dev* 157. On International Relations as originally a study of a 'world of races' prior to its present study of a 'world of states', see Robert Vitalis, *White World Order, Black Power Politics: The Birth of American International Relations* (Cornell University Press 2015).

56 Erik Christensen, *The Northern Crusades* (Penguin 1997).

57 SC Rowell, *Lithuania Ascending: A Pagan Empire within East-Central Europe, 1295–1345* (CUP 1994). There remains much controversy over whether the Grand Duchy was an 'empire'. Zenonas Norkus, *An Unproclaimed Empire: The Grand Duchy of Lithuania: From the Viewpoint of Comparative Historical Sociology of Empires* (Routledge 2017). On the predominant subjects of the Grand Duchy, see Serhii Plokhy, *The Origins of the Slavic Nations: Premodern Identities in Russia, Ukraine, and Belarus* (CUP 2006).

in the 900s largely shielded it from the Germanic Holy Roman Empire.[58] Initially aligned with the Teutonic Order, the ultimate betrayal of the Poles by these knights led to a new alliance with the Grand Duchy of Lithuania who joined with the Poles to decisively rout the Order at the Battle of Grunwald in 1410.[59] While the Polish-pagan alliance prompted no shortage of controversy despite the Lithuanian's conversion promise,[60] including the question of whether Christians aligned with infidels against other Christians could ever possess just cause in a just war under natural law,[61] the very nature of Lithuanian paganism allowed it to act as of something of a mediation zone amidst the contentious fault-line of Catholic and Orthodox Christian worlds.[62] Given these geopolitical circumstances, from the initial alliance grew increasing interdependence in the following centuries, and in 1569 the Lublin Union merged the Kingdom of Poland and the Grand Duchy of Lithuania as a singular commonwealth.[63]

Following the union, the Commonwealth continued its unique evolutionary trajectory as a unique divided sovereignty-based entity ruled by a non-hereditary elected monarchy and an extensive parliamentary authority known as the *Sejm* where, via the infamous *Liberum veto*, any member of the nobility had the power to unilaterally block legislation.[64] While its neighbours in all directions evolved along the lines of absolutist centralisation, the divergent Commonwealth viewed itself as a bastion of republican liberty against this backdrop.[65] Though Lithuania continued to exist as a geographic designation, and Lithuanian remained as a folk language along the Baltic coast, the widely dispersed Lithuanian elites, in adopting the culture of the greater Polish nobility, largely became Polish speakers who ruled over large

58 Roman Michałowski, 'Christianisation of the Piast Monarchy in the 10th and 11th Centuries' (2010) 101 *Acta Poloniae Historica* 5.

59 Christensen (n 56) 227–231.

60 Darius Baronas and SC Rowell, *The Conversion of Lithuania: From Pagan Barbarians to Late Medieval Christians* (Institute of Lithuanian Literature and Folklore 2015).

61 James Muldoon, *Popes, Lawyers, and Infidels: The Church and the Non-Christian World, 1250–1550* (University of Pennsylvania Press 1979) 107–19.

62 SC Rowell, 'Pagans, Peace and the Pope 1322–1324: Lithuania in the Centre of European Diplomacy' (1990) 28 *Archivum Historiae Pontificiae* 63; Jūratė Kiaupienė, *Between Rome and Byzantium. The Golden Age of the Grand Duchy of Lithuania's Political Culture. Second Half of the Fifteenth Century to First Half of the Seventeenth Century* (J Will tr, Academic Studies Press 2019).

63 Snyder (n 17) 19–20. On pre-union integration, see Robert Frost, *The Oxford History of Poland-Lithuania: The Making of the Polish-Lithuanian Union, 1385–1569* (OUP 2015).

64 Dalibor Roháč, 'The Unanimity Rule and Religious Fractionalisation in the Polish-Lithuanian Republic' (2008) 19 *Const Pol Econ* 111; "It Is by Unrule That Poland Stands': Institutions and Political Thought in the Polish-Lithuanian Republic' (2008) 13 *Independent Rev* 209.

65 Anna Grześkowiak-Krwawicz, *Queen Liberty: The Concept of Freedom in the Polish-Lithuanian Commonwealth* (Brill 2012).

estates of Eastern Slavic Orthodox subjects.[66] Yet despite the Commonwealth's affirmation of a unique identity, this divergence with its absolutist neighbours, especially as its lack of a hereditary monarchy limited the prospects of influence accumulation via dynastic marriage/inheritance, did not bode well for the Commonwealth's long-term survival.[67] In 1772 in pursuit of a more direct mode of accumulation, Russia, Prussia, and Austria initiated the first partition of the Commonwealth.[68] While this imposition prompted the Commonwealth to embrace Enlightenment-era ideals that were ultimately embedded in the 1791 Polish Constitution—the first written constitution in Europe.[69] However, within a broader political sphere defined by the 1789 outbreak of the French Revolution, the prospect of such anti-absolutist sentiments within their immediate proximity prompted the partitioning powers to end the Commonwealth's existence through two additional partitions in 1793 and 1795.[70] While the Polish cause lived on, especially through the championing of figures such as Jean-Jacque Rousseau;[71] what this meant for the Lithuanians largely depended on which partitioning empire they now found themselves to be the subjects of.

Most of historic Lithuania was absorbed by the Russian Empire and, in the early decades, resistance against Tsarist rule was typically cast as a quest to restore the republican institutions of the partitioned Commonwealth—a cause that many Lithuanian elites prominently championed.[72] However, the defeated 1863 Polish uprising and ensuing Russian suppression changed everything. With this event came a general abandonment of Commonwealth restoration efforts and a turn to Polish nationalism.[73] For the Lithuanians who blamed the Poles for this failure—and felt excluded by this new Polish nationalism—their new goal became building their own nationalist movement and, as a vital means to this end, abandoning Polish and reviving

66 Snyder (n 17) 22–24. Conforming with these patterns, Lithuanian peasants largely began speaking Belarussian. ibid 32.

67 Teschke (n 35) 236–37.

68 Herbert Kaplan, *The First Partition of Poland* (Columbia UP 2020).

69 Richard Butterwick, *The Polish-Lithuanian Commonwealth: Light and Flame* (Yale UP 2020).

70 Robert Lord, *The Second Partition of Poland: A Study in Diplomatic History* (Harvard UP 1915); 'The Third Partition of Poland' (1925) 3 *Slavonic Rev* 481.

71 Jean-Jacque Rousseau, 'Considerations on the Government of Poland' in *Of the Social Contract and Other Political Writings* (Quintin Hoare tr, Christopher Bertram ed, Penguin 2012) 241.

72 Jerzy Ochmański, 'The National Idea in Lithuania from the 16th to the First Half of the 19th Century: The Problem of Cultural-Linguistic Difference' (1986) 10 *Harv Ukrainian Stud* 301, 309–10.

73 On this turn in the context of Polish scepticism towards 'the West', see Jerzy Jedlicki, *A Suburb of Europe: Nineteenth-century Polish Approaches to Western Civilization* (Central European UP 1998).

Lithuanian as a language of literary and political culture.[74] As a Baltic language distinct from the surrounding Slavic languages, despite the narrow geographic scale in which it was still spoken in the mid-nineteenth century, Lithuanian provided a means of foundational distinction from both Russians and Poles.[75] Intimately related to linguistic revival, newfound national consciousness prompted great interest in Lithuania's pre-union era that, in depicting centuries of Polish influence as undue imposition, sought to bypass the early modern institutions of the Commonwealth and depict the medieval past as the maligned, yet inextinguishable, basis of Lithuanian national identity.[76] From Russia's perspective, the situation was complex. On the one hand, encouraging Lithuanian nationalism provided a means of undermining the more pressing threats of Polish nationalism and/or Commonwealth revival.[77] On the other hand, in these same lands, the Empire was engaging in an intensive process of 'Russification' that could privilege no national expression beyond Russian nationalism.[78] This tension was emblematic of Russia's unique status as both a multi-ethnic empire and a distinct nationalist/pan-nationalist project during a time of great institutional/ideological/juridical transformation on a global scale.[79]

As important as these contentions within the Russian Empire may have been to fully understand the sources of this modern Lithuanian nationalism and its corresponding disavowal of the Commonwealth and turn to deeper medieval histories, we must account for the Lithuanians who became subjects of another partitioning empire in the form of Prussia.[80] In the decades following the Napoleonic wars, this region was the leading site of Romantic nationalist conceptualisations positing that the essence of a 'people' could be determined through their unique histories and traditions.[81] This mode of

74 Snyder (n 17) 32.

75 As such, Lithuanian nationalism proved far more successful than Belarussian nationalism—the latter's language being largely between Polish and Russian. ibid 40–42, 46–47.

76 ibid 35; Rimantas Miknys and Darius Staliūnas, 'The "Old" and "New" Lithuanians: Collective Identity Types in Lithuania at the Turn of the Nineteenth and Twentieth Centuries' in Martyn Housden and David J Smith (eds), *Forgotten Pages in Baltic History: Diversity and Inclusion* (Brill 2011) 35; Moreno Bonda, *History of Lithuanian Historiography: Didactical Guidelines* (Vytautas Magnus University 2013).

77 Alfred Erich Senn, 'Tsarist Authorities and Lithuanian Book-Smuggling' (1980) 11 *J Baltic Stud* 334.

78 Darius Staliūnas, 'Between Russification and Divide and Rule: Russian Nationality Policy in the Western Borderlands in Mid-19th Century' (2007) 55 *Jahrbücher für Geschichte Osteuropas* 357.

79 See Eric Loefflad, 'Blood of Nations, Blood of Empire: Pan-Slavism as a Critique of International Law in Late Imperial Russia and Beyond' German Ybk Intl L (forthcoming).

80 Vasilijus Safronovas, *The Creation of National Spaces in a Pluricultural Region: The Case of Prussian Lithuania* (Academic Studies Press 2016).

81 Johann Gottfried von Herder, *Outlines of a Philosophy of the History of Man* (TO Churchill tr, Bergman Publishers 1966).

thinking also very much implicated German legal sciences as 'law' became viewed by many as the organic expression of fundamentally unique peoples.[82] In this milieu, Lithuanian, as an ancient language with almost no surviving relatives, became viewed by many scholars as the very key to unlocking the fabled origins of the newly identified Indo-European language family.[83] Relatedly, the status of the Lithuanians as Europe's last pagans, a source of much fascination in the early modern era,[84] gained renewed emphasis in this nineteenth-century moment as Romantic thinkers sought to uncover the pagan origins of discrete European nations.[85] Interestingly, in a manner that effectively inverted Lithuanian views of Polish-orchestrated marginalisation, this German fetishisation of Lithuanians occurred in roughly the same context as new German theories of Slavic inferiority justified increasingly harsh practices in the partitioned territories ultimately manifesting in concerted 'Germanisation' efforts.[86] Additionally, as the century progressed, medieval histories of the Teutonic Order and Northern Crusades so important to new Polish and Lithuanian national identities were ascribed with new meaning in the German cultural imagination.[87] While these events were long viewed by many as an embarrassment to be transcended by Enlightenment sensibilities, in the latter half of the nineteenth century prominent thinkers began to celebrate Crusader violence as a pure expression of the German character.[88]

Given these compounded backdrops, how might we gauge Pashukanis' consciousness of these politics of medieval history in connection to the emergent Lithuanian national consciousness of his era? One fascinating quote here related to his point that the 'order' international law creates is order between a common capitalist upper class maintaining relations across sovereign borders.[89] Analogously, he stated that: 'in the feudal period the knights of every European country had their codes of military honour and accordingly, their class law, which they applied in wars with one another; but they

82 Roger Berkowitz, *The Gift of Science: Leibniz and the Modern Legal Tradition* (Fordham UP 2010) 109–36.

83 Scott Spires, 'Lithuanian Linguistic Nationalism and the Cult of Antiquity' (1999) 5 *Nations and Nationalism* 485, 490–93.

84 Francis Young (ed), *Pagans in the Early Modern Baltic: Sixteenth-Century Ethnographic Accounts of Baltic Paganism* (Arc Humanities Press 2022).

85 Joep Leerssen, 'Gods, Heroes, and Mythologists: Romantic Scholars and the Pagan Roots of Europe's Nations' (2016) 1 *Hist Humanities* 71.

86 Lithuanians existed outside the particular German-Pole-Jew triad that defined this context, see William Hagen, *Germans, Poles and Jews: Nationality Conflict in the Prussian East, 1772–1914* (University of Chicago Press 1980).

87 Micheal Burleigh, 'The Knights, Nationalists and the Historians: Images of Medieval Prussia from the Enlightenment to 1945' (1987) 17 *Eur Hist Q* 35.

88 Vejas Gabriel Liulevicius, *The German Myth of the East: 1800 to the Present* (OUP 2009) 76. For an illustration, see Heinrich von Treitschke, *Treitschke's Origins of Prussianism: The Teutonic Knights* (Eden Paul and Cedar Paul trs, Routledge 2014).

89 Pashukanis, 'International Law' (n 34) 324.

did not apply in inter-class wars, for example, the suppression of burghers and the peasantry'.[90] Given the general lack of medieval knights as a cultural image in Pashukanis' Russia,[91] it is likely that his insight here can be linked to his background where images of knighthood symbolically connected medieval, early modern, and modern Lithuanian identity.[92]

It is revealing that Pashukanis characterises victims of the knights on the universal basis of class given the more standard invocations of victimhood by the Teutonic Order as a tool of parochial nationalist assertion—especially in narratives of Polish nationalism.[93] In this way, Pashukanis' Lithuanian background rendered him well-positioned to show how universality-invoking narratives of bourgeois nationalism amongst Poles were contradicted by their embedded marginalisation of the other national groups that inhabited the former Polish-Lithuanian Commonwealth. Here, an interesting parallel to Pashukanis' context was the Austrian portion of the Commonwealth where an emergent Ukrainian nationalism ascended within a similar timeframe and context to that of the Lithuanians.[94] Serving a dual function as the site of both the greatest post-partition Polish autonomy and the Ukrainian effort to distinguish itself from Russian identity, this common region of Galicia forced very different nationalist projects to confront one another.[95] According to Rosa Luxemburg's synthesis of these issues as informed by her broader materialist critique of the right of nations to self-determination: 'Polish bourgeois nationalism is directed as much against the Ruthenians [Ukrainians] as against the Lithuanians. The very nationality which had to endure the bitter policy of extermination by the partitioning powers . . . now refuses the right of independent existence to other nationalities'.[96] Yet how precisely did these

90 ibid.

91 In Russian/Ukrainian cultural consciousness, the Cossack plays a far greater role as the romanticised figure on horseback, see Anna Kovalchuk, 'Narrating the National Future: The Cossacks in Ukrainian and Russian Literature' (doctoral thesis, University of Oregon 2017).

92 Rimvydas Petrauskas, 'Knighthood in the Grand Duchy of Lithuania from the Late Fourteenth to the Early Sixteenth Centuries' (2006) 11 *Lithuanian Hist Stud* 39; Agnė Railaitė-Bardė, 'The Triumphant Genealogical Awareness of the Nobility in the Grand Duchy of Lithuania in the 17th and 18th Centuries' (2018) 22 *Lithuanian Hist Stud* 29; Giedrė Jankevičiūtė, 'Constructing National Identity: The Image of the Medieval Grand Duchy of Lithuania in Lithuanian Art from the 1920s to the 1990s' (2010) 8 *Central Eur* 158.

93 Adam Kożuchowski, 'The Devil Wears White: Teutonic Knights and the Problem of Evil in Polish Historiography' (2019) 46 *E Cen Eur* 133. Condemning the Teutonic Order Is coupled with veneration of Poland's own knights, see Norman Davies, 'Polish National Mythologies' in Geoffrey Hosking and George Schopflin (eds), *Myths and Nationhood* (Hurst 1997) 141.

94 Piotr S Wandycz, *The Lands of Partitioned Poland, 1795–1918* (University of Washington Press 1974) 239–259.

95 Larry Wolff, *The Idea of Galicia: History and Fantasy in Habsburg Political Culture* (Stanford University Press 2010).

96 Rosa Luxemburg, 'The National Question and Autonomy' in Horace Davis (ed), *The National Question: Selected Writings* (Monthly Review Press 1976) 101, 164.

historic questions of nationality, empire, constitutionalism, and statehood—quintessential issues of public law—shape Pashukanis' theory of the legal form that, in depicting juridified individuals as base-level capitalist subjects, was largely focused on matters of private law?

The Pashukanis-Stučka Debate as Lithuanian-Latvian Difference

When analysing Pashukanis' theory through these vast inter-connected histories, there are numerous options. Much can be said in relation to Lenin's particular endorsement of the 'right of nations to self-determination' as a revolutionary imperative within the inter-imperial rivalry defined international system—an analysis with a clear entry point given Pashukanis' application of Lenin's imperialism framework to international law.[97] Much can also be said about the intense contestation between the restored post-First World War Polish and Lithuanian states, particularly in their struggle over Vilnius (the old capital of the Lithuanian Grand Duchy that since became predominantly Polish/Jewish[98]), that were occurring roughly contemporaneously with Pashukanis' diplomatic mission in Germany.[99] However, in raising the question of 'legal form' within this analysis, I centre a narrow, yet significant, point of disagreement between Pashukanis and his fellow Soviet jurist Pēteris Stučka. Famously, for Pashukanis, to recognise law as the 'legal form', one must conclude that technical administrative matters cannot, contrary to common perception, be deemed 'law' properly understood.[100] He illustrated this through his point that train schedules, surgical procedures, and beehives, though functioning according to distinct administrative procedures, are too far removed from the abstracted structure of individualised rights/obligation holders (i.e. legal forms) to be 'law'.[101] However, as Anna Lukina has shown, for Stučka (contra Pashukanis), technical administrations could in fact be law.[102] This premise was well-suited to his view that 'law' was that which was determined to be law by the dominant class and, on that basis, was not necessarily bourgeois; proletarian law could in fact exist should workers become the dominant class.[103] In Pashukanis' critical assessment, Stučka's 'definition

97 Pashukanis, 'International Law' (n 34) 322–23.

98 Snyder (n 17) 53–57.

99 Post-imperial property redistribution questions here were deeply connected to assertions of national identity, see Klaus Richter, '"An Orgy of Licence?" Democracy and Property Redistribution in Poland and the Baltics in their International Context, 1918–1926' (2018) 46 Nationalities Papers 791.

100 Pashukanis, *General Theory* (n 20) 78–84.

101 ibid 79.

102 Anna Lukina in this volume.

103 ibid; Pēteris Stučka, 'Proletarian Law' in Robert Sharlet, Peter B Maggs, and Piers Beirne (eds), *Selected Writings on Soviet Law and Marxism* (ME Sharpe 1988) 9.

uncovers the class content concealed within legal forms, but does not explain why this content assumes that particular form'.[104]

In interpreting this divergence in light of the broader patterns of history and identity detailed above, I argue that, in short, the divergence between Pashukanis and Stučka on whether administration was 'law' can be explained at least in part by the fact that, while Pashukanis was Lithuanian, Stučka was Latvian. Making this claim necessarily invites much inquiry on the nature of the relationship between Latvians and Lithuanians, especially as they are speakers of the only two surviving Baltic languages. Yet despite this commonality, immense historical difference renders comparison of pre-statehood Latvians and Lithuanians rather difficult. However, in an important intervention, Saulius Pivoras shows that the emergence of Latvian national consciousness played a profound role in the Lithuanian transition from a civic nationalism to an ethnic nationalism after the failed 1863 Polish uprising.[105] While the legacies of the Commonwealth bequeathed the Lithuanians with numerous challenges when it came to constitutionalism, republicanism, and the reality of partition, the Latvians had no experience of any such structures and could thus bypass such issues when defining themselves in purely ethnic terms.[106] In addition to providing an ethnic emulation model, identifying Latvians as ethnolinguistic kin despite religious differences, allowed Lithuanians to escape the grasp of Roman Catholicism as an identity medium that bound them to the Poles.[107] In the context of Russian rule, this distinction was all more important given that Russians were apt to conflate 'Polishness' with Catholicism.[108]

Important as these interactions may be, to understand how Latvian-Lithuanian differences might explain the difference between Stučka and Pashukanis' jurisprudence demands a deeper historical exploration. In once again revisiting the medieval Northern Crusades, the lands inhabited by the Latvians' ancestors were thoroughly subjugated and converted by Germanic invaders.[109] In stark contrast to the Lithuanians, these peoples were unable to organise into a resistance-capable polity to anything near the extent of the Lithuanian Grand Duchy. Following these conquests, the initial invaders and later waves of Germanic migrants established feudal lordships that imposed regimes of serfdom upon the indigenous Baltic inhabitants while

104 Pashukanis (n 20) 84.

105 Saulius Pivoras, 'The Role of Latvian Nationalism in the Transformation of Lithuanian Nationalism during the Long 19th Century' (2021) 27 Nations and Nationalism 566.

106 ibid 570.

107 ibid 575.

108 Darius Staliūnas, 'The Pole' in the Policy of the Russian Government: Semantics and Praxis in the Mid-Nineteenth Century' (2000) 5 Lithuanian Hist Stud 45, 53–54.

109 Christensen (n 56) 93–104. For the defining first person account, see Henricus Lettus, *The Chronicle of Henry of Livonia* (James Brundage tr, Columbia UP 2004).

also developing lucrative commercial ports, namely Riga, that connected the Baltic Sea to the network of rivers in Eastern Europe that extended to the Black Sea in the south.[110] The strategic importance of this region brought about much great power competition in the early modern era between the Polish-Lithuanian Commonwealth, the Kingdom of Sweeden and the newly westward expanding Russian Tsardom who waged a long series of wars that were only conclusively ended in 1721 when the Treaty of Nystad formalised Russia as the region's dominant power.[111] For the Baltic peasants, foreign powers were typically looked upon with favour as they provided a counter-balance to the local Baltic German lords in a manner that helped to preserve local languages and cultures.[112] In situating this material meta-context as Stučka's formative backdrop, we gain many insights into why it was that he theorised 'law' as the command of the dominant class in a manner that could not exclude technical administration.

Stučka's approach towards this end is well depicted in his text on 'The State' where, as a prelude to discussing 'bourgeois revolution and the state', he details a variety of historical state formations that are quite easy to connect to the modes of rule endured by Latvians and their forebears.[113] In beginning with 'the primitive state' whereby '[t]he direct successor of the clan is the so-called *patriarchal* state', he then goes to describe 'the patrimonial and feudal state' that, while phrased in general terms, nevertheless depicts the Germanic feudal colonisation of the eastern Baltic very well.[114] Here Stučka claims that the feudal state entails a union of owners under the common banner of class which in turn sets the stage for a division between countryside and city-based modes of production.[115] In the history of Stučka's formative context, this occurred in the long unravelling of the Northern Crusades where, following the Polish-Lithuanian victory at Grunwald, the various conquerors of today's Latvia and Estonia formed the 'Livonian Confederation' which provided a foundation for enhanced Baltic commerce.[116] The next stage for Stučka is 'absolutism' whereby the decentralised configuration of feudalism

110 Michael North, *The Baltic: A History* (Kenneth Kronenberg tr, Harvard UP) 35–37; see also Kevin O'Conner, *The House of Hemp and Butter: A History of Old Riga* (Northern Illinois University 2019).

111 Robert Frost, *The Northern Wars: War, State and Society in Northeastern Europe, 1558–1721* (Routledge 2014).

112 Rein Taagepera, 'Albert, Martin, and Peter too: Their Roles in Creating the Estonian and Latvian Nations' (2011) 42 *J Baltic Stud* 125, 132–35.

113 Pēteris Stučka, 'The State' in Sharlet, Maggs, and Beirne (n 103) 108.

114 ibid 114.

115 ibid 114–15.

116 Muntis Auns, 'Acquisition of the Acquired: The Establishing of a Real Administration in Livonia' in Nils Blomkvist (ed), *Culture Clash or Compromise: The Europeanisation of the Baltic Sea Area, 1100–1400 AD* (Gotland Centre for Baltic Studies 1998) 259.

is replaced by centralisation around a singular monarchical figure.[117] This could easily be related to the Latvian experience of rule by Swedish Kings and Russian Tsars who represented something very different from the rule of the old Baltic German lords who came to question their belonging under these new authorities, particularly under Russian rule.[118] Interestingly, he names the 'police state' as a sub-category of absolutism but only lists Prussia as an illustration—a designation that is perhaps intended to exclude the Swedes and Russians who alleviated the Latvian burdens of Germanic tyranny.[119] Throughout these various iterations of authority, command and administration would be easy to characterise as 'law'. Given this framing, it is easy to understand his exasperated claim

> that Comrade Pashukanis' conception encompasses only bourgeois law and, by declaring it to be *law in general*, he blurs the *class nature* of law, i.e., he denies the existence of feudal law and now the law of the transition period, Soviet law, as well.[120]

The Lithuanian 'Secret' of Pashukanis' Critique of Legal Form

In light of Stučka's admonishment, when drawing upon the multilayered backdrops detailed above, we are well-positioned to theorise why Pashukanis' Lithuanian background might have led him to critique law as bourgeois law in a manner that confounded his Latvian interlocutor. As a preliminary matter, while Pashukanis occasion to consider his Lithuanian heritage as a minority in Russian and German-dominated worlds, in stark contrast, Stučka was not only deeply enmeshed within Latvian culture and politics but was the leader of the short-lived Latvian Socialist Soviet Republic (1918–1920).[121] On this basis, Stučka's task of justifying revolutionary order as law in relation to a discrete political community was far more immanent relative to Pashukanis.[122] However, this biographical consideration must not conceal the deeper materiality that shaped defining differences between the Latvian and Lithuanian experiences. This is especially important in light of how nationalist proclamations of affinities between Latvians and Lithuanians, however

117 Stučka, 'The State' (n 113) 115.

118 Ulrike Plath, 'Heimat: Rethinking Baltic German Spaces of Belonging' (2014) 3/4 Kunstiteaduslikke Uurimusi 55, 60, 64.

119 Stučka, 'The State' (n 113) 115–16.

120 Pēteris Stučka, 'My Journey and My Mistakes' in Sharlet, Maggs, and Beirne (n 103) 219, 223.

121 Marina Germane, 'Pēteris Stučka and the National Question' (2013) 44 *J Baltic Stud* 375.

122 Pashukanis certainly recognised Stučka professional need for a more pragmatic approach to law. Pashukanis, *General Theory* (n 20) 84.

powerful they were rhetorically, were prone to reproducing grave material distortions. To provide a profound illustration, by the late nineteenth century, nationalists of both groups claimed that the Baltic German repression of the Latvians was analogous to the Polish repression of Lithuanians.[123] Such a parallel, though certainly validating to Lithuanians wishing to disavow their historical connections to Poles, is difficult to sustain at any material level. As detailed above, while Baltic Germans long defined themselves as incontestably distinct and superior to local populations,[124] designations of 'Polish' and 'Lithuanian' were historically far more fluid and intertwined.[125] On this basis, even after the rise of ethnonationalism, Polish attitude towards Lithuanians was far more multifaceted in their temporal and emphatically variable measures of admiration, assimilation, and ultimate consternation at the prospect of disunion.[126] These differing attitudes reflected differing material histories and social relations as they existed between Baltic Germans/Latvians and Poles/ Lithuanians. Unifying these animosities on a nationalist basis—especially as they might affirm the sovereign state as an object of desire—exemplified the type of juridical abstraction that Pashukanis condemned as a grave barrier to uncovering historical sociological truth.[127]

What then might the *longue durée* of the Lithuanian Question have meant for Pashukanis as a materialist theorist of the legal form whose heritage connected him to this history? Drawing upon the pasts detailed above, it can be argued that, since the rise of global capitalism, Lithuania and Poland—both together and apart—had been defined by one legal fetishisation after another. This being the case, such fetishisation was understandable for it was in the precapitalist moment of the early 1400s that the allied Poles and Lithuanians triumphed over a despised invader and, through novel assertions of reason via natural law, justified their Catholic-pagan union against existing religious dogmas.[128] In the ensuing 'Golden Age' that was the sixteenth century, the nascent Polish-Lithuanian Commonwealth was the recipient of no small amount of luck, namely the fact that it was only minimally affected

123 Pivoras (n 105) 573.

124 Liina Lukas, "Who Holds the Right to the Land?' Narratives of Colonization in Baltic-German and Estonian Literatures' in Andreas Beer and Gesa Mackenthun (eds), *Fugitive Knowledge: The Loss and Preservation of Knowledge in Cultural Contact Zones* (Waxmann 2015) 65.

125 Snyder (n 17) 15–51.

126 Wandycz (n 94) 239

127 Pashukanis, *General Theory* (n 20) 146. On this point, he was highly critical of the Austro-Marxists who placed much faith in international law. Pashukanis, 'International Law' (n 34) 322.

128 On the contingent non-reception of this history into international legal origin narratives, see Eric Loefflad, 'In Search of Paulus Vladimiri: Canon, Reception, and the (In)Conceivability of an Eastern European "Founding Father" of International Law' (2023) 36 *Leiden J Intl L* 833.

by the Black Death, and this momentary strength formed the groundings of its unique institutions.[129]

However, as new capitalist rationalities and effects began to proliferate from the seventeenth century onwards, adherence to identity-defining pre-capitalist legacies became a liability as Commonwealth elites maintained debilitating institutional forms and failed to adopt advantageous ones.[130] This included continued adherence to a *Liberum veto* that made legislation virtually impossible via its ability to be rejected by any individual member of a large social class, and (in an intimately related capacity) a disavowal of the Roman Law that was rapidly increasing as a medium of interaction and exchange throughout Europe.[131] The Commonwealth thus deployed the core private law concept of individual consent to uphold a fetishised conception of public law/constitutional heritage in a feudal manner that undermined consciousness of how the true core of legal power was private law. This all occurred at a time when the public law/private law divide was entrenching as capitalism was expanding—something Pashukanis was very much aware of.[132]

However, even when the Commonwealth nobility sought to reform their system (including the abandonment of the *Liberum veto*[133]), in embracing liberal constitutionalist conceptions following the first partition, they replaced one legal fetishisation with another. This proved exceptionally perilous as the Enlightenment mirage of 'universal liberty' created a false sense of commonality between the feudal Commonwealth and increasingly capitalist Western societies in a manner that, by sparking anxiety in its neighbours, hastened the Commonwealth's death by two more partitions.[134] Relatedly, in adhering to the continued truth of lost juridical realities, the post-partition efforts to restore the Commonwealth proved a means of marginalising early nineteenth-century resistance efforts much more grounded in the material conditions of primary producers.[135] However, these restoration efforts paled in comparison to the rise of post-1863 rival Polish and Lithuanian ethno-nationalism when it came to destructive potential. Seeking independence from empire, these nationalists affirmed the premises of the hopelessly

129 Loefflad, 'Unpartitionable' (n 26) 926.

130 Jacek Kochanowicz, 'The Polish Economy and the Evolution of Dependency' in Daniel Chirot (ed), *The Origins of Backwardness in Eastern Europe: Economics and Politics from the Middle Ages Until the Early Twentieth Century* (University of California Press 1989) 92.

131 Tomasz Giaro, 'Legal Tradition of Eastern Europe: Its Rise and Demise' (2011) 2 *Comp L Rev* 1, 6–7.

132 Pashukanis, *General Theory* (n 20) 58–59, 95–97.

133 Jerzy Lukowski, 'Machines of Government': Replacing the Liberum Veto in the Eighteenth-Century Polish-Lithuanian Commonwealth' (2012) 90 *Slavonic and Eastern Eur Rev* 65.

134 Loefflad, 'Unpartitionable' (n 26) 930–32.

135 Peter Brock, *Polish Revolutionary Populism: A Study in Agrarian Socialist Thought From the 1830s to the 1850s* (University of Toronto Press 1977).

abstracted mode of nineteenth-century positivist statehood that certain German Volk theories imbued with the pathologically delusional hope that a nation's true organic substance could be achieved through this empty truth-concealing juridical vessel.[136]

It was this basic belief structure that, in the aftermath of the First World War, fuelled intense armed clashes between Lithuanians and Poles over the city of Vilnius/Wilno, a space that both sides viewed as integral to their identity according to mutually excluding nationalist ideologies.[137] Freed from the old bounds of Commonwealth and empire, and armed with arguments on the legal form of sovereignty, both sides were now capable of deploying the type of violence that only a nation-state could.[138] It is not difficult to see how Pashukanis, akin to Walter Benjamin's latter observations, might have viewed this Polish-Lithuanian violence as just the tip of a massive rubble pile assembled by the belief that an idealised concept of 'law' could transcend social contradictions and social domination.[139] Given the Polish-Lithuanian saga of tragedy upon tragedy, and the perpetual rise of false juridical messiahs in their wake, law needed to be exposed for what it actually was as opposed to what it purported itself to be and was understood to be in light of its popular disseminations as such. For Pashukanis, this actuality of law was the legal form that only became universalised upon the triumph of capitalist social relations. To misunderstand this truth of the legal form was to repeat endless cycles of dashed hope giving rise to naïve redemption arcs that could never succeed on their own terms. This provides an important insight into why Pashukanis was so adamant that under communism law would 'wither away' and that the Soviet law of the Transition Period should strive to be something other than 'law'—a position that Stučka could not abide.

In contrast to the critical Lithuanian view Pashukanis possibly possessed, from Stučka's materialist Latvian perspective it was far more possible to merge a belief in progress through law with a materialist analysis of history and society. After all, it was under Russian rule that Latvian peasants were emancipated from Germanic-imposed feudal serfdom in the early nineteenth century.[140] Here, a new regime of law imposed by a new ruler meant

136 On the entrenchment of this presumption in international legal thought via its under-theorisation of 'customary international law' and its organicist premise of state 'consent', see Carty (n 24) 74–74.

137 Dangiras Mačiulis and Darius Staliūnas, *Lithuanian Nationalism and the Vilnius Question, 1883–1940* (Verlag Herder-Institut 2015).

138 Tomas Balkelis, 'The Logic of Violence in the Polish-Lithuanian Conflict, 1920–1923' (2021) 49 *Nationalities Papers* 911.

139 Walter Benjamin, 'Theses on the Philosophy of History' in Stephen Eric Bronner and Douglas MacKay Kellner (eds), *Critical Theory and Society: A Reader* (Routledge 1990) 255.

140 Marju Luts-Sootak and Hesi Siimets-Gross, 'Baltic Peasants after Emancipation—Free and Equal People or a New Social Estate in the Estate-Based Society' in *Legal Science: Functions, Significance and Future in Legal Systems II* (University of Latvia Press 2020) 158.

progress as it contributed, in conjoined measure, to both freedom for the Latvians and a more enlightened re-invention of Baltic German identity.[141] From Stučka's perspective, there was no reason why this improvement could not continue into the new era that bore witness to the near-simultaneous Russian Revolution and the rise of an independent Latvia. Even when his socialist government was overthrown with aide from the proto-Nazi Freikorps, German First World War veterans who continued to fight communists in the Baltic,[142] the presence of the newly established Soviet Union provided a barrier to reactionary politics and an opportunity to merge Latvian national identity with the ends of the Bolshevik Revolution.[143] This meant placing a great deal of trust in the belief that new class configurations would bring new emancipatory legal realities, and, on this basis, bourgeois law should not be the totality of 'law'. Passing away in 1932, Stučka did not live to see the Soviet purge of the Latvian National Communists that occurred after the Second World War.[144]

Yet this was not the only Latvian-related disjuncture that Stučka did not live to see. Against the backdrop of the Russian Revolution, much discourse on the nationality question was deeply connected to Lenin's influential dichotomy between 'oppressed' and 'oppressor' nations that underpinned his theory of national self-determination.[145] In Stučka's Latvia, violence conformed to this model, especially as the Freikorps-backed overthrow of his government fit seamlessly within a narrative of centuries-long German oppression of the Latvian nation. What then was to be made of violence between two different oppressed nations, as was the case with Poles and Lithuanians? The answer depended, in great measure, on the faith one was willing to place in the medium of law. While post-Stučka Latvia may have been the site of a Polish-Lithuanian ceasefire via the 1921 Treaty of Riga, Pashukanis, himself no stranger to treaty negotiations, may have had much reason to believe that building durable peace through such legalistic means was grossly insufficient at best.[146] Though his 1937 execution prevented him from seeing it, the legal

141 Andrew James Blumbergs, *The Nationalization of Latvians and the Issue of Serfdom: The Baltic German Literary Contribution in the 1780s and 1790s* (Cambria Press 2008); Ivars Ijabs, 'Another Baltic Postcolonialism: Young Latvians, Baltic Germans, and the emergence of Latvian National Movement' (2014) 42 *Nationalities Papers* 88.

142 Charles Sulivan, 'German Freecorps in the Baltic, 1918–1919' (1976) 7 *J Baltic Stud* 124, 126–28.

143 Germane (n 121) 387–88.

144 William D Prigge, *Bearslayers: The Rise and Fall of the Latvian National Communists* (Peter Lang 2015).

145 Vladimir Lenin, 'The Revolutionary Proletariat and the Right of Nations to Self-Determination' in *Collected Works, Volume XXI* (Foreign Languages Publishing House 1964) 407, 409; see also Stanely Page, 'Lenin, the National Question and the Baltic States, 1917–19' (1948) 7 *Am Slavic and East Eur Rev* 15.

146 On this settlement, see Stanisław Dąbrowski, 'The Peace Treaty of Riga' (1960) 5 *Polish Rev* 3.

form—especially as it was applied to the prospect of ethnic peace—could not prevent, and arguably accelerated, the ethnic violence of the Second World War.[147] While of course, the greatest acts of destruction were those of the Nazis,[148] under such conditions of total rupture, Leninist distinctions between 'oppressed' and 'oppressor' nations provided little meaningful indication of who would commit grave acts of violence against whom—this included Latvia where numerous local factions participated in the Holocaust.[149] Framed this way, Pashukanis' legal scepticism proves darkly prophetic in retrospect. The grave limits of faith in law derived from an analysis of Pashukanis' theory in relation to Lithuania (and its dismal record of dashed juridified hope) thus provide much opportunity to theorise the violence endemic to the legal form he identified.[150] Owing to perceptions made possible by his unique material-cum-juridical contexts, for Pashukanis, in a manner far more acute than Stučka, the bloody and chaotic world around him *was the rule of law*.[151]

147 Hitler iconically manipulated the minority rights protection system by demanding territorial concessions to protect externally located German speakers. Mark Mazower, 'The Strange Triumph of Human Rights, 1933–1950' (2004) 47 *Hist J* 379, 384–85.

148 Often divided by victim identity, integrated studies of Nazi mass violence are relatively recent, see Alex Kay, *Empire of Destruction: A History of Nazi Mass Killing* (Yale UP 2021).

149 Timothy Snyder, *Black Earth: The Holocaust as History and Warning* (Vintage 2015) 169–72.

150 This is especially true regarding Lithuania where the wartime transformation of demographics created new realities in the Soviet era, see Violeta Davoliūtė, *The Making and Breaking of Soviet Lithuania: Memory and Modernity in the Wake of War* (Routledge 2014).

151 Miéville (n 27) 319.

Chapter 4

Pašukanis on Ideology and the Juridical (A Note on *The General Theory of Law and Marxism*)*

Rafał Mańko

Introduction

Forty years ago, in a preface to the Polish translation of *The General Theory of Law and Marxism*, Professor Jerzy Kowalski remarked that anyone reading Evgenij Bronislavovič Pašukanis[1] 'has the impression of dealing with a contemporary legal theorist who joined the currently ongoing jurisprudential debates', given that the Bolshevik jurist's 'views on many key questions do not depart from contemporary positions. They do not seem to be merely [part of] history, but, on the contrary, they appear to participate in the ongoing discussion.'[2] Today, 100 years after the publication of the first edition of *The General Theory*, Pašukanis's distinctly hylomorphic[3] concept of law still strikes us as fresh and innovative. This undoubtedly stems from the fact that the essence of his intellectual endeavour was not so much to mechanically transpose Marx's theory onto the domain of jurisprudence, but rather to build a new, critical jurisprudence using Marxian methods.[4] Against the background of other Marxists attempting to venture into the juridical domain, Pašukanis' work was remarkable in that it was 'essentially a radical and thoroughgoing critique of any attempt to treat law as mere

* I would like to thank Gian-Giacomo Fusco for reading and commenting on an earlier version of this paper and to Cosmin Cercel for inspiring discussions on Pašukanis. The present paper presents exclusively my personal views.

1 The surname Pašukanis is Lithuanian, I have therefore opted for retaining its original spelling which is, incidentally, identical to the ISO 9 transliteration of its Cyrillic version into Latin characters.

2 Jerzy Kowalski, 'Słowo wstępne' in Jewgienij Bronisławowicz Paszukanis, *Ogólna teoria prawa a marksizm* (Ludwika Lisiakiewicz tr, PWN 1985) 10.

3 I.e. based on the form vs. content distinction. On hylomorphism in general see for example, William MR Simpson, *Hylomorphism* (CUP 2023). Cf. Mathew Dimick, 'Pashukanis' Commodity-form Theory of Law' in Paul O'Connell and Umut Özsu (eds), *Research Handbook on Law and Marxism* (Edward Elgar 2021) 122–26.

4 Artur Kozak, 'Poglądy Jewgenija B. Paszukanisa na istotę prawa' (1988) 24 *Przegląd Prawa i Administracji* 5, 17. Cf. Wiesław Staśkiewicz, 'Koncepcja prawa J.B. Paszukanisa—dylematy teorii i praktyki' (1982) 8 *Państwo i Prawo* 41, 54.

DOI: 10.4324/9781032724522-5

class ideology'.[5] By adopting an epistemologically internal point of view, Pašukanis was able to show that juridical form is not merely one of many parts of a broader 'ideological superstructure', but rather has its own history which is ontologically real and parallel to economic history.[6]

This chapter examines Pašukanis' discussion of the law-ideology nexus—which remains a central question for critical legal theory[7]—based on a close reading of *The General Theory of Law and Marxism*.[8] Obviously, a lot has been written on law and ideology during the last century, and new theories have emerged in their own right. However, before those concepts are compared with Pašukanis', it is necessary, as a preliminary step, to prepare what Artur Kozak called for as an 'astute elaboration of Pašukanis's achievements'.[9] Therefore, I focus on reconstructing and analytically generalising Pašukanis' views on law and ideology, as expressed on the pages of *The General Theory*, leaving for another occasion their creative development in confrontation with what has been written on the subject subsequently.

Given that questions of law and ideology are scattered across *The General Theory*, occurring in all chapters and the preface to the second edition and in diverse contexts, I will not follow the order of Pašukanis' book, but rather an analytical order of treatment. Thus, the next section discusses the distinction of law and ideology according to Pašukanis, focusing on his insistence on law's ontological autonomy in contrast to "orthodox" Marxist interpretations.[10] The following section analyses Pašukanis' critique of juridical ideology, first discussing his critique of the *ideology of*

5 Eugene Kamenka, 'Marxism, Economics and Law' (1981) 20 *Bulletin of the Australian Society of Legal Philosophy* 14, 26.

6 Евгений Брониславович Пашуканис, *Избранные произведения по общей теории права и государства* (Наука 1980) (hereinafter: "*Избранные*") 61. Due to their unsatisfactory quality (terminological errors), I have refrained from citing the available English versions. All translations from the Russian are my own, double-checked against the Polish translation.

7 Cf. Costas Douzinas, 'A Short History of the British Critical Legal Conference or, the Responsibility of the Critic' (2014) 25(2) *Law and Critique* 187, 188.

8 In this chapter I refer to the theory of Pašukanis as contained in *The General Theory*, omitting later works. This is because I assume, following Robert Sharlet and China Miélville, that the further development of the views contained in his publications—leading, in fact, to their reversal within the framework of auto-critique—did not flow from their free development, but was dictated by a desire to fit into the changed intellectual conditions resulting from the development of Stalinism. See China Miéville, *Between Equal Rights: A Marxist Theory of International Law* (Brill 2005) 76 with reference to Robert Sharlet, 'Pashukanis and the Commodity Exchange Theory of Law, 1924–1930: A Study in Soviet Marxist Legal Thought' (Unpublished PhD thesis, Indiana University 1968) 268–87.

9 Kozak, 'Poglądy' (n 4) 17.

10 Martijn Hesselink, 'Alienation Commodification: A Critique of the Role of EU Consumer Law' (2023) 2 *European Law Open* 405, 407 n. 12.

juridical form in its most general and abstract manifestations,[11] secondly, the critique of *legal*[12] *ideology* understood as the ideological presuppositions and implications of a concrete system of positive law (on the example of bourgeois legality); and thirdly, the critique of *juristic ideology* understood as the ideological beliefs of the juristic community in a given time and place. In the conclusions to this chapter, I sketch a synthesis of Pašukanis's methodological approach to ideology critique which, arguably, can be of inspiration for contemporary critical legal thinkers.

'A Parallel, Real History': Ideology and the Juridical

From Law as Ideology to Law Versus Ideology

For Pašukanis, the concept of ideology was synonymous to 'ideas, views',[13] that is, phenomena of individual or collective consciousness, as opposed to objective and material social phenomena. In contrast to many Marxists who considered law as being a purely ideological phenomenon, Pašukanis forcefully argued in favour of treating both concepts as ontologically and analytically distinct:

> The law, taken in its broadest definition, the law as form, exists not only in the heads and theories of learned jurists. It has a parallel, real history which develops not as a system of thoughts, but as a specific system of relationships, into which people enter not because they have consciously chosen them, but because they are forced to do so by the conditions of production. A human being becomes transformed into a juridical subject due to the same necessity which transforms a natural product into a commodity with its puzzling property of value.[14]

What is important in this statement is not only the deliberate conceptual and stylistic parallel to Marx's definition of a commodity but above all Pašukanis' emphasis on the objective existence of the juridical quite apart from its representations within ideology or social consciousness. Juridical form, in his words, exists 'as a specific system of relationships' and has its own history, which is *parallel* to that of the economy. That is, the juridical is

11 Pašukanis' understanding of the notion of juridical form is deeply historical, in opposition to Stammler's aprioric conception; juridical form *in abstracto*, therefore, is the result of abstraction or sedimentation from concrete legal forms. See Andreas Harms, *Warenform und Rechtsform. Zur Rechtstheorie von Eugen Paschukanis* (ça ira-Verlag 2009) 65–67. Cf. Maria Zmierczak, 'Jewgienij Bronisławowicz Paszukanis i jego marksistowska teoria prawa—kilka refleksji krytycznych' (2019) 12 *Z Dziejów Prawa* 587, 590.

12 I am drawing here on the *lex-ius* distinction and using 'juridical' to refer to the law in its most general sense, contrasted with 'legal' as denoting a concrete system of positive law.

13 *Избранные*, 36.

14 ibid 61. Emphasis added.

an objective and material phenomenon which can be studied sociologically and historically,[15] and not merely an ideological phenomenon which exists only in the consciousness of individuals (and thus is subjective or, at best, intersubjective but not objective and material).

Pašukanis emphasises the specificity of the juridical relationships which do not allow them to be dissolved in the general category of the ideological superstructure.[16] In his social ontology of the juridical, Pašukanis consciously draws on Marx's hylomorphism[17] (where the content is a material product which, by the imposition of the value form, becomes a new substance—the commodity)[18] to explain *inter alia* the way in which a human being (the material content) is transformed into a juridical subject due to the imposition of juridical form.[19] Incidentally, it would not be an exaggeration to say that—by employing Marxian conceptual tools—Pašukanis, in fact, defended the autonomy[20] of the juridical.[21]

15 Artur Kozak, '[book review of:] J.B. Paszukanis, *Ogólna teoria prawa a marksizm*, Warszawa 1985' (1989) 25 *Przegląd Prawa i Administracji* 238, 239. Cf. Cosmin Cercel, *Towards a Jurisprudence of State Communism: Law and the Failure of Revolution* (Routledge 2018) 89.

16 Cf. Márcio Bilharinho Naves, *Marxismo e direito: um estudo sobre Pachukanis* (Boitempo Editorial 2000) 56–57; Adolfo Sánchez Vázques, 'Pashukanis, teorico marxista del derecho' (1977) 2(2) *Dialéctica* 99, 104–5.

17 Harms (n 11) 66–67. Cf. Andreas Arndt, 'Rechtsform gleich Warenform? Zur Methode in Paschukanis' *Allgemeine Rechtslehre und Marxismus*' in *Rechtst- und Staatskritik nach Marx und Paschukanis* (Bertz + Fischer 2021). Hylomorphism was already present in Marx's dissertation and arguably influenced his later thinking about the value-form, use-form and capital as such. See Gabriele Schimmenti, 'Marx's Dissertation in Light of the Value-Form' (2023) 31(4) *Historical Materialism* 206.

18 See e.g. Karl Marx and Frederick Engels, *35 Collected Works* (Lawrence and Wishart 1996) 57.

19 Marx also applied a hylomorphic approach to law, differentiating between law *qua* legal form and law *qua* social relationships (Staśkiewicz (n 4) 50). By contrast, the 'hyperpositivist' legal theory associated with Andrej Vyšinskij, was 'essentially contrary to the Marxian method, assuming a unity of juridical form and social relationships' (ibid 53), and therefore collapsing the refined hylomorphic analysis. I do not agree with Melkevik's non-hylomorphic interpretation of Pashukanis (if I understand it correctly), according to which the juridical form has no corresponding content (Bjarne Melkevik, *Marxisme et philosophie du droit: Le cas Pasukanis* [Buenos Books 2010] 58–59).

20 Cf. Felipe Araújo Castro, 'Bourdieu Meets Pachukanis' (2020) 11(1) *Revista Direito e Práxis* 117, 127, 139–40.

21 As judge of the Cassation Division of the Revolutionary Tribunal, he was one of the co-signatories of the Circular of 6 October 1918 which, for the first time after the Revolution, provided for a fairly detailed list of crimes, thus restoring elements of the *nullum crimen sine lege* principle. Prior to that, as judge of one of district tribunals in Moscow, in March 1918 he gave a lecture in which he criticised the decision of a local Council of Delegates to change a court judgment, thus defending judicial independence. See Adam Bosiacki, *Utopia. Władza. Prawo. Doktryna i koncepcje prawne bolszewickiej Rosji 1917–1921* (2nd edn, Liber 2012) 220–22.

To grasp the full significance of the fragment quoted above, it needs to be put in the context of two important *loci* within the Marxist *corpus*. Firstly, in the context of the definition of ideology in *The German Ideology* (1845) where the latter is described as being entirely epiphenomenal:

> Morality, religion, metaphysics, and all the rest of ideology as well as the forms of consciousness corresponding to these, thus no longer retain the semblance of independence. *They have no history, no development*; but people *(Menschen)*, developing their material production and their material intercourse, alter, along with this their actual world, also their thinking and the products of their thinking. It is not consciousness that determines life, but life that determines consciousness.[22]

Although this specific sentence in *The German Ideology* which contains the famous phrase, 'they have no history, no development' ('*sie haben keine Geschichte, keine Entwicklung*') does not enumerate the law *expressis verbis*, it is absolutely clear from the context that law is treated by Marx and Engels as part of their understanding of ideology,[23] enumerated there alongside 'politics, laws (*Gesetze*), morality, religion, metaphysics, etc., of a people'[24] in the previous paragraph of the same text. Fourteen years later, in the *Contribution to the Critique of Political Economy* (1859), Marx spoke of 'the juristic (*juristisch*), political, religious, artistic or philosophic—in short, ideological forms in which people (*Menschen*) become conscious of this [class] conflict and fight it out'.[25] In both quotes from Marx (which, characteristically, have been consciously followed in terms of style by Pašukanis) the law appears alongside other 'ideological forms', and is not ascribed any specific, autonomous status. The *keine Geschichte* thesis means that they are entirely epiphenomenal, that is, that the ideological superstructure is simply a reflection of the economic base and the class struggle which occur within it. By contrast, Pašukanis—by using Marxian hylomorphic method—goes beyond or, to be precise, even contrary to Marx because, in the fragment quoted above, he countenanced the *materiality* of the juridical, that is, the fact that—in contrast to *purely ideological* phenomena as religion or metaphysics—the

22 Karl Marx and Friedrich Engels, 'The German Ideology' in Marx and Engels, 5 *Collected Works* (1976) 36–37. Translation corrected after Karl Marx and Friedrich Engels, 'Die Deutsche Ideologie' in Marx and Engels, 3 *Werke* (Dietz Verlag 1978) 26–27. Emphasis added.

23 See for example, Булат В. Назмутдинов, 'Постмарксистская критика права в XX веке: Введение в проблематику' in ЕН Тонков and ИИ Осветимская (eds), *Критические теории права* (Алетейя 2023) 63.

24 Marx and Engels, 'The German Ideology' (n 22) 36.

25 Marx, 'A Contribution to the Critique of Political Economy' in Marx and Engels, 29 *Collected Works* (2010) 263. Translation altered after Marx, 'Zur Kritik der politischen Ökonomie' in Marx and Engels, 13 *Werke* (Dietz 1961) 9.

juridical does in fact have its own history and development, and is itself a historically determined phenomenon.[26] To wit: the obvious stylistic parallel to *The German Ideology* and the departure from the views espoused there could not have been accidental in a text written by someone as familiar with Marx and Engels as Pašukanis, and ostensibly seeking to construct a *Marxist* theory of law.

The second *locus* in the Marxist *corpus* at which Pašukanis hints, both stylistically and semantically, is the famous passage from the already quoted preface to Marx's *Contribution to a Critique of Political Economy*, where we read:

> In the social production of their existence, people (*Menschen*) inevitably enter into *definite relations, which are independent of their will*, namely relations of production appropriate to a given stage in the development of their material forces of production. The totality of these relations of production constitutes the economic structure of society, the real base, on which arises a juristic and political superstructure and to which correspond certain forms of social consciousness. The mode of production of material life conditions, in general, the social, political and intellectual life process. It is not the consciousness of people that determines their existence, but their social existence that determines their consciousness.[27]

According to Marx, the relations in which people enter 'independent[ly] of their will' are the relations of production, that is, economic relations between workers and the owners of the means of production. He does not mention juridical relationships as such but places them in the superstructure. By contrast, according to Pašukanis, people *also* enter into juridical relationships, 'not because they have consciously chosen them, but because they are forced to do so by the conditions of production'. For Marx, the statement about relationships of production is a starting point for discerning between the 'real' base, on the one hand, and the 'juristic and political superstructure' (*ein juristischer und politischer Überbau*),[28] on the other hand. Indeed, it is in the Preface to the *Critique of Political Economy*, a text written in preparation for the *opus magnum* of *Das Kapital*,[29] that the famous base-superstructure theorem takes its origin, notoriously assigning the law a place within the

26 Cercel (n 15) 89.

27 ibid. Emphasis added.

28 Characteristically, the juridical component of the 'superstructure' is described as juristic (*juristisch*), and and not as 'juridical' (*rechtlich*) or 'legal' (*gesetzlich*). In this way, Marx emphasises the role of the legal profession—the jurists—in creating, upholding and developing the *juristischer Überbau*.

29 Cf. Karl Marx, 'Preface to the First Edition' in Marx, 1 *Capital: A Critique of Political Economy* (Penguin 1990) 89.

ontologically inferior superstructure. But Pašukanis, in carefully drawing both on this metaphor, and the 'ideology has no history' thesis, consciously entered into a polemic with Marx or, at the very least,—presumably for the sake of building a Marxist legal theory 'with Marx, but going beyond Marx'—considered it necessary to correct the classical Marxist view and upgrade the place of law in the broader scheme of (a revised) Marxist social ontology.

Juridical Form Versus Juridical Superstructure

At this point, a note needs to be made on the use of the term 'juridical superstructure' (*юридическая надтройка*) by Pašukanis and its relation to juridical and legal form. Undoubtedly, Pašukanis countenances the existence of the juridical superstructure 'with its formal laws, courts, procedures, advocates, etc.'[30] but according to Miéville it is possible conceptually to differentiate it, in his understanding, from juridical form as such.[31] A characteristic passage where the distinction is made is, for instance, this:

> The basic prerequisite of legal regulation is thus the opposition of private interests. This is at the same time the logical prerequisite of the legal form and the real reason for the development of the juridical superstructure.[32]

However, there are places in *The General Theory* where Pašukanis uses the terms 'form of law' (*форма права*) and 'juridical superstructure' (*юридическая надстройка*) as synonyms, following each other.[33] We have to keep in mind, though, that *The General Theory* was intended just as an exploratory essay and not a definitive statement,[34] and, thus, its terminology was not necessarily precisely chosen. The distinction between juridical form and juridical superstructure sits well with the overarching features of Pašukanis' hylomorphic theory which presupposes the logical and historical primacy of the autonomous subject of private law over the sovereign of public law, of the subjective right over objective law and of the juridical relationship over the legal norm established by the state.[35] An alternative reading to the form versus superstructure distinction thesis assumed by Miéville is the interpretation provided by Cosmin Cercel who claims that for Pašukanis 'the

30 *Избранные*, 37; cf. ibid 85–86.

31 See Miéville (n 8) 88–89, 95–96, Gian-Giacomo Fusco 'Legal Subjectivity and Abstraction: Tracing the Past of the Legal Form,' in this volume, 131.

32 *Избранные*, 73.

33 See e.g. *Избранные*, 85.

34 Cf. Kozak, 'J.B. Paszukanis' (n 15) 238.

35 Rafał Mańko, 'Problem autonomii prawa w świetle hylemorficznej teorii J.B. Paszukanisa' [The Problem of Law's Autonomy in the Light of E.B. Pašukanis's Hylomorphic Theory] (2024) *Archiwum Filozofii Prawa i Filozofii Społecznej* (forthcoming).

paradigmatic legal relationship is to be sought . . . in the *contiguous zone* between the material base and the deepest layer of the legal superstructure where "property relations" are instituted'.[36] Thus, for Cercel, juridical form does belong to the superstructure but occupies within it a special place—'the deepest layer'—and the juridical form as such arises within a 'contiguous zone' between that deepest layer of the superstructure and the underlying economic base. Regardless of whether we consider that juridical form and juridical superstructure need to be conceptually differentiated (which, in my view, finds certain support in the text of *The General Theory*, as claimed by Miéville) or that the juridical form is part of the superstructure (or perhaps its foundation), what is crucial is the relation between the juridical, on one hand, and what is external to it. After all, the concept of a 'superstructure' is, in the last instance, nothing more than a conceptual metaphor which is aimed at expressing a certain real social relationship.

Law and the Political Superstructure

This brings us to the second zone of distinction, put forward by Pašukanis, namely that between law and politics—he sought to show that the juridical superstructure was not genetically subordinated to the political superstructure.[37] Within his theory, he conceptualised this question, in a 'logical and systemic' dimension, as one concerning the relationship between *ius obiectivum*, the objective law, and *ius subiectivum*, the subjective right.[38] In the controversy, which engaged many jurists of his times, such as notably Duguit, Bierling and Petrażycki, Pašukanis clearly took the view about the primacy and originality of the *ius subiectivum* over the *ius obiectivum*.[39] In this vein, he also rejected the view of the primacy of the political before the juridical:

> If in all [juridical] relationships we will consider the [juridical] norm to be the dominant element, then before we start looking for the juridical superstructure, we have to countenance the existence of a norm-setting authority, i.e., in other words, of a political organisation. This way we should arrive at the conclusion that the juridical superstructure is a consequence of the political superstructure.
>
> However, Marx himself emphasises the fact that the basic, most deep layer of the legal superstructure—the relationships of ownership, are so closely connected with the base that they are only 'the same relationships

36 Cercel (n 15) 90, emphasis added.

37 Kozak, 'Poglądy' (n 4) 12–13.

38 *Избранные*, 89. The Russian terms are '*объективное право*' and '*субъективное право*' where the signifier '*право*' (*ius*, *Recht*, *droit*) is used for both its objective and subjective emanation. Due to the lack of the *ius*/*lex* distinction in English, I have opted for the Latin terms.

39 *Избранные*, 83.

> of production, expressed in juristic language'. The state, i.e. the organisation of political class rule, stems from the given relationships of production or relationships of ownership. The relationships of production and their juridical expression constitute that what Marx, following in Hegel's footsteps, called civil society. The political superstructure, particularly official statedom, is a secondary, derived element.[40]

In this fragment, Pašukanis very clearly underscores the intimate relationship between the relationships of production and the relationships of ownership—both of which express the same reality, but one in economic terms, whereas the other one—in juristic, or—to put it in hylomorphic terms—they are two different forms which are built upon the same material content.[41] Pašukanis quotes Marx who describes the relations of ownership (*Eigentumsverhältnisse*) as a merely 'juristic expression' (*juristischer Ausdruck*) of relations of production (*Produktionsverhältnisse*).[42] To say that the relationships of ownership are a juristic way of describing production relationships amounts to saying that the object of description (the phenomenon at stake) is the same, only the terminology differs. But whereas Marx was using this expression *from the point of view of a philosopher and historian*, that he considered himself to be,[43] Pašukanis seems to employ it from the perspective of a jurist, that is—from within the juridical institutional world.[44] Thus, when the (social) philosopher and (economic) historian Marx says that a given legal concept is but the 'juristic expression' of an underlying economic concept, he makes the impression of seeking to downplay the importance of jurisprudence and conveying the message that jurists employ their technical guild language in order describe, in cryptic terms, the economic reality, which is the only real one. But when the jurist Pašukanis quotes Marx in the early days of the Soviet state and law, he wants to emphasise something else, namely that lawyers are actually working *on the same key economic concepts* as Marx did, that their legal conceptual framework is not an ideological fantasy, detached from reality, but an actual description of the economic core of social ontology. The juridical form is not, therefore, an ideological mirage but rather a form of the same objective, social content which is also expressed through economic form.[45] Or, to put it in other words, that the

40 ibid. The quotation from Marx is from 'A Contribution,' 263, translation altered after original (Marx, 'Zur Kritik' (n 25) 9) and syntactically adapted to the Russian version.

41 Cf. Mańko, 'Problem autonomii' (n 35).

42 Marx, 'Zur Kritik'(n 25) 9.

43 ibid 7.

44 Cf. B Peckham, 'Pashukanis in Perspective' (1987) 12(1) *Journal of Juridical Science* 80.

45 This follows Marx's sophisticated social hylomorphism which allows the same content to be expressed by different forms. For instance, the same material product can be expressed through value form or through use form. See for example, Marx, *Capital* (n 29) 57.

same relations of exchange are endowed with 'a double character: economic and juridical'.[46]

This allows to conclude that for Pašukanis, the juristic reader of Marx, the law is, indeed, phenomenologically subordinated to the economy (in this sense, it is a 'juridical *superstructure*') but it is a special kind of superstructure, one which, on an ontological plane, is endowed with a 'parallel history and development', thus with a proper, self-sustained existence, in contrast to the ideological mirages which are merely the more or less distorted reproductions of reality in human consciousness taken in its social dimension. Therefore, the juridical is not just like any other superstructural phenomenon, not even like politics, but it is 'a special social relationship'.[47] As B Peckham put it, for Pašukanis, '[t]he legal system is not merely a form into which the dominant class "injects" its ideology. It is an integral and necessary element of the overall structure of that society'.[48]

Perhaps the most powerful plea for treating the juridical—the form of law—as an objectively existing, substantial form of legal relationships *qua* economic relationships cloaked in juridical form was provided by Pašukanis in the following paragraph from the preface to the second Russian edition of *The General Theory*:

> The more or less free flow of social production and reproduction which, in a society producing commodities takes place formally through a number of private juridical acts—this is the *deeply practical purpose* of the juridical bond. It cannot be attained exclusively through forms of consciousness, i.e. purely subjective moments: there is the need for scales, for laws, there is the need for their interpretation, there is the need for casuistry, there is the need for courts and enforcement of judgments. For this reason only one cannot, when discussing the form of law limit oneself to "pure ideology" and not take into account this entire, objectively existing apparatus. Any juridical effect, for instance the resolution of a juridical dispute, is an objective fact, situated outside the consciousness of the participants, just like that economic phenomenon which is, in the given case, mediated through law.[49]

Pašukanis' hylomorphic ontology of law[50] is clearly at work in this formulation. The production of commodities 'takes place formally' via contract law and the economic phenomena are 'mediated through law'. Importantly, Pašukanis does not deny or exclude the psychological or ideological

46 Staśkiewicz (n 4) 43.
47 ibid.
48 Peckham (n 44) 72, 79.
49 *Избранные*, 39–40.
50 Cf. ibid 47–48.

aspects of the law: the 'practical purpose of the juridical bond', he writes, 'cannot be attained *exclusively* through forms of consciousness', through '*purely subjective* moments', but this formulation does not, of course, negate the fact that juridical phenomena, just like economic phenomena, have their reflection both in individual consciousness and in social imaginaries, that is—in ideology.[51] The important point is that neither economic, nor juridical phenomena are purely psychological or ideological, but rather material and objective.[52] Both sides of the hylomorphic relation—the form and the content of law—correspond to the conditions of a society of commodity producers.[53]

However, the fact that law *is not ideology* does not deny the fact that it has *ideological implications*. However, such implications should not overshadow the law's proper ontological status because:

> The recognition of the ideological character of those or other concepts does not liberate us at all from the efforts to find the objective reality, i.e. existing in the external world, and not only in consciousness. Otherwise we will be forced to obliterate any border between the world of afterlife which also exists in the imaginations of some people, and, let us say—the state.[54]

Therefore, the fact that the juridical is an ideological phenomenon—which, importantly, Pašukanis does not deny—needs to be distinguished from the claim that law is *exclusively* ('*лишь*') an ideological phenomenon, that is, that law *is* ideology and *nothing but* ideology. For Pašukanis, there is nothing objectionable in the statement that 'general juridical concepts may become part and actually do become part of ideological processes and ideological systems'.[55] What is important for him, is that this ideological dimension of the juridical should not overshadow its actual ontological dimension as a distinct dimension of social being. To support his argument, he draws attention to the concept of state:

> The state is not only an ideological form, but simultaneously it is also a form of social being. The ideological character of the concept does not obliterate the reality and materiality of those relationships which it expresses.[56]

In the preface to the second edition of *The General Theory*, Pašukanis responded to critique by Pëtr Ivanovič Stučka who—rather surprisingly—claimed that for Pašukanis the juridical form is allegedly 'a simple reflection

51 ibid 39.
52 ibid. Cf. Harms (n 11) 52; Linda Lilith Obermayr, *Die Kritik der marxistischen Rechtstheorie: Zur Paschukanis' Begriff der Rechtsform* (Velbrück 2022) 148.
53 Sánchez Vázques (n 16) 106.
54 *Избранные*, 66.
55 ibid 67.
56 ibid 68.

of purest ideology'.[57] Responding to this claim which he considered to be an unfounded accusation, Pašukanis reiterated his statement about the 'parallel history' of the law, quoted already, and explained:

> To put it otherwise, the form of law expressed through logical abstractions, is the product of a real or concrete (this is the expression used by Comrade Stučka) juridical form, of a real mediation of the relations of production. I not only showed that the genesis of juridical form should be searched for in the relations of exchange, but also identified that moment which, from my point of view, constitutes the fullest realisation of juridical form, namely the court and the judicial process.[58]

Three crucial points should be noted with regard to this fragment. Firstly, it is the distinction between the form of law (*форма права*) on one hand, and the juridical (or legal) form (*правовая форма*) on the other.[59] The former—which I will refer to as 'juridical form'—denotes the form of law in the abstract and general, that is, the operation of law vis-à-vis its socio-economic content. In Pašukanis' own words, the form of law is 'expressed through logical abstractions', that is, it is a system of formally abstracted concepts that represent the legal system in the abstract. The form of law in this sense is not any concretely existing legal system, but the abstract idea of law in the juristic sense; in other words, it is 'pure juridicity' at the highest level of conceptual abstraction. By contrast, the concept of *legal form* denotes concrete, empirically existing legal systems which express, in legal terms, the relations of production existing in concrete states (legality). This distinction will be relevant to understanding Pašukanis's critique of juridical form that I discuss in the next section.

Towards a Critique of Juridical Ideology

Theoretical Foundations

In the previous section, I drew attention to Pašukanis' distinction between the form of law (*форма права*) and legal form (*правовая форма*), interpreting it as a distinction between *juridical form* in its most general terms, as opposed to the *legal form* of a concretely existing system of positive law. An analysis of

57 Петр Иванович Стучка, *Революционная роль права и государства: Общее учение о праве* (3rd edn, Издательство Коммунистической Академии 1924) V. Although Stučka placed this phrase in a quotation mark, as if quoting directly from Pašukanis, in fact this is not the case and such a sentence cannot be found in *The General Theory*.

58 *Избранные*, 39.

59 The two concepts bear a resemblance to the external versus internal legal form, proposed by Lev Yavich. See Лев С Явич, *Общая теория права* (Издательство Ленинградского Университета 1976) 97–99. Cf. Rafał Mańko, 'Legal Form, Ideology and the Political' in Adam Sulikowski, Rafał Mańko and Jakub Łakomy (eds), *Legal Scholarship and the Political: In Search of a New Paradigm* (C.H. Beck 2020) 28.

Pašukanis' critique of juridical ideology on the pages of *The General Theory* seems to confirm this reading. Additionally, Pašukanis devotes quite some attention to an ideology critique which is focused specifically on the views of jurists, that is, juristic ideology which he treats as distinct from the law as such, although perceives them as closely intertwined.[60] Drawing on this tripartite distinction—not formulated explicitly by Pašukanis, though plausible as an interpretive frame for reading *The General Theory*—I will, in this section, distinguish between three phenomenal forms of juristic ideology: firstly, the *ideology of juridical form* as such, that is the objective ideological content of the very form of law in its most generalised abstractions;[61] secondly, the *legal ideology* understood as the ideological underpinnings and implications of concretely existing legal forms in connection to their socio-economic content; and, thirdly the *juristic ideology*, that is, the professional or guild ideology of lawyers.

Critique of Ideology of the Juridical Form

First of all, Pašukanis never claimed that juridical form is a faithful reflection of social reality. To the contrary, he called it 'a mystified form of a certain specific social relationship'.[62] Regarding the purpose of the critique of juridical ideology, Pašukanis provided a hylomorphic answer, pointing to the need to exploit bourgeois forms, 'exhausting them to the end' which requires to subject them to an ideology critique:

> One has, therefore, to remember that morality, law and the state are forms of a bourgeois society. If the proletariat is forced to make use of them, it does not at all mean the possibility of any further development of those forms with the purpose of filling them with socialist content. Nonetheless, in the current transitory period the proletariat should, in its own class interest, make use of those forms inherited from a bourgeois society, and thereby exhaust them to the end. In order to do so, it must first of all have a completely clear, free from ideological fog, understanding of the historical origin of these forms.[63]

Ideology critique, in this perspective, is perceived as a means towards a precise end, namely that of arriving at a 'completely clear . . . understanding' of

60 Cf. Obermayr (n 52) 155–60.

61 This is consistent with the fact that *The General Theory* addresses the juridical as such, even if it focuses on bourgeois law (Sánchez Vázques (n 16) 104). Although Pašukanis emphasises the perfection of bourgeois legal form *qua* juridical form *par excellence*, nonetheless the latter arises 'whenever private exchange or private property exist, in however rudimentary form' (Dimick, 'Pashukanis' (n 3) 120).

62 *Избранные*, 71.

63 ibid 152.

juridical form, one that will be 'free from ideological fog', that is, distortions which separate the subject of cognition from its object. A critique of the fundamental features of juridical form as such is, in Pašukanis' case, inevitably entangled with the critique of the legal form of bourgeois, capitalist law given that he considered the latter to be the fullest emanation of juridical form.[64] However, for analytical purposes, it is possible to disentangle them, discussing under the heading of critique of the ideology of juridical form those passages in *The General Theory* which address ideological distortions of juridical form as such, separately from those which specifically address bourgeois law.

The gist of any juridical form is its reductionist, selective and abstracting approach to social reality which is subject to juridification.[65] Hence, a primary direction of ideology critique directed at the juridical is to emphasise this process and draw attention to it.

> Just as the natural multiplicity of use-values of a product is, in a commodity, a simple shell of value, and the concrete types of human labour are dissolved into abstract human labour as the creator of value—so too the concrete multiplicity of the relations between of the human to a thing appears as the abstract will of the owner, and all concrete characteristics which distinguish one representative of the genus *homo sapiens* genus from one another dissolve into the abstraction of human being in general—as a juridical subject.[66]

Indeed, one of the key features of juridical form is the interchangeability of subjects and objects of juridical relationships, that is, of *personae* and *res* which are, legally speaking, all of the same abstract quality, they are all *fungibiles*, juridically interchangeable.[67] As Costas Douzinas puts it, juridical '[p]ersonhood abstracts from the specific characteristics of the human being, brackets its history, needs, desires, treating humans as calculable and comparable units'.[68] What is more, *iura in rem* and *in personam* are equally abstract, conflating ownership of the means of production with ownership of consumer

64 Staśkiewicz (n 4) 44; Dimick, 'Pashukanis' (n 3) 120.

65 Costas Douzinas, *The Radical Philosophy of Rights* (Routledge 2019) 122; Mańko, 'Legal Form' (n 59) 29–30. Cf. Hugh Collins, *Regulating Contracts* (OUP 2003) 15–16.

66 *Избранные*, 106.

67 Cf. Aldo Schiavone, 'La produzione normativa' in idem (ed), *Storia giuridica di Roma* (Giapichelli 2016) 135–36; idem, *The Invention of Law in the West* (Belknap Press 2012) 202–6; idem, 'Singularity and Impersonality in the Thought of Roman Jurists' in Fara Nasti and Aldo Schiavone (eds), *Jurists and Legal Science in the History of Roman Law* (Routledge 2022) 8. See also Dan Swain, 'Justice as Fetish: Marx, Pashukanis, and the Form of Justice' (2018) 2(2) *Contradictions: A Journal for Critical Thought* 13, 20.

68 Douzinas, *Radical* (n 65) 122. Cf. Gian-Giacomo Fusco, 'Notes on the Person and the Anthropological Machine of Law' in Thanos Zartaloudis (ed), *Law and Philosophical Theory: Critical Intersections* (Rowman and Littlefield 2018) 85.

goods and other personal possessions.[69] This approach—which is an effect of juridical ideology[70]—belongs to the fundamental core of juridical form as such, although, obviously, it becomes more pronounced in some legal forms (such as in bourgeois legal form), whereas it can be less pronounced or even *prima facie* difficult to discern in legal forms which put an emphasis on the specificity of various classes of subjects and objects (such as feudal law). Of course, the same *persona* can sometimes act as an *emptor* or *venditor*, *locator* or *conductor*, *actor* or *reus*,[71] the same *res* can be acquired, alienated, onerated, transformed, lost, destroyed, etc., but the pure potentiality of all *personae* and *res* to become subjects and objects of such more detailed legal *figurae*, or—more precisely—their fundamental abstract quality of being *potentially* involved in any kind of juridical relationship belongs to the very fundamental core of the concepts of *persona* and *res* in their essential abstraction.[72] Pašukanis was well aware of this 'juridical metaphysics'[73] and subjected it to an ideology critique:

> There is no doubt that the concept of a moral or equally valuable individual is an ideological creation and, as such, it is inadequate of reality. A no less ideological distortion of actual reality is also the egoistic, managing subject. Nonetheless both those descriptions correspond to one specific social relationship but express it abstractly and therefore one-sidedly.[74]

Pašukanis is critical also of one of the other concepts which are the *naturalia* of any juridical form such as notably the concept of justice which, following Marx, he considers as being inherently linked to commodity exchange:

> the very concept of justice is derived from the relationship of exchange and does not express anything outside it. In essence, the very concept of justice does not contain anything new compared to the concept of equality of people. . . . Therefore, it is ridiculous to see in the idea of justice some independent and absolute criterion. True, if used skilfully, it gives more possibility to explain inequalities than equality and therefore is particularly useful to mask the ambiguity of ethical form.[75]

Finally, in line with his sceptical approach to the juridicity[76] of public law, and his consideration of private law as the 'prototype of juridical form in

69 Douzinas, *Radical* (n 65) 125.
70 ibid.
71 Cf. Fusco (n 68) 85.
72 Cf. Dimick, 'Pashukanis' (n 3) 119–23.
73 Cf. Schiavone, *Invention* (n 67) 202.
74 *Избранные*, 146.
75 ibid 153.
76 I borrow the term from Paul Amselek, *Methode phénoménologique et théorie du droit* (Librairie générale de droit et de jurisprudence 1964) 49, English translation after: Neil

general',[77] Pašukanis seemingly approached the form of public law *as such* as an ideological phenomenon which distorted the picture of the reality of political relationships *as if* they were juridical in nature (i.e. based on exchange), whereas they are not:

> The 'juridical' demands emanating from the state authorities, are nothing less than a juridical stylisation of facts of political life. A demand of the state appears as an impartial and disinterested law. In this case one almost cannot imagine the state as a subject—to such a degree it is deprived of any substance and transformed into an abstract guarantee of relations between real subjects—the owners of goods.[78]

In the same vein, Pašukanis was sceptical of any legal theories of statehood:

> the logic of relations of power and subjection only partly arrange themselves into a system of juridical concepts. Therefore, the juridical conception of state can never become a theory, it will always be an ideological distortion of facts.[79]

His sociological, deeply realist consciousness that politics cannot be fully symbolised within the juridical order, that they escape full juridical symbolisation,[80] always leaving a certain unjuridified surplus, led Pašukanis to reject legal-formalist theories of statehood[81] as an ideological fiction.

Critique of (Bourgeois) Legal Ideology

The Generalisation of Juridical Ideology

Whereas the ideology critique of juridical form as such, in its most general outlines, was not the main point of focus in *The General Theory*, there is much more to be found as regards to the critique of legal ideology—and specifically bourgeois legal ideology. This does not come as a surprise for two reasons: firstly, Pašukanis repeatedly claimed that the bourgeois legal form is the most accomplished type of juridical form; and secondly, it was the

Duxbury, 'Normativity and Technique in the Legal Philosophy of Paul Amselek' (1989) 75(1) *Archiv für Rechts- und Sozialphilosophie* 104, 105.

77 *Избранные*, 158, n. 11.

78 ibid.

79 ibid 88.

80 Cf. Mathew Bolton, 'Three theories of separation: Kelsen, Schmitt and Pashukanis and the historical development of the legal form' (2023) *Philosophy & Social Criticism*, online first https://doi.org/10.1177/01914537231170908l4, 14.

81 For example, Hans Kelsen, *Communist Theory of Law* (Praeger 1955) 95–96.

legal form he knew the best from his own education, research and everyday experience in the times of NEP.[82] But there is also a third reason, connected to juridical ideology under the bourgeois system, exposed by Pašukanis in the following terms:

> in bourgeois society, as opposed to a society of slave-owners and feudal society, that juridical form attains a universal meaning, that juridical ideology becomes above all ideology, and the protection of class interests of exploiters is realised most effectively as the protection of abstract principles of juridical subjectivity.[83]

Under the capitalist mode of production, the place of law and legal ideology differs from other formations for two reasons. Firstly, because the juridical ideology 'attains a universal meaning'—it is not only relevant for the law but for the entire society in all of its dimensions. This universality of juridical ideology makes it 'above all ideology', in the sense that it becomes the general ideology of society; or, to put it in other words, that ideology becomes juridified, that society adopts juridical ideology as its own ideology. Secondly, because the 'abstract principles of juridical subjectivity', that is, the foundational building block of *any* juridical form, within the legal ideology of a bourgeois society gain a new important function of upholding the protection of class interests of exploiters. Indeed, the juridification of human relationships in capitalism goes hand in hand with their commodification,[84] and the theoretical possibility of class mobility finds its juridical expression in emergent positivistic conceptions of law.[85] One could add here that the presence of such principles in other legal ideologies, notably those of feudal or slave-holding societies, could have been counter-hegemonic because members of legally repressed groups (slaves or serfs) could refer to the abstractness of the *persona* as an argument in favour of their political and juridical emancipation (by contrast with the law of their times which formally made them slaves or serfs, depriving them of juridical personhood and simultaneously subjecting them to reification).[86] In capitalism, by contrast, the exploited classes are juridically emancipated, but remain economically oppressed: however, the juridical ideology plays an opposite role—it preserves the unequal relationships in the name of equal possibilities.[87] Juridical subjectivity—legal personhood—becomes central to the ideological setup of capitalist societies.

82 Cf. Sánchez Vázques (n 16) 107–8; Michael Head, *Evgeny Pashukanis: A Critical Reappraisal* (Routledge-Cavendish 2008) 157–60.

83 *Избраные*, 41.

84 Kamenka, 'Marxism', 27–8.

85 Назмутдинов, 'Постмарксистская,' 78.

86 Cf. Dimick, 'Pashukanis' (n 3) 130; Fusco (n 68) 87.

87 Douzinas, *Radical* (n 65) 124.

As Costas Douzinas put it, '[t]the person belongs to law as the most prominent characteristic of modernity's nomophilia'.[88]

Critique of the Rule of Law

Mature bourgeois legal form introduces, under the influence of liberal legal ideology, the concept of the rule of law, known in the Civilian tradition as *Rechtsstaat/état de droit*, literally translated into Russian as *правовое государство*.[89] For Pašukanis, this concept was not so much a juridical concept, but a question of an ideological 'mirage':

> The rule of law is a mirage, but a mirage which is very comfortable for the bourgeoisie because it replaces the weathered religious ideology, it conceals from the masses the fact of the bourgeoisie's domination. The rule of law ideology is more convenient than the religious one because whilst not fully reflecting the objective reality, it is nonetheless based on it. Power as the 'general will', as the 'power of law' is fulfilled in a bourgeois society to the extent that the latter is a market.[90]

In Pašukanis' perspective, the function of the rule of law is not so much to limit the powers of state organs (as the liberal narrative has it), but rather to conceal the domination of the bourgeoisie over the exploited classes. In this role, the 'rule of law ideology' is more effective than 'state religious ideology' because of its more intimate relationship to reality: whilst it partly distorts reality, it is still 'based on it'.[91] What is more, the supremacy of law is indeed a fact, but only to the extent that the law is identified with the outcomes of capitalist market exchange, which for inherent structural reasons privilege the bourgeoisie over the exploited classes.[92] One could therefore say that the rule of law ideology contains a reflection of reality *plus a surplus of distortion*; in other words, it contains truthful elements *enriched by a lie*. In a footnote to this fragment, Pašukanis refers to the *Communist Manifesto* to say that '[i]n historical reality the rule of law, i.e. the state standing above society is realised only as its own opposition, i.e. as the "executive committee for the affairs of the bourgeoisie" '.[93] To summarise: the rule of law ideology

88 ibid 122.

89 I have opted for rendering the Russian *правовe государство* (*Rechtstaat*) as 'rule of law'. On the (subtle) historical and conceptual distinctions between *Rechtstaat* and rule of law see, for example, Jens Meierhenrich, '*Rechtsstaat* versus the Rule of Law' in Jens Meierhenrich and Martin Loughlin (eds), *The Cambridge Companion to the Rule of Law* (CUP 2021) 39–67.

90 *Избранные*, 138.

91 Cf. ibid 133.

92 Cf. Douzinas, *Radical* (n 65) 124.

93 *Избранные*, 143 n. 15. I retained the Russian wording of the quote from the Communist Manifesto which is slightly different from the German original (cf. Marx and Engels, 4 *Werke* [Dietz 1977], 464).

is true insofar as the legal apparatus indeed wields power over society but it is false insofar as it conceals how this apparatus depends on the ruling class. Thus, the false element in the rule of law ideology is its focus on form with a simultaneous concealment of its class content.

Pašukanis also addressed the crisis of the rule of law ideology, ultimately leading to the 'falling of masks' and the emergence of open violence:

> The state as a factor of force both in internal and external policy—this is the correction that the bourgeoisie was forced to make with regard to its theory and practice of the 'rule of law'. The more uncertain the rule of the bourgeoisie was becoming, the faster the 'rule of law' was becoming transformed into its immaterial shadow, until the extreme exacerbation of class struggle forced the bourgeoisie to throw aside the masks of the rule of law and reveal the essence of power as the organised violence of one class over another.[94]

What he hints at here, is the well-known figure of the state of exception as the moment in which the bourgeoisie decides to give up the rule of law ideology altogether and use direct force against the proletariat. As Pašukanis notes, the exception takes over from the rule of law once the class struggle becomes exacerbated to the extreme: one could think, for instance, of the uses of the *état de siège* in France to crush worker's protests[95] or Bismarck's infamous *Sozialistengesetz*.[96]

Critique of Ideological Distortion of the Capitalist Relations of Production

Juridical form with its interchangeable abstractions of the legal subject endowed with a free will to enter into contractual relations and exchange commodities, including commodified labour, is particularly apt to mask the inequalities of capitalist society.[97] Pašukanis focused a significant part of his critique of bourgeois legal form on the discrepancies between the juridical fictions of equality and freedom, on one hand, and the reality of economic inequality and exploitation, on the other. In other words, he noted how the same content (the social reality relationships of production and exchange) is cloaked in a legal form which for the purpose of the proper functioning of the 'social technology' of the juridical[98] conceals and distorts a certain part of that content. For instance, he noted the discrepancy between the protection

94 *Избранные*, 141.
95 Cercel (n 15) 63.
96 RGBl. 1878, S. 351.
97 Douzinas, *Radical* (n 65) 124.
98 Cf. Schiavone, *Invention*, 200.

of ownership in bourgeois law, on one hand, and the 'expropriation of ownership' of an entire class of people, the proletarians, which is a hidden *condicio sine qua non* of the functioning of the entire mechanism for which ownership exists in capitalism:

> Capitalist ownership is, in essence, the freedom to transform capital from one form into another. This freedom to dispose of capitalist ownership is impossible without the presence of individuals deprived of ownership, i.e. proletarians. The juridical form of ownership does not contravene the fact of expropriation of ownership (*экспроприация собственности*) of a large number of citizens. This is because the characteristic of being the subject of rights is a purely formal feature. It qualifies all people as equally 'worthy' of ownership but it does not in any way make them owners.[99]

What is characteristic of bourgeois legal form, in line with the general features of juridical form, is that it treats bourgeois and proletarians 'equally' in juridical terms, that is, both are juridical subjects, 'equally "worthy" of ownership'.[100] Thus, the bourgeois legal form *ex definitione* masks the social class antagonism of the capitalist mode of production by refusing to acknowledge—on a juridical plane—its existence and pretending that members of both classes are the same 'equal' legal subjects which, in economic reality, is not true.[101] But the ideological assumption of equality justifies and legitimises the deployment of the public authority of the state against the workers:

> a hired worker is not politically and juridically forced to work for a given enterpreneur, but alienates onto him his workforce formally, on the basis of a free contract. Because the relation of exploitation is formally realised as a relationship of two 'independent' and 'equal' owners of commodities, from among which one, the proletarian, sells the workforce, and another, the capitalist, purchases it, therefore the political class power can assume the form of public authority.[102]

Pašukanis noted not only the actual inequalities between capitalists and workers but also between various capitalists depending on their market power:

> A powerful capitalist 'acting in good faith', *bona fide* ruins a small one, not endangering for a minute the absolute value of the latter's personality. The personality of a proletarian is 'in principle equal' to the personality of a capitalist; this finds its expression in the fact of a 'free' contract of hire.

99 *Избранные*, 118–19.
100 Cf. Douzinas, *Radical* (n 65) 125.
101 *Избранные*, 138.
102 ibid 134.

> But that same 'materialised freedom' means, for the proletarian, the possibility to peacefully die of hunger.[103]

Importantly, the subordination of workers to the capitalists is not explicitly accounted for in legal terms:

> The domination of the bourgeoisie is expressed both in the dependance of government from banks and capitalist groupings, and in the dependance of every worker on his employer, and in the fact that the members of the state apparatus are personally linked to the ruling class. All these facts—and their number can be multiplied to infinitude—are in no official way legally expressed. But in a certain wonderful way they coincide on account of their significance with those facts which do find their legal, official expression and subordinate the same workers to the laws of the bourgeois state, the orders and decisions of its organs, judgments of its courts, etc.[104]

The officially proclaimed freedom of contract serves to conceal the despotic reality of worker-capitalist relationships:

> exploitation assumes the forms of a 'free contract'. This view lies at the basis of the critique which communism has directed and directs against the bourgeois ideology of freedom and equality, and against formal bourgeois democracy, in which the 'market republic' conceals the '*despotia* of the factory'.[105]

Pašukanis also notes the transformation of capital into an 'impersonal class force' and its consequence—further ideological mystification of the notion of ownership:

> As the capitalist mode of production develops, the owner becomes gradually liberated from technical-productive functions, and together with that, he loses full control over capital. The basic mass of capital entirely becomes an impersonal class force. Because it participates in market transactions, which presupposes the autonomy of its separate parts, those parts appear as the ownership of legal persons. In reality, it is managed by a relatively small group of the most powerful capitalists, acting through their hired representatives or proxies. The juridically distinct form of private

103 ibid 150.

104 ibid 131

105 ibid 35. This opposition was already described in similar terms by Marx and Engels (*Communist Manifesto*, 40) and Vladimir I Lenin, *The State and Revolution* (Robert Service tr, Penguin 1992) 78.

> ownership no longer reflects the actual state of things because by relying on methods of participation and control, factual domination exceeds the purely juridical framework.[106]

Indeed, especially today, when entire structures involving 'parent' companies and their subsidiaries are involved, the mystification of bourgeois ownership reaches, at times, a new peak, concealing the fact that most of the global wealth is held by a handful of individuals. The classical right of ownership, in that context, is approached, even by capitalists themselves, with cynicism.[107]

Critique of Bourgeois Criminal Law

Pašukanis devoted an entire (last) chapter to criminal law, exposing its historical genesis and not shunning away from subjecting bourgeois criminal law to a thorough critique, including ideology critique. He starts by underlining the social reality, in which the criminal courts functioned as a mere appendix to the police apparatus and inflicted 'organised class terror'.[108] This form of critique of law is based on showing the discrepancy between the official narrative of criminal law (based, as it is, on equality before the law, etc.) with the reality of the police and judicial apparatus as a mechanism protecting the rule of the bourgeoisie. Pašukanis also criticised criminal procedure, noting that it is characterised by the presence of an 'irrational, mystified, absurd element [which] is the specifically juridical one'[109]—this element is, according to Pašukanis, the underlying contractual ideology of the criminal process, whereby the victim demands retribution, the prosecutor demands a high price, the indictee seeks to get a discount, and—at the end—'the court decides "according to justice"'. If one sets entirely aside this form of a contract—he noted—one will entirely deprive the criminal procedure of its 'juristic soul'.[110]

The ideological character of criminal law manifests itself in the types of penalties. Pašukanis draws attention to the popularisation of the penalty of imprisonment in the 19th century and links it to the understanding of 'abstract freedom' as a form exchange for the commission of a crime, insightfully noting that the 'necessary precondition of the appearance of the view that a crime can be settled by a pre-determined amount of abstract freedom was the reduction of all concrete forms of social wealth to the simplest and

106 *Избранные*, 120.
107 ibid 92.
108 ibid 165.
109 ibid 169.
110 ibid 168–69.

most abstract form—human labour measured by time'.[111] In this optic, the criminal process is *per se* ideological and mystified: it is, in fact, a form of private law settlement which only externally pretends to be the penal reaction of an impersonal state, but in reality—if we subject it to an ideology critique—it appears to be an extension of the commodity form.[112]

Critique of Juristic Ideology

Pašukanis' critique of legal ideology, discussed above, can be analytically distinguished from his critique of the ideological presuppositions and implications of the common beliefs and assumptions of the juristic community, with particular emphasis on its more intellectually refined representatives. Thus, for instance, he wrote that the 'bourgeois jurists deduct the universalism of juridical form from the eternal and absolute properties of human nature'[113] and noted that 'bourgeois legal philosophy . . . considers juridical relationships as the eternal and natural form of any human relationships'.[114] He criticised jurists for 'naturalising' legal form, for concealing the fact that it expresses the economic relations between owners of goods, and for abstracting from the historical process which gave rise to the emergence of juridical form.[115]

As a Russian scholar who completed his doctorate in Germany, Pašukanis was well-versed in the abstract, conceptual jurisprudence of the Pandectist school (*Pandektistik*) which enjoyed immense influence upon Russian legal culture.[116] Among the chief theoretical achievements of the Pandectists are the abstract and generalised concepts of the 'juridical act' (*Rechtsgeschäft*; *сделка*) and 'declaration of will' (*Willenserklärung*; *волеизъявление*). These concepts are, indeed, highly abstract, and their application throughout private law (and even beyond it, i.e. in administrative law) is based on the acceptance of a number of ideological premises mystifying the reality of legal transactions. Pašukanis approaches the problem from a genealogico-archaeological perspective, noting that the abstract concepts of juridical act and declaration of will are, as such, abstracted from the notion of the contract but in the Pandectist system the logic is turned upside down—the contract is a specific type of a juridical act. What is more, '[o]utside the contract the very concept of a

111 ibid 172.

112 ibid 176. Cf. Zbigniew Cywiński, 'Społeczno-ekonomiczna interpretacja prawa karnego J.B. Paszukanisa' (1987) 4 *Nowe Prawo* 78, 81–82.

113 ibid 74.

114 ibid 75–76.

115 ibid 74–75.

116 Cf. Anton Rudokvas and Alexej Kartsov, 'The Development of Civil Law Doctrine in Imperial Russia Under the Aspect of Legal Transplants (1800–1917)' in Zoran Pokrovac (ed), *Rechtswissenschaft in Osteuropa: Studien zum 19. und frühen 20. Jahrhundert* (Vittorio Klostermann 2010).

subject and will in the juridical sense exist only as dead abstractions'.[117] By resorting to the genealogy and archaeology of the abstract legal concepts of the *Pandektistik*, and showing that the more abstract concepts (juridical act) are only generalisations of more concrete concepts, Pašukanis explores the ideological dimension of Pandectist legal form, its departure from socio-legal reality in the name of an abstract, systemic-logical approach.[118] His critique shows us that not only are these concepts abstract to the extreme, but that they also rely on counter-factual premises,[119] such as that all juridical acts—the commercial contract and the prenuptial agreement, for instance—share the same nature, which, from a socio-legal perspective, is obviously untrue.

Pašukanis is also a critic of the ideology of legal dogmatics with its formal-juridical method, writing that it 'works only with norms, only with what "one is entitled to according to the law"' but in fact '[i]n the material reality [it is] the relationship [that] enjoys primacy over the norm',[120] thus *vice versa* with regard to the formal-juridical approach. He goes on to criticise doctrinal jurists 'for abstracting from real life and focusing only on logical connections between norms',[121] and, more generally, for claiming that the legal norm precedes the legal relationship.[122] This is in general, a critique of legal formalism undertaken from legal realist premises, not uncommon among the jurists of that epoch.

Discussing the question of the juridical subject, Pašukanis notes the moments in which juristic ideology necessarily departs from social reality. He does so, for instance, in the context of the volitional theory of subjective rights which, despite its counter-factuality (e.g. the 'legal capacity of idiots, babies, legal persons'[123]), remains part of the legal thinking about subjectivity. Pašukanis ascribes this to the fact that it is the market exchange which lies at the foundation of the notions of legal subject and legal object, and this remains part and parcel of the juristic ideological consciousness:

> The formal and perfected concept of the subject, which retains only juridical capacity, pulls us farther way from the true historical significance of this juridical category. That is why the *jurists find it so difficult to do without the active, volitional element* in the concepts of subject and subjective right.[124]

117 *Избранные*, 113.
118 Cf. Konrad Zweigert and Hein Kötz, *Introduction to Comparative Law* (Tony Weir tr, 3rd edn, Clarendon Press 1998) 146–47.
119 Cf. Uwe Kischel, *Comparative Law* (OUP 2019) 387.
120 *Избранные*, 79.
121 ibid 82–83.
122 Cf. Kozak, 'Poglądy' (n 4) 10–11.
123 *Избранные*, 109.
124 ibid.

What is interesting in the above fragment is the way in which Pašukanis discerns between the objective content of the juridical form, on one hand, and the collective ideological consciousness of the juristic community, on the other hand. The idea of a volitional subject, a subject endowed with and exercising their 'free will' persists in juristic thinking as a kind of dogmatic legal survival.[125]

Pašukanis provides also an insightful critique of the dogmatic concept of a *contrat d'adhésion*, developed in his times by private lawyers to account for the developing phenomenon of mass, unnegotiated 'contracts'. He pierces the ideological veil to show that, in reality, those 'adhesion contracts' are, in fact, a form of neo-feudal 'private legislation', and the conceptual notion of 'adhesion' is merely a legal fiction.[126] The legal fiction has of course its primary, juridical function of making the internal factory rules legally binding and enforceable vis-à-vis the workers but it also has an ideological function of concealing the reality of a neo-feudal form of law-making which would be too embarrassing for jurists to admit. As a consequence:

> relationships of subordination and domination in the capitalist mode of production may exist, without detaching themselves from that concrete form in which they occur as the domination of the conditions of production over producers. But this precise fact that they do not appear in a masked form, as in the period of slavery and serfdom, makes them imperceptible for the jurist.[127]

What Pašukanis hints at here is the epistemological hindrance effected by juristic ideology: by insisting on 'subsuming' the harsh reality of the factory 'under modernity', bourgeois jurists invent juridical categories (such as *contrat d'adhésion*) which, in effect, make them blind towards the actual reality of genuine subordination and domination, directly comparable to slavery and serfdom. The relationships between capitalist owners and proletarian workers are, in effect, a legal survival of feudalism, but a survival too embarrassing to be accounted for (symbolised) within the juridical order. In his incisive critique, Pašukanis brings those cracks or symptoms of bourgeois juristic ideology to the fore, confronting the convenient legal fiction with actual socio-legal reality on the ground.

Pašukanis goes on to explain why direct domination of human beings over human beings—which is the reality of capitalist relationships of production—cannot be accounted for within bourgeois legal form because direct coercion would be incompatible with the basic premise of that form, which rests on the concept of free commodity owners interacting with each other.

125 On legal survivals see e.g. Rafał Mańko, 'Legal Survivals and the Resilience of Juridical Form' (2023) *Law and Critique* <https://doi.org/10.1007/s10978-023-09357-2>.

126 *Избранные*, 134.

127 ibid 135.

For this fundamental and structural reason, coercion needs to be masked as 'emanating from some abstract, general person, as coercion realised not in the interests of the individual from which it originates . . . but in the interests of all participants in juridical transactions. The power of a human being over a human being is realised as the power of law itself, i.e. as the power of an objective, impartial norm'.[128] This is a very insightful explanation for the ideological blackout described earlier on which shows how the first ideological premises of bourgeois legal form—namely, that all juridical subjects are free and equal—lead to further ideological consequences.

Conclusions

Although the law-ideology nexus is not the main subject-matter of *The General Theory*, nonetheless Pašukanis laid down on its pages important methodological premises for the critique of ideology in the field of the juridical. The *first* premise is ontological: Pašukanis clearly insisted on the distinction between law and ideology. Although he used the expression 'juridical superstructure', he meant by it the relationship between law and the economy which he rendered through a sophisticated hylomorphic social ontology of the juridical. The juridical form, which expresses (*alongside* economic form[129]) the content of relationships of commodity exchange, has—as he insisted—its own, independent but no less real history. This objective and material reality of juridical form has its own existence which is parallel to but independent from the material reality of its underlying economic content.

The *second* premise of Pašukanis's ideology critique is based on the juridical form's selective and one-sided reflection of the underlying social reality. The juridical form is not equal to its content—there is a certain surplus of content which escapes symbolisation as a result of the juridical form's essentially selective and abstract way of operation, which transforms human beings and material objects in interchangeable *res* and *personae*, and their relations into abstracted *iura in rem* and *iura in personam*. Thus, the juridical form reflects only part of the truth of the content it expresses. Therefore, the role of ideology critique, following this premise, is to expose the 'symptoms', that is points of breakdown of the juridical ideology, those points at which the fabric of its ideological presuppositions cracks, allowing to gaze into the abyss of the Real—the *de facto* slavery in the factory, cloaked *de iure* into the form of a *contrat d'adhésion*; the *de facto* direct coercion of workers, dominated by the capitalists, cloaked *de iure* into the form of an impersonal rule

128 ibid 135–36.

129 Cf. Isaac D Balbus, 'Commodity Form and Legal Form: An Essay on the "Relative Autonomy" of Law' (1977) 11(3) *Law and Society Review* 571, 573 who claimed that there is 'identity or homology' between juridical and economic form. But see Dimick, 'Pashukanis' (n 3) 120 (rejecting the homology thesis).

of equal law for all; the *de facto* deep inequalities of bourgeois and proletarians, cloaked *de iure* into the legal form of commodified labour exchanged for money, and so forth. Therefore, Pašukanis' ideology critique encompasses both the element of an immanent critique (focused on internal inconsistencies of juridical ideology) and an external critique (comparison between ideology and social reality).[130]

The *third* premise is the analytical distinction of juridical ideology into its three phenomenal forms—the *ideology of juridical form* as such, the *legal ideology* of a given concretely existing form of legality (such as bourgeois law) or branch of the legal system (such as criminal law), and the *juristic ideology* of the legal community. Although Pašukanis does not formulate this division explicitly, his incisive critique addresses these three spheres of juridical ideology in a distinct fashion.

The analysis of Pašukanis' approach to law and ideology confirms Jerzy Kowalski's thesis that reading *The General Theory of Law and Marxism* one 'has the impression of dealing with a contemporary legal theorist who joined the currently on-going jurisprudential debates'.[131] The reconstruction of his views, which I presented in this chapter are, therefore, only a first step towards integrating them into contemporary debates in critical legal theory, interpretive sociology of law and legal philosophy.

130 Cf. Obermayr (n 52) 153–55.
131 Kowalski (n 2) 10.

Chapter 5

Fetishes of Criminal Law

Reading Pashukanis with Hegel and de Lagasnerie

Linda Lilith Obermayr

Introduction[1]

For the past century, Evgeny Pashukanis' theory of criminal law has either remained unnoticed, has been dismissed as insignificant or was considered a flaw and set aside.[2] It was Norbert Reich who prominently raised the predominant objection of so-called civil law reductionism (*Zivilrechtsreduktionismus*) against Pashukanis, which has been restated for the realm of criminal law by Wolf Rosenbaum.[3] The accusation of civil law reductionism suggests that within Pashukanis' theory of the legal form, all law is reduced to the legal mediation of commodity exchange. To the extent that legal relations are identified with the exchange relation of two commodity owners, Pashukanis' theory would, hence, lack an understanding and proper reflection of public law.[4] By critically engaging with the accusation of civil law reductionism, we will discuss whether Pashukanis' critique of criminal law truly reveals a blind spot of his theory: the state and its interplay with capitalist domination. The significance and originality of Pashukanis' thoughts on criminal law, however, have been recently highlighted, and even considered the key

1 The following considerations build upon my previous work, especially in the chapter 'Äquivalenzprinzip der Strafe' in Linda Lilith Obermayr (ed), *Die Kritik der marxistischen Rechtstheorie: Zu Paschukanis' Begriff der Rechtsform* (Velbrück Wissenschaft 2022) 204–18.

2 For a comprehensive overview of the reception history of Evgeny Bronislavovich Pashukanis, *The General Theory of Law and Marxism* (Dragan Milovanovic new intro, Transaction Publishers 2003) see Andreas Harms, *Warenform und Rechtsform: Zur Rechtstheorie von Eugen Pashukanis* (Nomos 2000).

3 Norbert Reich, 'Marxistische Rechtstheorie zwischen Revolution und Stalinismus: Das Beispiel Pašukanis' [1972] *Kritische Justiz* 154, 156; Wolf Rosenbaum, 'Zum Rechtsbegriff bei Stučka und Pašukanis' [1971] *Kritische Justiz* 148.

4 In *Die Kritik der marxistischen Rechtstheorie*, I attempt to show that, contrary to the objection of civil law reductionism, Pashukanis does not postulate an identity between private law and public law but rather argues that bourgeois legal form exclusively appears in this very duality. It is precisely the division into the sphere of privacy, the *bourgeois*, and the sphere of the public, the *citoyen*, that reoccurs in this prominent accusation.

DOI: 10.4324/9781032724522-6

question of his legal philosophy.[5] Although it is arguable if his theory of criminal law truly depicts the epitome of the legal form critique, both the strengths and weaknesses of Pashukanis' thought become apparent, when engaging with the pertinent last chapter 'Law and the Violation of the Law' of *The General Theory of Law and Marxism*.

Pashukanis' theory of criminal law is worth discussing not only because it yet again provokes the objection of civil law reductionism and thus contributes to a much more granular analysis of his work, but especially because it questions prevailing narratives of penal policy and thus contributes to a more differentiated understanding of present criminal justice systems. Pashukanis' thoughts on the form of criminal law particularly affect the rather naïve belief in progress, when identifying the historical shift from retribution to prevention with the humanization of criminal justice. The critical core of Pashukanis' theory, however, lies in carving out the class character of bourgeois criminal law without reducing it to a mere instrument of the ruling class, that is without relinquishing his form-theoretical claim. Bourgeois criminal justice and its penal politics of punishment as the proportional deprivation of freedom rely on the real abstraction of concrete human labour to abstract labour: their operational centrepiece is the principle of equivalent retaliation.

However, by emphasising the retributive character of modern criminal law, Pashukanis has been accused of falling short of his very own methodological core principles. For *The General Theory of Law and Marxism* never simply posits otherworldly ideals and principles, which are not (yet) met by reality, but rather shows how the reality of modern law is, in itself, positing its very own norms and, with necessity, contradicts them. As I've argued elsewhere,[6] Pashukanis' theory of the legal form must be regarded as a type of immanent critique of bourgeois law, a depiction of its contradictory and ideological truth. This strong dialectical and anti-idealistic approach is reminiscent of Hegel's argument against the 'perennial ought'[7] (*perennierendes Sollen*) presented in the early chapters of his *Science of Logic*. Hegel shows how the 'perennial ought' in seeking to overcome finitude by simply negating

5 See Daria Bayer, *Tragödie des Rechts* (Duncker & Humblot 2021) 110, 115; Jochen Bung, 'Geheimnisse der gesellschaftlichen Formen—Rechtsformanalyse und Rechtskritik bei Pashukanis' in Georg Steinberg (ed), *Sozialistische Straftheorie und -praxis in Europa* (Nomos 2018) 55.

6 Apart from Obermayr (n 1), I've made a case for interpreting Pashukanis' critique of the legal form as a type of *immanent critique* in Linda Lilith Obermayr, 'Warenform, Rechtsform und immanente Kritik: Überlegungen zur Wertförmigkeit des Rechtssubjekts im Ausgang von Paschukanis *Allgemeine Rechtslehre und Marxismus*' (2022) 108(1) *Archiv für Rechts und Sozialphilosophie* 36–61.

7 GWF Hegel, *Science of Logic* (Routledge 2002) 136, 142. For a discussion of Hegel's critique of the 'perennial ought' also see Ernst Bloch, *Subjekt—Objekt: Erläuterungen zu Hegel* (Suhrkamp 1972) 419 et seqq. and Odo Marquard, 'Hegel und das Sollen' [1964] *Philosophisches Jahrbuch* 103–19.

it is bound to finiteness eternally. This separation of 'is' and 'ought', which is initiated by the 'ought' itself, eventually leads to a concept of reality that undercuts reality in its totality. If bourgeois criminal law and its practice of proportionate punishment are simply obfuscating their actual archaic, retributive quality and lack an autonomous logic then the notions of prevention, social protection and resocialization are mere (i.e., false and unreal) ideologies and could still function as normative ideals, yet to be realized. With this, the 'ought' would slip back in. With a close reading of contemporary philosopher Geoffroy de Lagasnerie's *Judge and Punish*, however, we can avoid this recurrence of the 'ought' in Marxist criminal law critique and attain a more refined concept of bourgeois criminal justice as well as its core principles of *equivalent retaliation* and the *violation of the general interest*. De Lagasnerie points out the fragmentating mechanisms of modern criminal justice systems, that is the individualization of the accused and the socialization of the convict and, thereby, elaborates on a thought that remains quite vague in Pashukanis. This twofold movement within criminal proceedings makes up the core of the 'mysterious character' of the criminal justice, the fetish of criminal law.

Form and Fetish of Bourgeois Criminal Law

a. Abstract Labour and Punishment: The Principle of Equivalent Retaliation

While polemically denouncing criminal justice in the bourgeois state as 'organised class terror',[8] Pashukanis' analysis of modern criminal law begins with a rather sober diagnosis. He states that criminal justice has indeed striven to replace cruel medieval and ancient methods of punishment such as corporal punishment, torture, family liability, exile and sentence to public humiliation, with the rather austere penalties of fines and custodial sentences.[9] In place of chastisement, punishment appears as a specific form of equivalent exchange within capitalist societies. This exchange is, in contrast to the contractual exchange between capital and double free wage labour (*doppelt freier Lohnarbeiter*), concluded 'involuntarily' and 'retrospectively, after arbitrary action by one of the parties'.[10] Within the realm of criminal law, not working hours for wages, but the 'ratio between offence and retribution' is negotiated. Drawing on the Aristotelian differentiation within commutative

8 Pashukanis, *The General Theory* (n 2) 173.

9 In respect of present penal policy, I would like to emphasize the wording *striven to replace* for the existence of Guantanamo Bay detention camp or the human rights-violating detention of Julian Assange in solitary confinement for over five years reveals the selectivity and relativity of the Western rule of law.

10 Pashukanis, *The General Theory* (n 2) 168.

justice, the equalization through voluntary action (contracts in the characteristic sense of a mutual consent) and the equalization through involuntary action (any form of crime or offense that results in a penalty), Pashukanis considers the modern criminal justice system's idea of 'just punishment' as a type of equivalent exchange for which punishment functions as the compensation for the damage suffered by the victim and becomes a 'currency of criminal justice'.[11] Thus, it's the victim and the damage inflicted on it which underlies the entire criminal process as its foundation; albeit in the distorted form of a higher public interest.[12]

Pashukanis admits that this construction may seem naïve at first glance but if we follow along the prevailing narrative of modern criminal law overcoming retribution in favour of prevention and in doing so sharing the idea of modern criminal law fulfilling the purpose of protecting society from the offender (general and special prevention), then 'the whole meaning of the term "punishment" evaporates at once'.[13] The questionable and pathologizing interest in 'influencing' or 'resocializing' the delinquent is infinitesimal compared to the 'telling moment of the verdict'[14] and the determination of the sentence. Pashukanis does not deny that modern substantial and formal criminal law is influenced by preventive considerations, and recognizes achievements of the modern rule of law in relation to criminal justice. Principles, such as the presumption of innocence or *audi alteram partem*, limitations to life imprisonment, partial prohibitions of capital punishment etc. have, indeed, improved the overall status of the defendant, the convict or the prisoner. However, as Pashukanis stresses, the logic of modern criminal law cannot be boiled down to preventive considerations or a general drive towards human progress. In addition to the social purpose of prevention, there is an 'irrational, mystified, absurd element'[15] to bourgeois criminal law and it is precisely at this point that the specificity of the legal form, of abstract legal subjectivity, emerges yet again: The deprivation of freedom for a certain period of time determined in advance by a court sentence is the specific form in which modern criminal law realizes the principle of *equivalent retaliation*. This form is unconsciously but profoundly connected to the idea of abstract men and of abstract human labour measurable by time:

> For it to be possible for the idea to emerge that one could make recompense for an offence with a piece of abstract freedom determined in advance, it

11 Peter Ramsay, 'Pashukanis and Public Protection' in Markus D Dubber (ed), *Foundational Texts in Modern Criminal Law* (OUP 2014) 206.

12 Pashukanis, *The General Theory* (n 2) 169.

13 ibid 177.

14 ibid 182.

15 ibid 177.

> was necessary for all concrete forms of social wealth to be reduced to the most abstract and simple form, to human labour measured in time.[16]

Pashukanis breaks with the modernist narrative in which the false and retrogressive idea of retribution is replaced by the progressive, enlightened idea of social protection. Pashukanis provides empirical examples to caution against the unquestioning praise of significant advancements in the humanization of methods of punishment, revealing that these advancements are often quite limited upon closer inspection. For instance, corporal punishment has only been partially abolished, and the use of physical punishment as a disciplinary method for deviant labourers persisted in England during Pashukanis' lifetime.[17] It is a merit of the contemporary German social historian Heide Gersternberger to have shown how practices of direct violence have accompanied the historical emergence of capitalism ever since. In *Markt und Gewalt*, Gerstenberger questions the idea that there is an inherent tendency within capitalism to eliminate direct violence; that is, the belief that it is the functioning of capitalist economies themselves that encourages the abandonment of direct violence. While with capitalism rationalized relationships between legal subjects in the form of contracts are established, they are not implemented necessarily universally. Forms of 'unbounded exploitation' ('*entgrenzte Ausbeutung*') have historically accompanied and supported the establishment of modern statehood and bourgeois-capitalist relations.[18] Disciplining individual labourers became increasingly privatized towards the end of the 19th century and was enforced through factory regulations, strict supervisory measures, terminations, and blacklists. This type of direct and violent control over labour power, however, has ever since been cynically labelled 'free wage labour'.[19] Hence, for the realm of criminal law and against the naïve idea of a linear and continuous progress towards a humanization of penal practices, Pashukanis emphasizes that development must not be identified with a mere change in people's ideas but is tied to the material economic and social basis.

The retribution of the commission of a crime with a pre-determined 'piece of abstract freedom'[20] must be understood in connection with the freedom and equality of the abstract legal subject, the abstract commodity owner and the alienated wage worker. The 'arithmetical expression of the severity of the sentence'[21] corresponds to the exact accounting of the remuneration

16 ibid 181.
17 ibid 75.
18 Heide Gerstenberger, *Markt und Gewalt: Die Funktionsweise des historischen Kapitalismus* (Westfälisches Dampfboot 2017).
19 ibid 68.
20 Pashukanis, *The General Theory* (n 2) 181.
21 ibid 180.

corresponding to the damage. Therein lies the *class character* of modern criminal law: the (re-)production of the reduction of humankind to abstract labour and abstract labour time. Similar to human labour, shedding its particularities to the point of mere expenditure of abstract human labour power within a capitalist mode of production, punishment as the proportional deprivation of freedom, time and/or money abstracts from the particular criminal action and translates it into the comparable and equal violation of the 'general interest'.[22] By tracing modern criminal justice's punishment methods back to the capitalist reduction of human labour to abstract labour and by showing how the idea of abstract freedom and its penal disposal is rooted in the capitalist control of abstract human labour power, Pashukanis formulates a critique of the class character of criminal law without abandoning his form-theoretical claim. Allegorically, Pashukanis delineates the 'mercantile logic'[23] of substantive and formal criminal law: 'The public prosecutor demands, as befits a "party", a "high" price, that is to say, a severe sentence. The offender pleads for leniency, for a "discount", and the court passes sentence "in equity"'.[24] In this sense, Pashukanis highlights the other side of procedural principles under the rule of law which reflects mercantile logic as well. The bourgeois judiciary 'sees to it that the transaction with the offender should be concluded according to all the rules of the game':[25] the public nature of the proceedings serves to control and affirm the legitimacy of the fair determination of the 'payment' (whether it's a sentence of imprisonment or a fine), the adversary form of the trial allows the offender to 'bargain for his liberty without hindrance' and the defense by lawyers is akin to the services of an experienced court broker. With the same sobriety, Pashukanis points out the logic of the principle of legality (*nulla poena sine lege*), which, in line with a proper framework of fair trading, enables the offender to know beforehand what quantum of abstract freedom he has to pay as equivalent to the crime committed (i.e., the transaction concluded before the court) and under which conditions this payment will be demanded.[26] But this must not be misunderstood: by showing how the rule of law and its basic principles of a fair trial play a central role in mediating domination and power the actual improvements in terms of the rights of the accused and/or convict in criminal proceedings are not liquidated. Procedural principles do indeed ensure a 'fair trial' but it is precisely this 'fair trial' that sets the described fetishization in motion. Procedural principles are, in fact, ideology but in being ideology, they harbour a true representation of reality as well: 'Thus the discovery of

22 See for this explicit analogy Ramsay (n 11) 206.
23 See Bung (n 5) 56.
24 Pashukanis, *The General Theory* (n 2) 177.
25 ibid 183.
26 ibid 184.

the ideological nature of a concept was merely the reverse side of establishing its accuracy'.[27]

The absurd principle of equivalent retaliation, superficially appearing to be a form of progress, demonstrates an ideological reversal and obfuscation similar to that of the commodity form and legal form:

> Yet while the equivalence of the punishment in its crude, brutal, physical-material form (infliction of a physical injury, or exacting expiatory payment) maintains its simple meaning, accessible to everyone precisely through this crudity, it loses this clear meaning in its abstract form (deprivation of freedom for a stipulated period) even though people continue to describe the degree of punishment here too as *proportionate* to the gravity of the deed.[28]

What Pashukanis delineates here can be referred to as a fetish of the form of criminal justice. In place of the archaic *lex talionis*, where passionate revenge led to bloody retribution, in bourgeois criminal justice there is the 'rational' administration of abstract freedom as the legal consequence of meeting the elements of a crime. In the following, we will see, however, that even in the bourgeois constitutional state, a yearning for retribution persists.

At this point, we encounter the first interpretative difficulties: if the imposed penalty is considered the equivalent of the damage suffered by the victim and criminal law, thus, a specific form of exchange, then (1) criminal law should primarily concern liabilities stemming from actions between private parties (*ex contractu* as well as *ex delicto*) and (2) the victim should play a central role in the criminal process. Regarding (1), one could counter that criminal law does not concern itself at all with the relationship between private individuals, that is, subjective rights and claims resulting from legal subjects asserting their legal entitlements and interests. This objection, of course, repeats the aforementioned prevailing allegation of civil law reductionism. However, as Pashukanis shows, the objective body of norms (such as criminal provisions or other general laws) cannot be decoupled from subjective claims in a way that views subjective claims as a mere 'consequence' of objective norms. This is Hans Kelsen's position, which, although it has an ideological critical point in showing how an emphasis on subjective rights creates a dualism between private law and public law—with private law as a space of freedom opposed to public law as a space of power and coercion—ultimately rejects subjective rights as a false conception and thus fails to see the dialectic between subjective and objective law altogether. Just as the sphere of privacy and subjective rights is absolutized against the sphere of the state and public law by theories

27 ibid 54.
28 ibid 181.

of natural law, the Kelsenian legal-positivist perspective tends to reduce the existence of subjective rights entirely to the objective, positive, that is state-enacted body of norms. While the state does indeed to fulfil a protective and regulatory function in guaranteeing and ensuring the commodity form of exchange and the wage labour through the coercive protection of private property, these subjective rights, or more precisely, the freedom of property, do not arise from state guarantees. It is rather the opposite: the law emanates from the legal relation between commodity owners, encountering each other with opposing interests, which necessitates the existence of a public authority endowed with coercive force to guarantee peaceful trade. Peaceful trade in commodities depends on general peace in civil society so that the safeguarding of property rights gives rise to a general need for order and security:

> The materialisation of this exchange relation in criminal law is one aspect of the constitutional state as the embodiment of the ideal form of transaction between independent and equal commodity producers meeting in market. However, since social relations are not confined to abstract relations between abstract commodity owners, so too the criminal court is not only an embodiment of the abstract legal form, but is also a weapon in the immediate class struggle.[29]

Beyond this mediating and reproductive relationship between the bourgeois state, its penal power and economic exploitation relations, Pashukanis does not delve into the bourgeois state form in more detail. It is worth noting that Pashukanis refers to the bourgeois state as both the rule of law and as a class state, therefore not reducing the state to either the instrument of the ruling class or the general unification of a common and rational act of will.

Regarding (2), unlike compensation for damages by contract or tort, modern criminal law differs from civil law in that the victim and its harm largely fade into the background. This is because the criminal judicial process can in several ways abstain from a real victim of the delinquent act. For example, the authority to initiate criminal proceedings lies not with the victim but with the prosecution (*principle of ex officio proceedings*). In the realm of modern criminal law and in stark contrast to archaic forms of revenge, criminal prosecution is not the victims' but the states' sole responsibility. If not joining the criminal proceedings as a private party with a civil action, the role of the victim is limited to that of a witness. With regard to the broad criminal liability of the mere attempt to commit a crime or the abstract endangerment of protected interests and goods, thus encompassing 'unsuccessful' yet punishable acts, the existence of a victim is conceptually and logically excluded. To avoid misunderstandings: speaking of a victim of a crime means speaking of

29 ibid 176.

the victim of a *particular* crime, thus a specific delict with certain constituent elements of a crime. The fact that attempted murder has no (murder) victim does not exclude the possibility that attempted murder may be preceded by a 'successful' bodily injury, for which a correspondingly injured victim exists. However, this victim is the victim of bodily harm and not the—conceptually impossible—victim of attempted murder. Hence, it is doubtful whether the injured public interest materialized in the prosecution relates to a real victim or if the criminal conduct can be truly reduced to the harm inflicted on the victim. As Pashukanis himself writes, a mystification occurs in punishment that goes beyond the just compensation for the actual harm caused.[30]

b. The Violation of the General

But what does Pashukanis exactly mean when stating that the victim forms the foundation of criminal proceedings? Let's take a closer look at a central passage in the chapter 'Law and the Violation of Law':

> The abstraction of injured public interest is based on the perfectly real figure of the injured party, who takes part in the trial either personally or through a representative and gives the trial its living meaning. Furthermore, this abstraction is personified in a real way even in those cases where there is in fact no injured party, and only the law 'starts up in anger' in the person of the public prosecutor.[31]

In the form of public prosecution separated from jurisdiction, Pashukanis argues that the figure of the aggrieved party seeking retribution persists:

> This split, whereby state power appears not only in the role of plaintiff (public prosecutor), but also in the role of judge, illustrates that the criminal case as a legal form is inseparable from the figure of the injured party demanding 'satisfaction'.[32]

Firstly, Pashukanis states correctly, that criminal justice and prosecution do not depend on a victim at all. The injured party and/or the prosecutor as its representative seem to form nothing more than the living flesh for the abstract injured public interest to manifest and personify in. What otherwise could only be grasped in thought now attaches to the physical existence of the victim and/or the prosecutor. Pashukanis literally speaks of the 'figures' in the sense of chess pieces of the criminal procedure. Therefore, the

30 ibid 177.
31 ibid.
32 ibid.

violation of the *public interest* rather than the injury of the victim, is what the trial ultimately revolves around. This is made crystal clear by Enlightenment philosopher Cesare Beccaria, who, in his prominent *Dei Delitti e delle Pene* (1764), states that the actual crime is not the individual offense, but rather the harm inflicted upon society inherent in every single criminal act. In contrast to Peter Ramsay,[33] I argue that Pashukanis' theory of criminal law is, indeed, capable of grasping criminal justice's agenda to criminalize dangerousness. With Herbert Spencer, Pashukanis argues that defense actions taken by the bourgeois state against external attacks and defense actions taken against disruptive elements within the bourgeois state are identical. For this reason, the concept of war takes on an entirely new meaning.[34] However, what remains quite nebulous is the very public interest itself, its violation, and its relation to the bourgeois state. What is the public interest after all? Is it identical with the state's interest? How can the violation of public interest be further specified? What exactly is it that is being violated when committing a crime? Pashukanis writes:

> The first difficulty is that modern criminal law starts out, not at all from the damage suffered by the injured party, but from the violation of the norm established by the state. Yet if the injured party with his claim steps into the background, one might well ask what then has become of the equivalent form. Nevertheless, in the first place, however much the injured party may fade into the background, he does not disappear altogether. He continues to signify the context of the criminal action taking place.[35]

Pashukanis' observations regarding the ideological roles that are being assigned within criminal proceedings themselves remain rather abstract. In his *Pure Theory of Law*, Hans Kelsen stresses that the severity of the punishment primarily depends on the violation of a criminal *norm*, meaning the fulfilment of a criminal offence or the commission of a crime. For instance, with regard to the legal situation in Austria, the degree of harm is already taken into account in assessing which offence the criminal act fulfils in the first place (e.g., minor or severe bodily injury, embezzlement or theft, etc.). It also impacts the subsequent determination of the sanction (if the victim of a violent crime was exceptionally brutally harmed, etc.). Within the logic of criminal law, the 'harm' does not lie in the damage suffered by the victim, nor the criminal act committed against the victim, but

33 Ramsay (n 11) 201 et seqq.

34 Bernard E Harcourt's work on the current US states' counterrevolution against its own people depicts this expansion of war against external threats to war against actual and (more often) potential enemies within. See his *The Counterrevolution: How Our Government Went to War Against Its Own Citizens* (Basic Books 2018).

35 Pashukanis, *The General Theory* (n 2) 177.

rather in the damage suffered by the legal order as a whole. It is the criminal act committed precisely in *violating a legal norm* that matters with regard to the logic of criminal justice and prosecution. But if the victim or their claim recedes into the background, it may seem that the equivalent form has disappeared altogether. The imposed penalty is, in fact, the equivalent of the damage caused by violating a legal norm, that is, the legal order as a whole, and suffered by the state himself. Whether the injured public interest objectified in the victim and/or the prosecution refers to the real injured party at all and whether the damage can be linked to the harm inflicted on the real injured party remains doubtful. Pashukanis does not sufficiently acknowledge the fact that punishment constitutes a break with the civil law logic of compensation for damages and, thus, exceeds the mere equivalent form of exchange; that in punishment, as he writes, a mystification takes place that points beyond the just compensation of the damage actually caused.

With a reading of Hegel's *Philosophy of Right*, we can demystify this dynamic of the criminal justice process and its ambivalent relation to the victim. It is the law's very own process of verifying itself ('sich als ein notwendig vermitteltes Dasein *bewährt*'[36]) that unfolds in court. What Hegel is pointing out to us is the astonishing fact that within the logic of legal proceedings, it is not the victim but rather the Universal itself that is violated by the criminal:

> The place of the injured person is now taken by the injured universal, which is actualized in a special way in the court of justice. To pursue and punish crime is its function, which therefore ceases to be a mere subjective retaliation or revenge, and is in punishment transformed into a true reconciliation of right with itself. In the act of punishment, viewed objectively, right is reconciled to itself, and restores itself by superseding the crime and realizing its own inherent validity.[37]

The legal process in general and criminal proceedings in particular is, first and foremost, a process in which the Universal demonstrates its existence as a necessary self-mediation and verification against its violation:

> The criminal act is not the primary and positive, to which punishment comes as the negative. It is the negative, and punishment is only the negation of a negation. Actual right destroys and replaces injury, thus showing its validity and verifying itself as a necessary factor in reality.[38]

36 GWF Hegel, *Grundlinien der Philosophie des Rechts* (Suhrkamp 1986) 186, § 97 Zusatz (emphasis added).

37 GWF Hegel, *Outlines of the Philosophy of Right* (OUP 2008) 209, § 220.

38 ibid 100, § 97 Addition.

Perhaps Pashukanis can be corrected in the sense that the victim always forms the basis of the criminal justice trial, as it embodies the negativity (the violation of the universal), which is being negotiated in the legal proceedings and in which the '*Bewährungsprozess*' of law takes place in the form of a double negation. The interest of the victim both immediate and concrete as well as mediated and abstract in the form of public prosecution is itself the reification and the 'living sense' of the abstract violation of the Universal.

c. *The Dialectic of Individualization and Socialization*

Contemporary French philosopher Geoffroy de Lagasnerie astutely observes that the punishment system constructs a scenario in which the individual is held accountable to 'society'. In contrast to Pashukanis, he argues that it is initially less about the act of judgment and more about the act of accusation that defines the logic of criminal proceedings. De Lagasnerie inquires into the subtle preconditions and mechanisms of the criminal trial that enable the action of an individual to be charged with a criminal offence in the first place. In other words, de Lagasnerie is interested in what it means to transform human agency into criminal conduct by the very acts of accusation and punishment.[39] Without mentioning Pashukanis nor Hegel, de Lagasnerie draws a very similar conclusion regarding the peculiar moment of condemnation, which reveals the mystifying and self-referential nature of the criminal justice system:

> During the trials I attended, there was always one moment that struck me as indicative of the justice system's capacity to run on empty, so to speak, without examining its own operations: the moment when the prosecution discusses the defendant's sentence. This moment, so revelatory of the mysterious nature of any criminal justice system, is akin to ritual, social magic. But nobody seems to notice its arbitrariness because, in reality, isn't this merely the transformation of a crime into time and money? A robbery garners X number of years and/or such-and-such a fine; a rape, X number of years; a murder, X number of years; and so forth.[40]

In close alignment with Pashukanis, de Lagasnerie demonstrates the kinship of the moment of conviction with rituals or social magic and emphasizes the 'mysterious nature'[41] of criminal justice and proceedings.

Much like Pashukanis, de Lagasnerie defines the narrative legitimizing the modern criminal justice system as progress from retaliation to prevention,

39 Geoffroy de Lagasnerie, *Judge and Punish: The Penal State on Trial* (Stanford UP 2018) 145.
40 ibid 9.
41 ibid.

as an ideology. The ideological substitution of the relationship between the prosecution and the victim must be considered progressive in the sense that the response to a crime is relieved from the passionate and spontaneous logic of retaliation by the victim and placed within a dispassionate and rational framework of procedural rules. However, as de Lagasnerie stresses, the modern criminal justice apparatus merely suppresses the passions that arise from below, but rather indulges in a 'phantasmatic treatment of illegal activity', which once again reveals a 'desire for punishment'.[42] Against the narrative of progress, punishment can be seen as an abstract form of retribution. However, difficulties arise in the concept of guilt as the linchpin of modern criminal law theory. Drawing from the notion of causality, one can at least question why mental impairment, mental illness, youth or intoxication lead to a lack of accountability while the specific environment into which the defendant was born or in which they operated at the time of the crime leaves their guilt untouched. Pashukanis also points to the arbitrary and unscientific nature of causal explanations in criminal justice. He questions whether there is a rationally understandable, necessary reason to prefer one link in the causal chain to another.[43] This makes guilt appear as an immediately evident, natural quality of a person, independent of societal and historical circumstances, and their wrongdoing as a highly personal failure, a pathology.

With de Lagasnerie, we must shift our focus to two subtle mechanisms within the criminal process if we want to understand how domination and power articulate themselves in the realm of bourgeois criminal justice. These two mechanisms are the *individualization of the accused subject* and the *socialization of the convicted subject*. (However, de Lagasnerie refrains from describing this contradictory movement within the unity of the criminal process as dialectical.) At the beginning of a criminal procedure, once the investigative phase is complete, the defendant is charged with committing a crime and the criminal procedure begins. But what are the preconditions for this act of accusation? What must be posited to function as an accusation and to demand to convict the defendant for the commission of a crime? On what specific interpretation or, better yet, construction of reality does the accusation rely upon? De Lagasnerie identifies the construction of criminal reality with a particular way of thinking that rejects the concept of totality: criminal justice refuses to think in terms of totalities by detaching an action from its specific interaction context and the collective scene while reconstructing it as the isolated action of an individual, following a sequential logic.[44] The act of accusation is thus based on an 'atomistic vision of reality', in which agency is

42 ibid 148.
43 Pashukanis, *The General Theory* (n 2) 180.
44 De Lagasnerie (n 39) 105.

pressed into the general form of criminal norms, disregarding 'social causalities, collective structures, or historical logics'.[45]

However, this violent reinterpretation of an action hides behind the ideological rhetoric of a progressive and humane justice system that does not want to reduce the individual to their act, in other words, does not aim to substantialize the individual (punishing a person convicted of theft as a thief, or a person convicted of murder as a murderer). Instead, with the regular use of psychology, it strives to understand the individual and the motives behind its actions. Through the judicial reconstruction of the individual's biography, which includes questioning the defendant, de Lagasnerie exposes the hypocritical logic of modern criminal justice. This process, which involves collecting social information (such as origin, social class, childhood, gender, ethnicity, religion, education, etc.), does not seek to determine the social logic and conditions underlying the committed act whatsoever. Instead, it creates a personality profile that achieves a paradoxical but necessary reversal of cause-and-effect relationships according to the logic of accusation: the social and historical context is not seen as the cause of the action but only as its impact on the defendant. Moreover, the meaning of the reason or justification for an action is also inverted. Justifying an action no longer means identifying its reason in terms of an explanatory cause. Instead, the reason is considered as incriminating information within the context of a deviant character, whereby the committed act appears as a consistent and even necessary expression of this character. De Lagasnerie encapsulates this distorting mechanism of criminal justice as a ruse of criminal reason:

> Even as this logic eases the conscience by claiming to 'understand', it links the act being judged to a series of individual traits without ever evoking their objective causes or roots in actual social and political life. The criminal act is therefore spontaneously separate from the social, economic, and political context in which it occurred and in which actors were inserted alongside others. It is directly linked to the defendant's life and perceived as embedded within a series of behaviors displayed by the person being judged. The act in question is connected to the person on trial and to his life, not to the social structure in which that life story took form. In short, it is desociologized.[46]

By reconstructing the defendant's biography, reality is doubled. Alongside the legal description of the action as a crime, a psychological moral dimension is introduced, which is ascribed temporal priority over the legal dimension. Drawing a psychological picture of the defendant's personality through

45 ibid 103.
46 ibid 108 f.

the reconstruction of his social biography creates the peculiar impression that the criminal and the crime, somehow, already existed before the actual criminal conduct. This means that the person committing a crime is, so to speak, always and only a criminal, independently of the committed act, while the committed act itself already existed as a possibility, constantly pressing to break through into reality. De Lagasnerie stresses this argument precisely when he diagnoses an intermingling of inner and outer aspects: 'the world more or less disappears. Everything that is external becomes internal. Crime is no longer the translation of a relationship to the world but the exteriorization of a relationship to the self'.[47] What de Lagasnerie calls the 'endogenization' of the social world describes a conceptual movement similar to commodity fetishism and legal fetishism: the naturalization and reification of the social nature of the crime.[48]

The act of accusation is based on an individualizing and atomizing reconstruction of the multifaceted social reality, focusing on the action as a singular event at the expense of understanding the *whole*. The logical precondition initially enabling the judgement is the refusal to think totalities, 'the act of judging' thus emanates from a deep misconception. But what about the act of punishment? The act of punishment relies on a peculiar reconstruction and doubling of reality as well. While the act of accusation reverses the social mediation of a crime in the sense of isolating the criminal act from their social and socio-economic context and, by doing so, install a substantialist concept of 'the criminal', the act of punishment returns to precisely this point that the act of accusation had originally reversed, only to further reverse the initial inversion. As de Lagasnerie observes, the punishment of the accused 'rests on the performative construction of crime as a social act'.[49] The logic of criminal law is highly twisted at this point. While the act of accusation presupposes an individualizing negation of the crime as a socially mediated action, the act of punishment recontextualizes the action that was originally abstracted from the social context. The de-socialization of the crime in the act of accusation is followed by a re-socialization in the act of punishment. The isolated criminal act, now reconstructed as an attack on society, the public good, state and order, replaces what was previously 'only' a criminal act. As a result, punishment doubles reality, replacing the initial crime with a second one:

> What, then, does penal logic signify? It means that, when a crime occurs, the state dispossesses the victim of what has happened and takes his or her

47 ibid 117.

48 In fact, de Lagasnerie mentions the 'fetishization' of law once (de Lagasnerie (n 39) 183) and speaks of criminal justice as 'a rite of depoliticization, dehistoricization and desocialization' (de Lagasnerie (n 39) 103).

49 ibid 153.

> place; the state positions itself as the victim—and even, more precisely, as the primary victim. In short: it adds another crime to the one committed. It adds a victim. It creates two violent acts from one: the first occurs in the civil domain and the second, in parallel, in the penal one. The penal state creates two crimes where only one existed: one committed against the victim, the other against the state.[50]

The ideological background to the logic of punishment is the theory of social contract. For the crime can only be considered an attack against society itself, when the general will is taken as the representation of the will of all. Only with such an interpretation of the general will, which reproduces the ideological fiction of a harmonious and homogeneous community, can the criminal be punished as a 'defector' on behalf and for the protection of all. While guilt is assigned to the convicted based on a specific offense, the individual is simultaneously made guilty in the broader sense of an attack against society as such.

What Pashukanis vaguely alludes to with the concept of the violation of the public interest has now been articulated more precisely. At this very point, however, the analytical density of de Lagasnerie's work converges with Pashukanis'. Pashukanis explains how the violation of the public interest relies on the fiction of a 'society as a whole' that exists nowhere 'except in the fantasies of jurists'.[51] Thus, the meaning of criminal justice and the practice of punishment in the bourgeois (class) state can only be understood when one starts from its antagonistic nature, that is, from conflicting and opposing private interests. These antagonisms change and every system of criminal justice depends not only in form but also in content on the interests of the ruling class at any given time. The struggle for criminalization or decriminalization of specific actions and activities (from the organization of workers into unions to divorce initiated by women), is an expression of historically specific class struggles.

d. *The Third Hypostasis Within the Triune Bourgeois Subject*

We have seen that something mysterious is happening to the status of the accused and convicted subject in criminal proceedings. While the accused or convict is addressed as an abstract legal subject by criminal law and criminal procedure, he himself undergoes a duplication. By criminal law, one is accused and convicted not only as a legal but as a moral subject as well. The idea of guilt towards society as a whole thus transcends the legal form: 'the

50 ibid 148.
51 Pashukanis, *The General Theory* (n 2) 174.

juridicial concept of guilt is not a scientific concept'.[52] In the first five chapters of *The General Theory of Law*, the mutual and equiprimordial relation between the egoistic economic subject and the legal subject has been the object of Pashukanis' examination. In the sixth and seventh chapters, however, Pashukanis introduces a third dimension within bourgeois subjectivity: the 'moral subject' as an 'equivalent personality'[53] and its role in the functioning of capitalist production:

> Thus the three aspects mentioned above, or, as people used to call them, the three principles of egoism, freedom, and supremely equivalent worth of the personality are indivisibly linked and represented, in their totality, the rational expression of a single social relation. The egoistic subject, the legal subject and the moral personality are the three most important character masks assumed by people in commodity-producing society.[54]

Criminal justice and punishment give form to the bourgeois idea of equivalent exchange, not only by enforcing the principle of equivalent retaliation as a specific type of equivalent exchange but also by accusing and convicting legal as moral subjects. The concept of individual liability and responsibility truly encapsulates the penal logic of bourgeois criminal law, which 'is one institutional form of the ideology of the moral subject'.[55]

The reality enforced and constructed by criminal law is shattered: detaching human agency from its specific historical and social context and reconstructing it as the isolated action of an individual mimics criminal justice's fundamental refusal of the concept of totality. By both individualizing and desocializing the *accused*, as well as re-socializing the *convicted* subject, a fragmented reality is established in the centre of which the individually responsible, atomized moral subject grows lonely. Only in capitalist societies, governed by the principle of equivalent exchange contractually mediating exploitation of wage labour, does criminal justice address legal as moral subjects liable to equivalent retaliation and proportionate punishment. Only when individuals are forced into their egoism by the bourgeois-liberal ruling of private property the need for morality as an atomizing and desocializing individual responsibility arise. However, in capitalist societies moral obligation arrives late, for the egoistic economic subject precisely exists in the duality of *bourgeois*, directed towards the fulfilment of private interests, and *citoyen*, directed towards the sphere of the General as its condition of reproduction. The egoistic interest of the commodity owner is necessarily related to the general interest for its very own sake. The mediation between

52 ibid 179.
53 ibid 153.
54 ibid 52.
55 Ramsay (n 11) 208.

the individual and society, or between the Particular and the General, which morality is supposed to provide, is already inscribed in the functioning of bourgeois-capitalist domination. Thus, as Pashukanis paraphrasing Kautsky, the self-purpose formula of the Categorical Imperative only makes sense in a social setting in which people can be, must be and already are practically made into a means for another person:

> Moral fervour is inextricably bound up with and feeds on the immorality of social practice. Ethical doctrines claim to change and improve the world whereas, in reality, they are merely a distorted reflection of one aspect of this real world—the aspect which shows social relations to be subject to the law of value.[56]

In the following section, I would like to expand on this consideration and make a case for the methodological significance of a critique of morality and its logical pendant, the *mere ought*, with regard to Marxist social critique.

3. Methodological Remarks: From Pashukanis' Form Critique to Hegel's Critique of 'Perennial Ought'

As Ramsay states, Pashukanis' *The General Theory of Law and Marxism* 'is not a foundational text in criminal law. It is a foundational text in the *critique* of criminal law'.[57] To be more precise, Pashukanis' intervention is both an adequate delineation of bourgeois law and jurisprudence and their mediation and justification of capitalist power relations as well as a fundamental critique of them. This unity and simultaneity of delineation and critique is an essential feature of Pashukanis' form-critical approach. Marxist legal theory and, in particular, Pashukanis hold a special position within classical legal theory for they do not—at least not primarily—function as *positive* theories of law. The crucial difference lies in the peculiar way in which they treat their subject. Pashukanis' legal theory is not Marxist because it criticizes capitalism but rather because of the specific way it formulates this critique. To put it differently, the way in which the contradiction between capital and wage labour is understood and logically 'endured' marks the crucial difference. The contradiction resolves itself by itself, as both sides turn out to be themselves precisely by being the opposite of themselves. And only because each side of the contradiction is already the opposite of itself—capital and wage labour or private property and wage labour cannot be understood as two independent, self-contained entities that later come into conflict—the contradiction is

56 Pashukanis, *The General Theory* (n 2) 157.
57 Ramsay (n 11) 199.

resolved into unity. Pashukanis' legal theory is *negative* in the sense that its analysis and delineation of bourgeois legal reality is at the same time its very critique. It generates insights into modern law precisely by carving out the contradictions of social reality mediated by the capitalist legal form as well as the distorted ideas that become ingrained in our thinking.

This critical approach goes hand in hand with a particular way of thinking that can best be described through Hegel's distinction between 'understanding' (*Verstand*) and 'reason' (*Vernunft*).[58] As Przemysław Tacik points out in his contribution to the present volume, *Verstand* is the form of knowledge—and, as I would like to add, the form of thinking—intrinsic to the law, not capable of reflecting its very own presuppositions, and thus 'nothing less than jurisprudence', while it is *Vernunft* that 'offers recognition of the law's relation to the core of capitalist constitution of reality'.[59] *Verstand* always and only expresses its own necessity, namely, the necessity of its rational, analytical judgments that are faithful to formal logic and its laws of identity and contradiction. By finickily dissecting the world into rigid, well-arranged categories, *Verstand* not only demonstrates its greatest merit but also its greatest flaw by fixating and keeping apart contradicting categories, *Verstand* is per se the faculty of segregation.[60] In the third chapter 'Force and the Understanding' of his *Phenomenology of Spirit*, Hegel shows how *Verstand* operates cannot but lead to an abbreviated and tautological concept of reality: *explaining*[61] means asserting a force (e.g., gravity) as the substance of things, which eludes the philosophical glance, and thus splitting reality into two realms, a worldly one and an otherworldly one. This otherworldly realm is posited as the 'true reality', whereas the worldly realm is disparaged as mere appearance, forever admonished by yonder for not appropriately realizing its otherworldly ideals. One might already guess why Hegel's critique of *Verstandesdenken* is of utter epistemic and methodological relevance to materialist legal critique. In his

58 There is no adequate equivalent to 'Verstand' in the English language. In the standard translation of the *Phenomenology of Spirit* by AV Miller (OUP 1977) 'Verstand' is translated as 'understanding'. However, this can lead to some ambiguities, so I will retain the German term in the following discussion.

59 See Przemysław Tacik, 'Subjectification Through Normativity: Legal Form as a Modern Device' in P Tacik, G-G Fusco and C Cercel (eds), *Legal Form and the End of Law: Pashukanis' Legacy* (Routledge 2024).

60 In Linda Lilith Obermayr, 'Die, Drachensaat' des Hegelianismus. Widerständigkeit und Kritik spekulativen Denkens' in René Bohnstingl and others (eds), *Jahrbuch für marxistische Gesellschaftstheorie 1* (Mandelbaum 2022) 73–96, I exhaustively delve into the significance of Hegel's critique of *Verstand* for a subversive praxis of thinking in general and Marxist social critique in particular.

61 Hegel makes special use of the word 'Erklären' (to explain) as the *modus operandi* of *Verstand*.

Science of Logic, Hegel links the tautological and self-referential activity of *Verstand* with the fetishistic fixation on the ought as the not-yet:

> Those who attach such importance to the ought of morality and fancy that morality is destroyed if the ought is not recognized as ultimate truth, and those too who, reasoning from the level of the understanding, derive a perpetual satisfaction from being able to confront everything there is with an ought, that is, with a 'knowing better'—and for that very reason are just as loth to be robbed of the ought—do not see that as regards the finitude of their sphere the ought receives full recognition.[62]

Ought *is* and at the same time *is not*. On the one hand, what ought to be *is*, for what is posited as *in itself* (*an sich*), that is, what should be in the sense that it must be because it is the determination of something, *is* the truth; on the other hand, however, what ought to be *is not* and the posited *in itself* is a non-being for it only should be and is not yet. With the ought a determination is introduced that points beyond itself: what simply is, does not suffice, and there is a limitation to be surpassed concerning it. But at the same time, it does not point beyond itself, since something only has a limit as 'ought' in the first place. In other words, it's the ought itself that produces the very limit it seeks to surpass: 'the ought, as such, contains limitation, and limitation contains the ought. . . . limitation is determined as the negative of the ought and the ought likewise as the negative of limitation'.[63] In his *Encyclopedia*, Hegel writes that the 'ought always carries within itself the impotence of recognizing something as legitimate that nonetheless cannot maintain and uphold itself'.[64] The concept of the 'perennial ought' designates this 'standpoint which clings to finitude'.[65] Precisely because the 'ought' fixates the finite as what needs to be overcome, it lingers in this very finitude and establishes a reality of infinite progress, the realm of bad infinity.

What does Hegel's analysis of the concept of 'perennial ought' imply for Marxist social criticism? As long as 'what should be' remains a mere abstraction from reality, the standpoint of 'perennial ought' encounters social reality externally and heteronomously. Something that's not yet realized but merely should be, fails to function as a normative criterion of social critique. That means the normative criterion must be immanent to social reality itself. If so, the concept of a criterion or measure is no longer a benchmark for social change in its conventional sense but becomes a part of reality itself, which thus defines its own normative principles.

62 Hegel, *Science of Logic* (n 7) 136 et seqq.
63 ibid 136.
64 GWF Hegel, *Encyclopedia of the Philosophical Sciences in Basic Outline* (CUP 2021) 150, § 94 Addition.
65 Hegel, *Science of Logic* (n 7) 136, 142.

4. Conclusion

While I wouldn't go as far as to label Pashukanis' criminal law theory as the central question of his legal theory, it is in criminal law that the coercive character of the law, embodied and realized by the state, reaches its climax: the norm is 'immediately connected' with the threat of punishment.[66] It is in this sense that Pashukanis is to be understood when he writes that 'criminal law plays . . . the role of a representative of law as such', indeed 'it is a part which stands for the whole'.[67] In criminal law, as we have shown with de Lagasnerie, the violation of a legal norm becomes an autonomous problem. The criminal process revolves less around the specific individuals involved, as the prevailing narrative of modern criminal law suggests and more around the attack on the state and the legal order, which act as the overarching and primary victim of the offence. In this regard, the focus shifts away from criminal law as a substantive instrument for the preservation of the particular interests of the ruling class toward the preservation of the common interest of the state's coercive order.

I would like to close with a paragraph from *The General Theory of Law*, where Pashukanis not only stresses a highly relevant topic with regard to recent and current expansions of state coercive and punitive powers in so-called liberal democracies but also makes a necessary consideration and correction of his legal theory. From his detachment from contemporary instrumentalist theories and critiques of law (such as Stuchka, Lenin, Renner), a strong structural-functionalist trait in Pashukanis' legal theory arises, which, by highlighting the general-abstract form of bourgeois law and domination, tends to overshadow the cracks within bourgeois freedom and equality. To put it differently, Pashukanis' legal critique inclines one to miss all the nooks and crannies, all the covert but also overt actual instrumentalist interventions of the ruling class. The anti-instrumentalist dimension of his legal critique must not let us forget the crudely real legal instrumentalism enforced by the ruling class with all their might. And that's exactly what Pashukanis draws our attention to in the following passage:

> [T]he bourgeoisie has never, in favour of purity of theory, lost sight of the fact that class society is not only a market where autonomous owners of commodities meet, but is at the same time the battlefield of bitter class war, where the machinery of state represents a very powerful weapon. The more the hegemony of the bourgeoisie was shattered, . . . the more quickly the 'constitutional state' was transformed into a disembodied shadow, until finally the extraordinary sharpening of class struggle forced

66 Harms (n 2) 62.
67 Pashukanis, *The General Theory* (n 2) 168.

> the bourgeoisie to discard the mask of the constitutional state altogether, revealing the nature of state power as the organised power of one class of the other.[68]

At the very moment when bourgeois society, bourgeois state and capitalism are threatened, they abruptly bring their self-narrative of the linear progression of the humanization of criminal justice to an end and spare no means to reintroduce even the most heinous forms of punishment.

68 ibid 150.

Chapter 6

Legal Subjectivity and Abstraction

Tracing the Past of the Legal Form

Gian-Giacomo Fusco[1]

Introduction

One of the distinctive traits of Evgeny Pashukanis' legal theory is the radicality with which he has sustained the necessity to consider the forms of the law first and foremost in their concreteness, as an integral part of the material foundations of modern society. Far from being a mere political tool of class struggle (and oppression) or the ideological by-product of a bourgeoise society, for Pashukanis the law and its categorial abstract apparatus are objective facts, rooted in the materiality of human relationships of a society dominated by total commodification. As we read in his *The General Theory of Law and Marxism*, in the capitalist world,

> the social relations of production assume a doubly mysterious form. On the one hand, they appear as relations between things (commodities) and on the other, as relations between the wills of autonomous entities equal to each other—of legal subjects.

The law in this sense, represents an 'enigmatic phenomenon' complementing the 'mystical quality of value' that makes the practice of exchange to assume both economic and legal qualities.[2]

Here is the signature motif of Pashukanis' commodity-form [or commodity-exchange] theory of law: the [modern] 'form' of the law is not a peculiar version of some transhistorical/natural datum—or tendency—but represents the original product of a specific society with specific modes of production—those of capitalism. On the trail of the Marxian/materialist critique and methods, he elaborated a 'general' theory of law according to which

1 I would like to thank Rafał Mańko for the insightful comments and suggestions on the text. The English translation of the cited works has been at times adapted in adherence to the original text.

2 Evgeny Bronislavovich Pashukanis, *The General Theory of Law and Marxism* (Transaction Publishers 2002) 117.

DOI: 10.4324/9781032724522-7

legal categories emerge in strict symbiosis with the practice of commodity exchange. As Pashukanis puts it: 'the legal form, expressed in logical abstractions is a product of the actual or concrete legal form' whose genesis should be 'sought in the relations of exchange'.[3] The abstract features of the practice of exchange (value, labour) and its normative codification (the formal and abstract ownership rights) are grounded—dialectically—on the material-legal relationships of exchange And it is by being a 'reflection of the market' that the law could become part of the instruments of class domination.

Pashukanis' theoretical strategy consisted of tying closely 'commodity exchange with the time at which the human being becomes seen as a legal personality—the bearer of rights'.[4] To the extent that in exchange the relationship between commodities is a relationship between values, abstracted from the material features of the exchanged things, the relationship between commodity owners too becomes a relationship between abstract legal subjects (bearers of rights). In other words, the markets' proper functioning requires that 'legal fetishism complements commodity fetishism'.[5] The very existence of something like a subject of rights—the abstract quilting point of rights and corresponding duties—separated from the sphere of concrete human living, somehow emerges in the exchange transactions. 'Only the continual reshuffling of values in the market', Pashukanis writes, 'creates the idea of a fixed bearer of such rights', a 'generic concept' abstracting from the concrete differences between subjects.[6]

Legal form is the term Pashukanis conjured up to define the abstract-mystical legal complement to the concrete relationships established in and through commodity exchange. Each agent taking part in market relations must be an owner of the commodities and formally equal to the other agents. Such abstract formal equality is a prerequisite to, and at the same time a product of, the commodity exchange itself: and the legal form is consequently the form that such a relation between the equal owners must acquire to take part effectively in the market.[7] The abstract legal subject coalesces in the circulation of commodities and constitutes itself as a determinant element of market relations. For it is only as a legal subject that the commodity owner could make his product available in the market: and this implies that exchange, the market, and the development of legal subjectivity are involved in a process of self-constitution.

A recurring criticism of Pashukanis' commodity-form theory of law is that it denies the existence of pre-capitalist law.[8] True that his proposi-

3 ibid 43.

4 Chris Arthur, 'Editor's Introduction' to Pashukanis (n 2) xiii.

5 Michael Head, *Evgeny Pashukanis: A Critical Reappraisal* (Routledge 2008) 177.

6 Pashukanis, *The General Theory* (n 2) 118.

7 Head (n 5) 178.

8 Such criticism was first advanced by Petr Stuchka (as Pashukanis suggested in the 'Preface to the Second Russian Edition of his *General Theory*), then discussed, developed, and reinforced: see Ronnie Warrington, 'Pashukanis and the Commodity Form Theory' in David Sugarman (ed), *Legality, Ideology and the State* (Academic Press 1983) 59; Hugh Collins, *Marxism and Law* (OUP 1984) 110–11; Head (n 5) 214–15.

tion rests on the conviction that the [modern] legal form emerged with the bourgeois-capitalist society, however, he does not deny the existence of 'embryonic' forms of the law in previous epochs. In the 'Preface to the Second Russian Edition' to his *General Theory of Law and Marxism*, Pashukanis writes that 'the relations between commodity producers generate the most highly developed, most universal and most consummate legal mediation [but] a developed and consummate form does not of course exclude undeveloped and rudimentary forms rather to the contrary it presupposes them'.[9] The factual form of ownership-as-appropriation is part of every mode of production, but 'only within a particular social formation does property take on its logically simplest and most universal form as private property'; only in bourgeois society 'the legal form attains universal significance, legal ideology becomes the ideology par excellence, and defending the class interest of the exploiters appears with ever-increasing success as the defence of the abstract principle of legal subjectivity'.[10] Lon Fuller has poignantly expressed this point in this way:

> This analysis of law is not simply an analysis of bourgeois law, but of law generally. In truth, the only law is bourgeois law. To be sure, legal institutions in embryo can be found in a feudal or slave society, where they are intertwined with religious and military elements. Modem scholars are likely to misinterpret these rudimentary legal elements in pre-capitalistic society as the equivalent of modem law. Actually, these embryonic and undifferentiated legal elements are like the first tentative gropings toward a capitalistic organization that can be detected in even the most primitive societies. The full inner logic of the conception of law can assert itself only under capitalism. The ideal of law is realized at the same time as the ideal of the market; both present man as the trader, as an autonomous agent setting his relations with his fellows.[11]

What are these rudimentary and embryonic legal forms presupposed by the fully developed capitalist/bourgeois one? Pashukanis refrained from engaging properly with such a question: he limited himself to observe that

> there are two epochs when the general concepts of law reached their highest point of development: Rome, with its system of private law and the seventeenth and eighteenth centuries in Europe, during which time philosophical thought discovered the universal significance of the legal form as a possibility which bourgeois society was destined to embody.[12]

9 Pashukanis, *The General Theory* (n 2) 44.
10 ibid 45.
11 Lon L Fuller, 'Pashukanis and Vyshinsky: A Study in the Development of Marxian Legal Theory' (1949) 47 *Michigan Law Review* 1161.
12 Pashukanis, *The General Theory* (n 2) 71.

Taking its cue from these observations, this chapter will interrogate the past of the legal form, by tracing in a genealogical fashion the emergence of some embryonic elements of its modern fully developed version. To this purpose, this work will take into consideration two central aspects of Pashukanis' theory: i) the nature of the legal form, that is the actual formation of the abstract (the fact that the relationship between people in the market becomes a relationship between abstract owners devoid of specific characteristics except being possessors of rights) out of the practice of exchange; ii) when he acknowledged the existence of embryonic legal forms in the past he invites us not only to place his theory of law in a historical continuum but to look at the formation of the legal tradition (and jurisprudence as a field of knowledge) from the point of view of his materialist method. Overall taking into due consideration this will help effectively elucidate the relationship the legal form entertains with its past.

What is Legal Form the Name Of?

At the heart of Pashukanis' commodity-form theory of law lies a question of method—more precisely, the discernment of the more suitable materialist approach for unravelling law's objective reality. Early on in his *General Theory of Law and Marxism*, he unequivocally asserts that to provide an effective theory of law the more appropriate methodology to embrace is Marx's rising from the 'abstract to the concrete'. In an oft-cited passage of the *Grundrisse*, Marx has described this specific approach in this way:

> When we consider a given country politico-economically, we begin with its population, its distribution among classes, town, country, the coast, the different branches of production, export and import, annual production and consumption, commodity prices, etc. It seems to be correct to begin with the real and the concrete, with the real precondition, thus to begin, in economics, with e.g. the population, which is the foundation and the subject of the entire social act of production. However, on closer examination this proves false. The population is an abstraction if I leave out, for example, the classes of which it is composed. These classes in turn are an empty phrase if I am not familiar with the elements on which they rest. E.g. wage labour, capital, etc. These latter in turn presuppose exchange, division of labour, prices, etc. For example, capital is nothing without wage labour, without value, money, price, etc. Thus, if I were to begin with the population, this would be a chaotic conception [*Vorstellung*] of the whole, and I would then, by means of further determination, move analytically towards ever more simple concepts [*Begriff*], from the imagined concrete towards ever thinner abstractions until I had arrived at the simplest determinations. From there the journey would have to be

> retraced until I had finally arrived at the population again, but this time not as the chaotic conception of a whole, but as a rich totality of many determinations and relations.[13]

For Marx, social phenomena appear as the concentration of many determinations, and for this reason, the analysis of capital cannot but begin with the simpler and more abstract of such determinations: the commodity form, value, and labour—the basic elements whose composite relations form the concrete reality of the capitalist world. The scientific analysis of complex concrete realities should, therefore, proceed from the single abstract elements, deriving the fundamental determinations from the totality would produce in Marx's terms, a chaotic conception of the whole.

Following in the footsteps of the Marxian method, Pashukanis developed his own materialist theory of the law by looking at the basic legal elements of a society dominated by the commodity form; that is the legal relationships that allow commodities to exist as such and to be exchanged. In his general theory, the legal form emerged along with the establishment of the fundamental determinations for making the market operative: the conflicting acquisition of private interests. Indeed, it is the 'conflict of private interest' for Pashukanis that presents 'both the logical premise of the legal form and the actual origin of the development of the legal superstructure'.[14] The whole edifice of the law (private and public) is built upon the basic juridical factor of the differentiation and opposition of individual private interests, which emerges in exchange.[15] Commodities, Marx wrote 'cannot themselves go to market and perform exchange'; to make it happen—to make things into commodities through the exchange,

> their guardians must place themselves in relation to one another as a person whose will resides in those objects, and must behave in such a way that each does not appropriate the commodity of the other, and alienate his own, except through an act to which both parties consent.[16]

In the process of exchange, thus, things become commodities, bearers of value, and individuals acquire the 'capacity to be legal subject and a bearer of rights'.[17]

13 Karl Marx, *The Grundrisse (1857–1858)* (Random House 1973) 101.
14 Pashukanis, *The General Theory* (n 2) 81.
15 P Beirne and R Sharlet (eds), *Pashukanis: Selected Writings on Marxism and Law* (Academic Press 1980) 58, 81.
16 Karl Marx, *Capital Volume 1* (Penguin 1976) 178.
17 Pashukanis, *The General Theory* (n 2) 112.

Pashukanis describes the emergence of the legal form on the ground of commodity exchange as follows:

> Just as in the commodity, the multiplicity of use-values natural to a product appears simply as the shell of value, and the concrete types of human labour are dissolved into abstract human labour as the creator of value, so also the concrete multiplicity of the relations between humans and objects manifests itself as the abstract will of the owner. All concrete peculiarities which distinguish one representative of the genus homo sapiens from another dissolve into the abstraction of the human in general, and the human as a legal subject.[18]

The exchange of commodities, as Marx preconised, is geared of a series of abstractions whose effects are what makes the process assume the form we are accustomed to: use-value becomes the mere support of exchange value, human labour is dissolved in purely quantifiable abstract labour, the complexity of human relationships is reduced to relations between abstract legal subjects devoid of individual characteristics excepts their being holder of rights. The legal form is the form of a relationship between legal subjects, resulting from the abstraction of social relations determined by the total commodification of reality. As Matthew Dimick puts it, 'just as exchange is constitutive of the abstractness of value, so it is also constitutive of the legal subject, a "free and equal", abstract subject with the capacity to possess rights'.[19]

But abstractness does not exhaust the nature of the legal form and law as a whole: Pashukanis is rather clear in this regard when he claims that the law 'does not exist in the heads and the theories of learned jurists', but it has a 'real history which unfolds not as a set of ideas, but as a specific set of relations which humans enter into not by conscious choice, but because the relations of production compel them to do so'.[20] Here the enigmatic nature of the legal form emerges with clarity: the legal form is a 'concrete' and 'real' relation between abstract equal subjects (separated from their individual grounded existence, except their capacity to bear rights). The legal form seems—on the one hand—strictly tied and emerging through the process of exchange (and production)—but on the other—appears as the product of the encounter of the reality of exchange with a legal institutional superstructure. Indeed, as Pashukanis claims:

> It is dispute, conflict of interest, which creates the legal form, the legal superstructure. In the lawsuit, in court proceedings, the economically

18 ibid 113.

19 Matthew Dimick, 'Evgeny Pashukanis' Commodity-Form Theory of Law' in Umut Özsu and Paul O'Connell (eds), *Research Handbook on Law and Marxism* (Edward Elgar Publishing 2021) 119.

20 Pashukanis, *The General Theory* (n 2) 68.

> active subjects first appear in their capacity as parties, that is, as participants in the legal superstructure. Even in its most primitive form, the court is legal superstructure par excellence. The legal differentiates itself from the economic and appears as an autonomous element through legal proceedings. Historically, law begins with dispute, that is, with the lawsuit; only later did it embrace the preceding, purely economic or practical relations, which thus from the very beginning assumed a double-edged economic legal aspect. Dogmatic jurisprudence forgets this sequence of events, proceeding directly from the end result, from the abstract norms with which the state fills, so to speak, the whole social domain. It acknowledges as legal only those actions which are undertaken within that domain.[21]

In this passage, Pashukanis introduces a distinction that is vital for the understanding of his materialist strategy, the one between legal form and legal superstructure. The first refers to the actual relationship between commodity owners considered in their capacity as legal subjects; the latter, instead, refers to the whole institutional apparatus that sustains the application and enforcement of the law. Both are, for Pashukanis, emerging from the 'conflict of interests' and the 'dispute'; but their relationship cannot be reduced to a simple process of determination. Although grounded in the economic base of society, the legal form—and the juridical element of social relationships—becomes visible only through the 'legal proceeding', that is through the existence of legal institutions. As China Miéville rightly observes for Pashukanis, the

> juridical relation is partly constitutive of the fundamental social relation, but it can only become visible as itself, ie., as a legal form, through the medium of actually-existing law . . . A particular legal superstructure allows the legality of the legal form to become visible—and is necessarily thrown up by it.[22]

Far from being ascribable to traditional forms of historical materialism (or economic determinism), the materialist theory of law that Pashukanis elaborated is built upon a dialectical conception of the relationship between the materiality of social relationships and their legal determinations, according to which a specific legal superstructure is what makes the concrete legal forms to become visible and operative. The law in this picture, operates performatively to form relations exchange at the point of intersection between practice and abstraction. Legal form, thus, is the name that Pashukanis gave to the specific material/concrete relationships between humans—in the commodity

21 ibid 93–94.
22 China Miéville, *Between Equal Rights: A Marxist Theory of International Law* (Brill 2005) 96.

exchange—once they enter contact with the institutional superstructure that makes them juridical in their essence: once they become relationships between abstract legal subjects. And to the extent that the right to ownership is fundamental for exchange to take place, the law here takes (dialectically) part in the very formation of commodity exchange itself. Legal form names one of the basic processes of abstraction fundamental to the determination of commodities and capital, and in their operation of social synthesis.

Real Abstraction

The 'commodity-form theory of law' reveals that legal forms and the institutional superstructure are not merely ideological constructs or something imposed by a sovereign command. Instead, they are integral components in shaping the commodity form itself, rooted in the practical dynamics of exchange. Pashukanis' understanding of law, therefore, goes beyond a rigid structural relationship between the material base and legal superstructure, since it exposes the legal form as being both the product and the producer of exchange. The legal form is indeed both creating and emerging from the practice of exchange: the abstraction of the legal subject—the owner of the commodities—is a necessary element for commodity exchange that somehow emerges in the act of exchange itself. Pashukanis, however, did not delve into the specifics of how this abstraction is generated and functions.

By taking the cue from Marx's theorisation of the commodity form and the abstraction of value, the German philosopher Alfred Sohn-Rethel in his *Intellectual and Manual Labour*[23] elaborated a concept that might be helpful to understand the nature of the legal form: that of 'real abstraction'. Such a concept encapsulates the idea that the abstract categories dominating the way we think, and consequently how we organise the world emerged out of what he called 'exchange-abstraction'—that is, the activity of commodity exchange. For Sohn-Rethel exchange is a 'really abstract' practice that stands 'as a presupposition of mental or intellectual abstraction': it constitutes the spatiotemporal basis for developing thought formations that could abstract from both time and space. What makes abstractions real is the fact that they are an effect of the actions of humans and not of their thoughts.[24]

Sohn-Rethel advanced the hypothesis that not only the determinate fields of knowledge with their sets of foundational paradigms; but even the more abstract categories of thinking and the very human tendency towards abstract thought could be explained by referring to the determinate material conditions of the commodity exchange. As he claimed, even the 'transcendental

23 Alfred Sohn-Rethel, *Intellectual and Manual Labour: A Critique of Epistemology* (Brill 2020).

24 Brenna Bhandar and Alberto Toscano, 'Race, Real Estate and Real Abstraction' (November–December 2015) 194 *Radical Philosophy* 8–9.

unity of the self-consciousness, to use the Kantian expression for the phenomenon here involved, is itself an intellectual reflection of . . . the form of exchangeability of the commodities'.[25] From this perspective, the very form of abstract categories whose effects are shaping how humans interact with the outside world and consequently inform our modes of life is the product of practical life. Conceptual abstractions, 'seizing what is common to several objects without being visible in any of them, is not a given, a prius'; on the contrary, it is ultimately the 'result of the existence of real abstractions in the production and reproduction of human life'.[26]

Sohn-Rethel summarises the operation of the emergence of specific forms of real abstractions in exchange as follows:

> The form of commodity is abstract and abstractness governs its whole orbit. To begin with, exchange-value is itself abstract value in contrast to the use-value of commodities. The exchange-value is subject only to quantitative differentiation, and this quantification is again abstract compared with the quantity which measures use-values . . . The form in which commodity-value takes on its concrete appearance as money—be it as coinage or bank-notes—is an abstract thing which, strictly speaking, is a contradiction in terms. *In the form of money riches become abstract riches and, as owner of such riches, man himself becomes an abstract man, a private property-owner*. Lastly a society in which commodity exchange forms the nexus rerum is a purely abstract set of relations where everything concrete is in private hands.[27]

For Sohn-Rethel, not only abstractions are essentially not a product of the mind, but the very practice of exchange is (somehow) paradoxically abstract: 'It is the action of exchange, and the action alone, that is abstract'.[28]

Here we see how Sohn-Rethel's starting point is the same as that of Pashukanis: exchange produces, as its constitutive parts, a series of abstractions; the transaction itself, its subjects, and the object of rights. But contrary to Pashukanis, Sohn-Rethel made a step further in the investigation of how, from the action of exchange, abstractions could arise. The origin of abstraction, he sustains, should be identified with the separation that the commodity yields between the actions of use and exchange. 'Wherever commodity exchange takes place', he writes 'it does so in effective "abstraction" from use': this abstraction is not a representation of the mind, but it is a 'state of affairs prevailing at a definite place and lasting a definite time. It is the state

25 Sohn-Rethel (n 23) 64.
26 Anselm Jappe, 'Sohn-Rethel and the Origin of "Real Abstraction": A Critique of Production or a Critique of Circulation?' (2013) 21(1) *Historical Materialism* 4.
27 Sohn-Rethel (n 23) 16.
28 ibid 22.

of affairs which reigns on the market'.[29] When entering the market, 'things stand still', awaiting to change owner and, while waiting to be exchanged their use is precluded. But use and use-value, Sohn-Rethel claims, do not disappear from the picture; indeed, people exchange commodities with some purpose in mind to make a determinate use of it. Use-value, thus, in exchange becomes a matter of the individual mind—it becomes itself abstracted from reality, entering the psychological sphere of the intention. This is in a sense the engine of the development of abstract thought, that is, the separation of use and exchange that makes 'the consciousness and the action of the people part company and go different ways'.[30] With the development of commodity production, Sohn-Rethel writes, humans'

> imagination grows more and more separate from [their] actions and becomes increasingly individualised, eventually assuming the dimensions of a private consciousness. This is a phenomenon deriving its origin, not from the private sphere of use, but precisely from the public one of the market. The individualised consciousness also is beset by abstractness, but this is not the abstractness of the act of exchange at its source. For the abstractness of that action cannot be noted when it happens, since it only happens because the consciousness of its agents is taken up with their business and with the empirical appearance of things which pertains to their use. One could say that the abstractness of their action is beyond realisation by the actors because their very consciousness stands in the way. Were the abstractness to catch their minds their action would cease to be exchange and the abstraction would not arise. Nevertheless the abstractness of exchange does enter their minds, but only after the event, when they are faced with the completed result of the circulation of the commodities. The chief result is money in which the abstractness assumes a separate embodiment.[31]

In use, the relationship between the subject and the thing is somehow practically immediate; and it is only by severing this immediacy that exchange could take place. Commodity exchange is nothing other than things changing ownership, through the separation between the owner and the possibility of using things. In this practical space of separation abstractions emerge: conceptual abstractions; money as quantification of value; and legal property as the attestation of property in separation from use. 'The state of reciprocal independence', Sohn-Rethel writes, 'exists on the basis of commodity production'; indeed, 'all commodities are used whether for production or

29 ibid 21.
30 ibid 22.
31 ibid.

consumption, exclusively in the private sphere of the commodity owners'.[32] Commodities can be exchanged only to the extent that they belong to different subjects claiming ownership, only if it's made 'impossible for a commodity to be owned simultaneously by two people in separate ownership',[33] and this of course is what the law guarantees.

Sohn-Rethel's theorisation of real abstractions exposes in a rather peculiar fashion the nature of the legal form. Indeed, the commodity form requires the separation of use and exchange; but while in use the relationship between the person and the thing is not at issue since it is somehow immediate, in exchange (when use is suspended) the relationship between the person and the thing becomes mediated by the very idea of ownership otherwise the exchange cannot take place. According to Pashukanis' idea of the legal form, such a relationship of ownership becomes (immediately) a legal one through the conflict of interests and the action of the legal superstructure (the court) that recognises the legal form as in place in the form of an abstract relationship between persons and things and between abstract legal subjects, owners of the commodities exchanged. In exchange, the abstraction from use makes the relationship between the person and the thing an abstract one; a claim to a right or a thing. With the notion of legal form, thus Pashukanis named the emergence out of the practical life of exchange of the real abstraction of the legal subject and the normative apparatus of private law, necessary for the commodity-exchange process to take place as such. The legal form names the artificial linkage between a subject and an object at the moment in which the practice of exchange separates the immediate and concrete relationship between humans and things: it is in a sense, the transposition on the abstract legal plane of a brute fact.

Legal Subjectivity

When Pashukanis discussed the emergence and definition of the modern legal form and noted that in modern capitalist societies, the natural person has been transformed into a juridical subject which assumed the form of a 'mathematical point, a centre in which a certain sum of rights is concentrated',[34] he was faced with the development of law and jurisprudence of the 18th and 19th century. It is at this moment that the idea of legal personality as an abstract point of concentration of rights and duties (that is the consolidated traditional idea of legal subjectivity) emerged in its more refined form.[35]

32 ibid 33.

33 ibid 35.

34 Pashukanis, *The General Theory* (n 2) 115.

35 Perhaps, as Visa Kurki claimed, 'Leibniz was the first to associate (legal) personhood with right-holding and duty-bearing' systematically. In his geometrical reconstructions of the law, Leibniz suggested that 'the elements of law are contained in the *Corpus Juris* . . . the

Although admittedly rather unique in its formulation, the Hegelian definition of (legal) personality and subjecthood is for Pashukanis indicative of such a 'speculative' conception of subjecthood.[36] Personality, we read in Hegel's *Philosophy of Right*, is that which 'contains in general the capacity for the right [*Rechtsfähigkeit*, i.e. legal capacity] and constitutes the concept and the (itself abstract) basis of abstract and hence formal right'.[37] Personality, he writes

> confers a right to things [*ein Recht an Sachen*, i.e. *ius in rem*], and consequently that personal right [*das persönliche Recht*, i.e. *ius in personam*] is in essence a right of things [*Sachenrecht*, i.e. property law]—'thing' [*Sache*] being understood in its general sense as everything external to my freedom, including even my body and my life.[38]

From this purely formal conception of rights and legal subjectivity the very idea of property, for Pashukanis, becomes ontologically evanescent and loses all ties with the 'organic natural principle of private appropriation resulting from personal expenditure of energy'; in exchange, he goes on, 'the bond between the property-owner and his property just as abstract, formal, qualified and rationalistic, as the relationship of a person to the product of his labour'.[39]

Naturally, the evolution of the modern conception of who is the juridical subject (of rights) was influenced by the political and social dynamics that have characterised the period, which saw the emergence of the liberal conception of rights—with its radically individualistic tone. Such a conception was based on the fundamental postulate/idea of human beings as rational and morally autonomous entities, with subjective (natural and legal) rights. The model for this image of the human was that of 'possessive individualism', that is individuals defined (somehow abstractly) by their capacity to be the owners (of things, their own bodies included). It is indeed this capacity

[simple] terms from whose complexion there arises the diversity of cases in the law are persons, things, acts, and rights'. This axiomatic reconstruction defines the subjects of the law (persons—which can be natural or artificial) essentially through the capacity to hold rights, which practically means that a 'person has the moral power to execute his or her will'; while a right 'imposes on some other person the moral necessity to forebear some right, which Leibniz terms an obligation (obligation)', see: Visa AJ Kurki, *A Theory of Legal Personhood* (OUP 2019) 38; Gottfried Wilhelm Leibniz, 'De Arte Combinatoria' in German (ed), *Samtliche Schriften und Briefe (Formerly Prussian)* (Academy of Sciences 1923, reprint Olms 1972-) cited in Alberto Artosi, Bernardo Pieri and Giovanni Sartor (eds), *Leibniz: Logico-Philosophical Puzzles in the Law: Philosophical Questions and Perplexing Cases in the Law* (Springer 2013) xxv.

36 Pashukanis, *The General Theory* (n 2) 111.

37 GWF Hegel, *Elements of the Philosophy of Right* (Allen W Wood ed, CUP 1991) § 36.

38 ibid § 40.

39 Pashukanis, *The General Theory* (n 2) 126.

that defines individuality in its own right, with the logical consequence of making relationships between individuals into relationships between proprietors—that is market relationships.[40]

Such a form of legal subject serves as the foundational element of the legal structure itself: it operates as a representation of the individual within the legal institutional sphere and works as that instrument granting access to the realm of the law, establishing the limits of social/political intervention and constituting the objects of governmental protection. Essentially designed to assert rights and fulfil duties, the abstract legal subject represents a bastion for safeguarding (and violently enforcing) the very function of property in the bourgeois-capitalist world. As Pashukanis puts it, with the full development of the legal form,

> property ceases to be unstable, precarious, purely factual property which may at any moment be contested and have to be defended, weapon in hand. It is transformed into an absolute, fixed right which follows the object wherever chance may take it, and which, ever since bourgeois civilisation extended its rule to encompass the whole globe, has been protected the world over by laws, police and lawcourts.[41]

The abstract legal subject operates a simplification of the real/concrete individual (or entity) to facilitate interactions and transactions, and to guarantee the formal equality of participants in the market so dear to the capitalist ideology. This abstraction ensures that activities carried out within the legal domain align with and exist within the symbolic universe of bourgeois law. On a practical level—that is at the level of its legal consequences—the legal subject can operate only through the removal of the physical, biological, and biographical specificities of the individual singularities, establishing a clear separation between our existence as the bearer of rights and duties and our substantial/concrete selves.

Although it might seem counterintuitive, legal subjectification (or personalisation) involves a process of denaturalisation, which appears vital for the construction of a normative order that can be enforced against equal parties. To the extent that legal subjects are construed entities—whose reality is measured by the concrete regulatory (often violent) effects they have on the lives of people—their existence depends entirely on the institutional reality they depend on. No wonder though if the legal conceptualisation of subjectivities allows for the personification of a multiplicity of non-human entities (from corporations to the more recent legal personality of environment and

40 Of course, here the reference is to CB Macpherson, *The Political Theory of Possessive Individualism: Hobbes to Locke* (OUP 1962).

41 Pashukanis, *The General Theory* (n 2) 115.

natural resources). From the point of view of the law, subjects (persons) are essentially 'empty forms, the most anonymous of masks, which can be distributed to everyone in the multitude (or even to such a multitude itself)',[42] to attribute rights, duties, and liabilities. Such a standardised abstraction has become, with the full development of capitalism and the state, an instrument fostering societal stability and substantial inequality through the enforcement of formal abstract equality.

Abstractness, for Pashukanis, is the main mode of existence of the legal subject in a society dominated and informed by commodities. For the law, the individual is a representation, a double, which interfaces and interacts with other subjects and with the legal system. Such a characteristic constitutes a core jurisprudential question in the historical development of legal and political theory. While the definition of legal subjectivity as that of 'bearing rights and duties' was not controversial, the question of what subject these legal relations belong to and are imputed has been the object of different interpretations.[43] However, as John Dewey once wrote: 'There is no general agreement regarding the nature *in se* of the jural subject; courts and legislators do their work without such agreement, sometimes without any conception or theory at all regarding its nature';[44] it seems, he goes on, that such a question is of no concern for the law. In the end, even when the law speaks of the difference between a natural (physical) person and a legal person (a corporation), the ontological abstract essence of the legal subject is not in question. Hans Kelsen explains clearly this points as follows:

> The legal order imposes obligations upon, or confers rights to, human beings, that is, that legal order makes human behaviour the content of obligation and rights. 'To be a person' or 'to have a legal personality' is identical with having legal obligations and subjective rights. The person as holder of obligations and rights is not something that is different from the obligations and rights, as whose holder the person is presented—just as a tree which is said to have a trunk, branches, and blossoms, is not a substance different from trunk, branches, and blossoms, but merely the totality of these elements. The physical [natural] or juristic [legal] person, who 'has' obligations and rights as their holder, is these obligations and rights—a complex of legal obligations and rights whose totality is

42 Niels van Dijk, 'In the Hall of Masks: Contrasting Modes of Personification' in M Hildebrandt and K O'Hara (eds), *Life and the Law in the Era of Data-Driven Agency* (Edward Elgar 2020) 247.

43 On this issue see: Ngaire Naffine, *Law's Meaning of Life: Philosophy, Religion, Darwin and the Legal Person* (Hart Publishing 2009).

44 John Dewey, 'The Historic Background of Corporate Legal Personality' (1926) 35(6) *The Yale Law Journal* 655, 660.

> expressed figuratively in the concept of 'person'. 'Person' is merely the personification of this totality.[45]

The person, as the subject of rights, is here portrayed as simply the sum or the totality of those incorporeal objects like rights and obligations and is substantially devoid of material connotation. In a sense, the legal subject is the abstract sum of the real effects of immaterial-legal elements.

From the historical/genealogical point of view, the idea of legal subjectivity as the abstract capacity of holding rights and duties, developed in modern times through the constant interplay between law, philosophical considerations and theological themes[46] and the decisive influence of the Roman law tradition. Indeed, the idea of the (law of the) person developed in Roman law jurisprudence represented the archetypal figure of a legal subject (a sort of *Ursubject*), the matrix over which subsequent theorisation evolved.[47] In a sense, the same Marx was aware of this when he wrote:

> In Roman law, the *servus* is therefore correctly defined as one who may not enter into exchange for the purpose of acquiring anything for himself. It is, consequently, equally clear that although this legal system corresponds to a social state in which exchange was by no means developed, nevertheless, in so far as it was developed in a limited sphere, it was able to develop the attributes of the juridical person, precisely of the individual engaged in exchange, and thus anticipate the legal relations of industrial society, and in particular the right which rising bourgeois society had necessarily to assert against medieval society[48]

If anything, this passage from the *Grundrisse* demonstrates, on the one hand, how for Marx the specificity of the legal form should be located in the economic sphere of exchange, and on the other hand the importance of the Roman law of person in anticipating (or the being an embryo) of the modern legal form.

45 Hans Kelsen, *Pure Theory of Law* (Max Knight tr, U of California P 1973) 173.

46 See: Adolf Trendelenburg, 'A Contribution to the History of the Word Person' (1910) 20(3) The Monist 336; Udo Thiel, *The Early Modern Subject: Self-Consciousness and Personal Identity from Descartes to Hume* (OUP 2011); Tomasz Pietrzykowski, *Personhood Beyond Humanism: Animals, Chimeras, Autonomous Agents and the Law* (Springer 2018); Kurki (n 35).

47 See: Yan Thomas, 'Le subject concret et sa personne. Essai d'histoire juridique retrospective' in Cayla Olivier and Yan Thomas (eds), *Du droit de ne pas naître: À propos de l'affaire Perruche* (Gallimard 2002) 91–175; Roberto Esposito, *Third Person* (Zakiya Hanafi tr, Polity Press 2012); Roberto Esposito, *The Machine of Political Theology and the Place of Thought* (Zakiya Hanafi tr, Fordham UP 2015); Kurki (n 35).

48 Marx (n 13) 245–46.

Person

Although it has been argued that the Romans did not possess a 'coherent theory of legal personality',[49] the influence of their juridical tradition upon the formation of the modern legal mindset cannot but lead us to consider the Roman law of persons as an paradigmatic figure for the subject of law. Not only did the term 'person' remain the key term in the discourses that founded the modern idea of legal subjectivity, but the Roman *ius personarum* constituted the base for the development of the modern legal personality.[50] It is not surprising, though, that many (if not all) attempts at reconstructing and historicising the very meaning/form of the (modern and contemporary) legal subject, begin with a reference to the Latin word *persona*—that is the root of the term person—and its meaning 'mask' (tragic, ritual, or ancestral),[51] as well as denoting the notions of part, duty, and dignity.[52]

Despite the word's contested etymology, one prevalent hypothesis suggests that 'person' (as a mask) is somehow the outcome of a 'Greek borrowing by the Etruscans' of the word *prosōpon* [πρόσωπον], meaning 'face' and 'theatrical mask'. However, as the philologist Giovanni Semeraro sustains, *persona* might evoke the meaning of *pars* (part), function, and office of a subject, with the association to mask as a secondary development. Semeraro indeed contends that the juxtaposition with the Greek *prosōpon* has obscured the etymological interpretation, somewhat concealing the juridical basis for the emergence of the term *persona*.[53] Amidst the obscure origin of the work, what remains indisputable is that for the Romans the person held a foundational position for the law.[54] The person, along with things (*res*), and actions (*actiones*), represented one of the basic categories sustaining the whole edifice of Roman law, as synthesised by Gaius in his *Institutiones*: 'the whole of the law by which we are

49 Barry Nicholas, *An Introduction to Roman Law* (OUP 1962) 60.
50 PW Duff, *Personality in Roman Private Law* (CUP 1938).
51 Marcel Mauss, 'A Category of the Human Mind: The Notion of Person; the Notion of Self' in Michael Carrithers, Steven Collins and Steven Lukes (eds), *The Category of the Person: Anthropology, Philosophy, History* (CUP 1985) 13.
52 Giovanni Semeraro, *Le origini della cultura europea, vol II, Dizionari etimologici, Basi semitiche delle lingue indeuropee* (Olschki 1994) 514. In Latin literature, the term *persona* has been employed to define the characters of dialogue and orations and more generally the social role and the function of an individual, as well as the temperament and personality of a subject. Throughout the centuries, the semantic sphere of such term gradually expanded: from the original meaning of a mask, the term 'person' began to signify the 'social role', the specific public function of an individual and subject, conceived from the point of view of his or her moral characteristics. See: Giuseppe Comerci, 'L'individuo e la cittá: L'idea di "persona" da Terenzio a Cicerone' (1997) XVIII Orpheus 29–65; Ulrico Agnati, '"Persona iuris vocabulum" Per un'interpretazione giuridica di "persona" nelle opere di Gaio' (2009) IX *Rivista di Diritto Romano* 1–41.
53 Semeraro (n 52) 514.
54 Mauss (n 51) 15.

governed relates either to persons, or to things, or actions'.[55] This tripartition, which has had an enduring influence on the development of the Western legal tradition identifies ideally the core elements of the law and legal rules with the subjects affected, the object (matter) of rights and duties, and the remedies.

In this basic categorisation, the person represents somehow the unitary notion epitomising human beings in the context of the law. The *persona* is the projection of the human subject in the theatre of the law, as a legal actor. As the Roman law historian Yan Thomas has pointed out, the juridical conception of the person is essentially a 'technical artefact', a legal mask, giving to the concrete person a 'unique and stable' identity (totally independent from the material individual attributes of the represented subject) to be deployed in the sphere of law.[56] Already in Roman antiquity, for the law, the person is nothing other than that side of human concrete living to which legal relationships, rights, duties, and imputation are related—and perhaps it is from this original legal definition that the word 'person' expanded its semantic reach and acquired further derived meanings. In practical terms, this means that rights and obligations were not 'properties' of the integral subjects but only of their *personae*; 'the person was first of all the creditor, the debtor, the proprietor, the actor, and the defendant, etc.'.[57] It is, therefore, possible for a single individual to embody different persons, and vice versa for a single *persona* to refer to more than one person: the law of persons is concerned with 'functional classes, the norms of which dictated the effect of the different juridical roles (*personae*)'[58] that the individuals could bear according to their social and legal positions, and not with the individuals in their singularity.

Legal personification is, therefore, that particular operation, according to which the acquisition of the capacity to act in the legal field happens as a result of a process of denaturalisation. Such a process, Thomas observed, consists in the concealment of 'the concrete individuality behind an abstract identity': these two modalities of being cannot be confused, since 'the first is biographic the second is statutory'.[59] For the legal person, the biographic, singular and concrete dimension of the lived existence is ultimately excluded and, at the same time, included as the necessary support to the mask/person and as the centre/subject of the legal consequences. The natural dimension of life appears for the law as something like a presupposition that must be institutionally excluded to become properly a foundational presupposition.[60]

55 *Omnes ius quo utimur, vel ad personas pertinent vel ad res vel ad actiones* (Gaius I.8).

56 Thomas, 'Le subject concret et sa personne' (n 47) 126.

57 ibid.

58 ibid 127.

59 ibid 135–36.

60 See: Gian-Giacomo Fusco, 'Notes on Person and the Anthropological Machine of Law' in T Zartaloudis (ed), *Law and Philosophical Theory: Critical Intersections* (Rowman and Littlefield International 2018).

What is more, the Roman law category of the person has an eminent economic dimension. Indeed, as Thomas has argued, the 'unity of the person does not refer . . . to that of the physical or psychological subject. It principally, originally at any rate, indicates the unity of an estate'; in Roman law, the *persona* represented 'the legal subject holding an estate as well as to the agents (sons, slaves) that it included', and this logically implies that the 'law recognised as many persons as there are estates, rather than as many as there are individuals'.[61] The person, in law, abstractly produces a unity of patrimony reducing several objects owned into a single point of implication. To explain this principle, Thomas makes the following example:

> A testator institutes his son and his grandson as heirs on one side, and his friend on the other. How should one interpret the testator's intention? Did he want to divide his inheritance into three equal parts, intended respectively for his son, his grandson and his friend? Or did he wish to divide it into two halves, one for his two descendants and the other for his friend? According to the text, which notes the rule that sons have no autonomy as to an estate, since 'father and son are one person', it is the second solution that prevails.[62]

This example reveals how a single estate (patrimony) can incorporate different subjects—the testator, the son, and the grandson. It then follows that one single individual, when part of two estates (like for instance, a slave owned by two masters) is split into two different persons. For this reason, Thomas could claim that the law 'to compose "persons", effectuates a genuine dissociation of subjects and bodies'.[63]

From the point of view of the materialist conception of the legal form, Thomas's interpretation of the Roman law category of the person is of the utmost interest since it confirms the genetic link between the material sphere of ownership and the abstraction of the legal subjectivity (between legal personality and the capacity to own an estate). The *ius personarum* here appears, in its own right, as a sphere in which the embryos of the legal form have been established and bequeathed to the Western legal tradition. By representing the unity of a patrimony, the Roman *persona* constitutes itself on the material ground of what is by definition owned and alienable: the objects forming the wealth of the individuals. And to the extent that what defined the most the objects—the *res*—composing the patrimony 'is their belonging to a social sphere of appropriability and exchange', the legal subjects of Roman law are by definition an abstract (immaterial) representation of the material association between a concrete individual and its property.

61 Yan Thomas, 'The Subject of Right, the Person, Nature: Remarks on the Current Criticism of the Legal Subject' in Yan Thomas (ed), C Schütz and A Schütz (trs), *Legal Artifices: Ten Essays on Roman Law in the Present Tense* (Edinburgh UP 2021) 128.

62 ibid 127–28.

63 ibid 127.

However, this sphere of exchange, which is what ultimately grants the very possibility of private property, is not a natural datum but, as the same Thomas has argued in the essay *La valeur des choses*,[64] the product of a fundamental legal operation. The patrimonial [*patrimoniel*] character of things (which determines the legitimate faculty to appropriate and exchange) is defined in Roman law, negatively. 'In order to make openly appear their juridical nature as evaluable, appropriable, and available things', Thomas writes, 'it is necessary that certain things are excluded from the area of appropriation and exchange, and then assigned to the Gods or the city'. These objects were defined 'through a paradoxical formula, which has not always been understood, as things belonging to a property that does not belong to anybody' (*res nullius in bonis*).[65] The act of taking out from private appropriation and commerce a certain amount of things renders what remains legally appropriable and exchangeable: 'It is the institution of sanctuarized reserves of things which renders via contrast the rest of the world—which is nothing but the sphere of private law—immune to sacrality and religion'.[66] However, the sphere of exchange and commerce does not appear as a derivative of this legal operation, on the contrary, the sphere of inappropriability seems to be carved out from things appropriable and affirmed as prior to the public/sacred inaccessible things. Thomas writes 'to formulate the patrimonial and commercial nature of *res*, Roman law took the detour of placing them in reserve, of their exceptional assignment to the city or the gods. Detour through the narrowly circumscribed areas of the public and the sacred to organise and think of the state of commerce as prior, and not the reverse'.[67] In the end, the *res nullius in bonis* is a further characterisation of the *res nullius*—those things not belonging to anyone and therefore open to absolute appropriability.[68]

Technique of Law

This chapter started by interrogating what Pashukanis intended as the legal form, and by raising the question of its past or origin for then moving in looking to the abstract nature of the legal form and legal subjectivity, and—following Pashukanis' suggestion—in considering Roman law as the primigenial place of emergence of proto-legal-forms. As a way of conclusion, (and considering the limit posed by a work of this kind) it is worth looking at the potential relationship between the early rudimental legal forms and the

64 Yan Thomas, 'La Valeur Des Choses: Le Droit Romain Hors La Religion' (2002) 57(6) *Annales. Histoire, Sciences Sociales* 1431–62.

65 ibid 1432.

66 ibid.

67 ibid 1433.

68 Max Kaser, *Römisches Privatrecht* (vol 1, 2nd ed, CH Beck 1971) 377 fn 15: "Nur dies ['privater Rechte unfähig'], nicht Herrenlosigkeit, bedeutet *nullius in bonis esse* bei Gai. 2,9; Marci D 1, 8, 6, 2 (Inst 2, 1, 7)."

modern fully developed one, at what survives[69] of the embryos into the mature forms.

Although Pashukanis has always been adamant about sustaining the unicity of the (fully developed) modern legal form, the question of the continuity of the law—and the banal fact that laws are related to a temporality that is never punctual but always grounded in a continuum were past experiences constitute the rationale for future applications—cannot be disregarded easily, especially when at stake there are old and established categories. In the end, the history of the European legal tradition, observed from the point of view of the longue durée, exposed how 'Roman juridical forms have constantly been superimposed on new historical contents', so much so that core paradigmatic breaks and legal innovations conserved rather than surpass the forms of the Roman legal classification. Indeed, it has been argued—perhaps not without a certain degree of approximation (or even exaggeration)—that for the modern capitalist world, the Roman private law provided a 'basic conceptual structure' through which it sustains its relentless evolution: the law of persons provided the basis for the limited company; the law of property provided the device, ownership, for controlling the assets; and the law of obligations provided the means for directing the labouring class (contract)'.[70]

Perhaps what constitutes the ground on which to consider the relationship between the past, present (and potentially the future) of the legal form is the status of the law as an art, a technique to produce (abstract) forms and categories. As Yan Thomas puts it, the law is a 'technique' (*ars* in Latin) among others 'like language', essentially devoted to 'abstraction' and 'denaturation', which is 'aimed at efficiency, at logics, and at building operational models able to conform to the goals to be achieved'.[71] The categorisation of reality operated by the law transfigures patterns of social relationships into images, and icons, for which the tangible aspects of life are condensed into specific archetypal models like the legal person, rights, obligation, ownership, loans, etc. The ontological status of these abstract concepts is uncertain and elusive, primarily perceived through the tangible impacts they exert on our ways of life and the (super)structures they create. The existential dimension of legal objects is not that of 'things'; rather their 'thingness' is resolved in the manifested effects they have on the reality they aim to order and from which they originate. The law as a technique, exists in the form of operativity and effectuality, manifested in classifications, procedures, and institutions without which the law's text would be confined to its immaculate impotentiality.

69 I use survive here in the sense developed in Rafał Mańko, 'Legal Survivals and the Resilience of Juridical Form' (2023) *Law and Critique* 1–23.

70 Geoffrey Samuel, 'Roman Law and Modern Capitalism' (1984) 4(2) *Legal Studies* 193.

71 Thomas, 'The Subject of Right, the Person' (n 61) 136.

Chapter 7

Exchange or Production? Poulantzas on the Legal Form and Pashukanis

Daniel McLoughlin

Evgeny Pashukanis famously argues that the legal form emerges from the process of exchange that dominates a commodity-producing economy and that there is a homology between the abstraction and equality of commodities and a legal subject that is treated as being free and equal. In his 2011 defence of "Pashukanism," Raymond Koen claims that Pashukanis should be understood as "*the* Marxist theoretician of the law" because "no subsequent Marxist jurisprudent has been able to match or even approximate"[1] his theoretical insights into the nature of law. Yet, he asserted, the critiques of his work meant that Pashukanis remained "anathema to . . . most jurisprudents, including many who would own to a more than a passing knowledge of and commitment to the tenets of Marxism."[2] Two critiques, in particular, have been common in the literature around Pashukanis. First, he stands accused of indulging in economic reductionism; Hugh Collins, for example, writes that Pashukanis' analysis of the legal form is characterised by a "crude materialism" that purports "to explain all legal rules as reflections of commodity exchange."[3] Second, Pashukanis is criticised for ignoring the relationship between law and the sphere of production: Karl Korsch was the first to make this claim when he argued that Pashukanis' work was characterised by a "rather odd overestimation of circulation" for a Marxist;[4] and, some

1 R Koen, 'In Defence of Pashukanism' (2011) 14 *Potchefstroom Electronic Law Journal* 104, 107–8.

2 ibid 108.

3 Hugh Collins, *Marxism and Law* (OUP 1984) 109. See also Dennis Davis, 'Legality and Struggle: Towards a Non-Instrumentalist View of Law' [Juta 1988] Essays on Law and Social Practice in South Africa 70–71; Hans Kelsen, *The Communist Theory of Law* (Stevens & Sons Limited 1955) 890–93; Alan Stone, 'The Place of Law in the Marxian Structure-Superstructure Analysis' (2017) 19 *Law and Society Review* 39, 45; Peter Binns, 'Review Article: Law and Marxism' (1980) 10 *Capital & Class* 100, 104; Colin Sumner, *Reading Ideologies* (Academic Press 1979); China Miéville, 'Between Equal Rights: A Marxist Theory of International Law' in *Between Equal Rights* (Brill 2004) 88–90.

4 Karl Korsch, 'Appendix: An Assessment by Karl Korsch' in *The General Theory of Law and Marxism* (Ink Links 1978) 195.

DOI: 10.4324/9781032724522-8

fifty years later, Alan Hunt would write that "the standard Marxist criticism" of Pashukanis was "that he reverses Marx's priority of production relations over commodity relations."[5]

What a difference a decade of economic stagnation and political turbulence makes. As Carl Wilen has recently noted, the renaissance of Marxist theory since the Global Financial Crisis has seen a renewed interest in the Marxist analysis of law, and "as Marxists increasingly explore the connections between rights, law, democracy and capitalism, one text in particular has taken centre stage: *The General Theory of Law and Marxism*."[6] Pashukanis' work has, of recent times, been much discussed by legal theorists, and has been deployed for the analysis of a range of legal fields, most notably, international law.[7] This revival of interest in Pashukanis is a welcome development given that the Marxist critique of law has tended to draw on the critique of political economy "to unveil the relations of domination and exploitation which constitute the content of the legal relation."[8] In doing so, however, it has tended to ignore "the fundamental task of the Marxist analysis of law," namely, to "explain why legal relations take the form they do."[9]

Yet Pashukanis is not, despite Koen's claims, the only Marxist thinker to develop a sophisticated analysis of the legal form. While Nicos Poulantzas

5 Alan Hunt, 'Marxist Theory of Law' in Dennis Patterson (ed), *A Companion to Philosophy of Law and Legal Theory* (Blackwell 1996) 355. For other examples of such criticisms, see Ronnie Warrington, 'Standing Pashukanis on His Head' (1980) 4 *Capital & Class* 102, 105; Robert Fine, *Democracy and the Rule of Law* (Pluto Press 1984) 157; Dennis Lloyd and Michael Freeman, *Lloyd's Introduction to Jurisprudence* (Stevens & Sons Limited 1985) 989; Andrew Norrie, 'Pashukanis and the Commodity Form Theory of Law: A Reply to Warrington' (1982) 10 *International Journal of the Sociology of Law* 419, 135; Ronnie Warrington, 'Pashukanis and the Commodity Form Theory' in David Sugarman (ed), *Legality, Ideology and the State* (Academic Press 1983) 53.

6 Carl Wilén, 'Why Pashukanis Was Right: Abstraction and Form in The General Theory of Law and Marxism' [2023] *Capital & Class* 2.

7 For recent work drawing on Pashukanis to theorise international law, see Robert Knox, 'Valuing Race? Stretched Marxism and the Logic of Imperialism' (2016) 4 *London Review of International Law* 81; Bill Bowring, 'Marx, Lenin and Pashukanis on Self-Determination: Response to Robert Knox in Historical Materialism' (2011) 19 *Historical Materialism* 113; Robert Knox, 'Marxism, International Law, and Political Strategy' (2009) 22 *Leiden Journal of International Law* 423; Bill Bowring, *The Degradation of the International Legal Order? The Rehabilitation of Law and the Possibility of Politics* (Taylor & Francis Group 2006); Miéville (n 3); Lee McConnell, 'Opportunity and Impasse: Social Change and the Limits of International Legal Strategy' (2022) 14 *International Theory* 25. For recent discussion of Pashukanis in other fields, see Raymond Koen, 'All Roads Lead to Property: Pashukanis, Christie and the Theory of Restorative Justice' (2017) 16 *Potchefstroom Electronic Law Journal* 187; Ruth Fletcher, 'Legal Forms and Reproductive Norms' (2003) 12 *Social and Legal Studies*; Raymond Koen, 'Pashukanis on Crime and Punishment' (2013) 46 *De Jure* 486; Noah Quastel, 'Pashukanis at Mount Polley: Law, Eco-Social Relations and Commodity Forms' (2017) 81 *Geoforum* 45.

8 Koen, 'In Defence of Pashukanism' (n 1) 114.

9 ibid 107.

is best known as a state theorist, he began his career as a legal thinker and continued to reflect on the nature and place of law in capitalist society over the course of his work.[10] Poulantzas' ideas on the legal form develop, in part, through a critical dialogue with the commodity form theory of law and the work of Pashukanis in particular. In one of his earliest essays, "Marxist Examination of the Contemporary State and Law and the Question of the 'Alternative,'" Poulantzas argues, much like Pashukanis, that the realm of exchange gives rise to the legal form. At the same time, however, he expresses some serious reservations about the Soviet jurist's thought, which he cites as an exemplar of the economism that has dogged Marxist thought and is to be avoided at all costs. In his later works, however, Poulantzas comes to argue that both the legal and state forms have their origins in the nature of capitalist production, and levels some quite severe criticisms at theorists who ground their analyses in the formal equality of exchange.[11] While he admits that commodity form theory has grasped a number of "important institutional mechanisms,"[12] he claims that it "misses what is essential," because the focus on the relationship between law and exchange makes it difficult to theorise the relationship between the state, class, and class struggle.[13] Poulantzas' later work also deepens his previous critique of Pashukanis' economism and claims that the commodity exchange theory of law and state as a whole is characterised by a methodological individualism that derives from the use of the concept of civil society.

This chapter interrogates Poulantzas' account of the legal form and his critique of Pashukanis. The first section explains and evaluates Poulantzas' argument that the legal form is intimately tied to the state form and that both have their origins in the capitalist organisation of production. It does so by focusing on the text in which Poulantzas most clearly articulates his "mature" account of the legal form, *Political Power and Social Classes*.[14] It also compares this analysis to Pashukanis' account of the relationship between law

10 See James Martin, 'Ontology and Law in the Early Poulantzas' (2009) 35 *History of European Ideas* 465.

11 In *State, Power Socialism*, this list includes including Pashukanis, Henri Lefebvre, the Italian Marxism of Della Volpe and Cerroni, and the theorists taking part in German State Derivation debates of the 1970s. See Nicos Poulantzas, *State, Power Socialism* (Verso 2000) 50.

12 ibid 51.

13 ibid.

14 Poulantzas' most developed account of the legal form appears in *State, Power, Socialism*. However, while *State, Power, Socialism* does see some development of Poulantzas thinking on the legal form, it largely recapitulates the arguments in *Political Power and Social Classes*, which is where the decisive break in Poulantzas thinking occurs. In this chapter, then, my analysis of Poulantzas' "mature" account of the legal form largely focuses on *Political Power and Social Classes*.

and the state form.[15] It shows that, for both thinkers, the separation between the economic and the political is fundamental to the capitalist mode of production, that it is enabled by the legal form, and is structurally necessary to capitalist exploitation. I argue, against some critiques of Pashukanis, that he does not simply ignore the problem of exploitation or the particular role that the wage contract plays under capitalism. However, I argue that Poulantzas thinks through the relationship between the legal form and production in far more detail, arguing that the commodification of labour power presupposes the separation of the worker from the means of production, and by theorising the relationship between the legal form, the state, and the class struggle that emerges from the sphere of production. The second part of the chapter explains the critique of Pashukanis' economism that runs throughout Poulantzas' work. It shows that the heart of this critique is the claim that Pashukanis is unable to adequately theorise the relative autonomy of the law.[16] The core of Poulantzas' critique of Pashukanis' economism is not, as it is for a critic such as Collins, that *The General Theory* explains all legal phenomena in economic terms, but rather, that he theorises the economic in juridical terms. It is the failure to distinguish between the economic and the juridical, that generates the problem that so many commentators have noted in Pashukanis' work; namely, the absence of an analysis of the relationship between the legal form, the sphere of production, and the class struggle. It is, then, the theory of the relative autonomy of the law that allows Poulantzas to develop his analysis of the relationship between the legal and state forms and the capitalist organisation of production.

This chapter makes two contributions to contemporary debates around the legal form. First, while there has recently been an explosion of interest in Poulantzas' work as a state theorist,[17] his analysis of law has played little role in recent discussions of the legal form, which are also expanding at a rate

15 Pashukanis' analysis of the state form was influential for the state derivation debates that took place in the 1970s: see John Holloway and Sol Picciotto (eds), *State and Capital: A Marxist Debate* (Edward Arnold 1978). For an excellent critique of Poulantzas from the perspective of State derivation theory, see Simon Clarke, 'Marxism, Sociology and Poulantzas's Theory of the State' in Simon Clarke (ed), *The State Debate* (Palgrave Macmillan 1991). In this essay, however, I focus on Poulantzas relationship to Pashukanis, rather than those whose analysis of the state is inspired by the Soviet jurist's work.

16 For an analysis of the development of the idea of the relative autonomy of law, Eduardo E Chia, 'On the 'relative' autonomy of the modern form of law: from Marx and Engels to Althusser' in Cosmin Cercel, Gian-Giacomo Fusco, Przemysław Tacik (eds) *Legal Form and the End of Law. Pashukanis' Legacy* (Routledge 2024).

17 Two important edited collections on Poulantzas work have been published in English over the past decade: Jean-Numa Ducange and Razmig Keucheyan, *The End of the Democratic State: Nicos Poulantzas, a Marxism for the 21st Century* (Springer International Publishing: Imprint: Palgrave Macmillan 2019); Alexander Gallas and others (eds), *Reading Poulantzas* (Merlin Press 2011). Poulantzas' analysis of authoritarian statism is also one of the most important theoretical reference points for recent debates around "authoritarian

of knots.[18] This chapter argues that Poulantzas account of the legal form provides us with an important alternative to the commodity exchange theory, one that avoids the problems commonly associated with Pashukanis' work. It should, therefore, be taken seriously by Marxists interested in the nature of legal relations. Second, while the critique of Pashukanis' economism, and his focus on exchange, have long been common in the critical literature, these points are rarely developed in a great deal of detail, and a number of important defences of Pashukanis have emerged in recent years. Poulantzas presents us with one of the most theoretically sophisticated versions of these criticisms, and this chapter both explains them in some detail and considers their implications for some of the recent defences of Pashukanis.

Production, Exchange, and the Origins of Law and State

The chapter of *Capital Volume 1* entitled "Exchange" opens by noting that "commodities cannot go to market and perform exchanges in their own right" and, as a result, we must "have recourse to their guardians, who are the possessors of commodities."[19] Capitalism thus presupposes the law of private property and contract, which attempt to ensure that their appropriation of commodities occurs through mutual consent, rather than theft and immediate violence. Marx then returns to the relationship between private law and exchange in his account of the buying and selling of labour power, which acts as the transition between his analysis of exchange and that of production. In this context, he notes that the law treats the worker and the capitalist as equals who are free to dispose of their property as they see fit, and who, in making a contract to exchange labour for a wage, seek only their self-interest: "this sphere . . . we are deserting," Marx writes, is "a very Eden of the innate rights of man. There alone rule Freedom, Equality, Property and Bentham."[20]

For Marx, however, the abstraction of exchange value is only a "hieroglyph" of the labour that has been expended in production—and if we want to understand how capitalism works, we need to turn our attention from the "noisy sphere" of exchange to the "hidden abode of production."[21] When

neoliberalism," which developed in response to Ian Bruff, 'The Rise of Authoritarian Neoliberalism' (2014) 26 *Rethinking Marxism* 113.

18 There is some work on Poulantzas' early legal theory: see Martin, 'Ontology and Law' (n 10); James Martin, 'Poulantzas: From Law to the State' in *The End of the Democratic State: Nicos Poulantzas, a Marxism for the 21st Century* (Palgrave Macmillan 2019); Sonja Buckel, 'The Juridical Condensation of Relations of Forces: Nicos Poulantzas and Law' in *Reading Poulantzas* (Merlin Press 2011).

19 Karl Marx, *Capital: A Critique of Political Economy* (vol 1, Ben Fowkes tr, Penguin 1990) 178.

20 ibid 280.

21 ibid 279.

we do, we find that there is a massive disjuncture between the equality and freedom that law attributes to all its subjects and the material inequality that characterises the employment relationship:

> he, who before was the money-owner, now strides in front as capitalist; the possessor of labour-power follows as his labourer. The one with an air of importance, smirking, intent on business; the other, timid and holding back, like one who is bringing his own hide to market and has nothing to expect but—a hiding.[22]

Having analysed the problem of exploitation, Marx goes on to demonstrate the range of social, economic, and political problems that arise from the capitalist organisation of production, from the reserve army of labour to the tendency of the rate of profit to fall. However, the most fundamental of these problems is the class struggle that arises from the antagonism between the interests of capitalists and workers. Law plays a central role in this analysis, as Marx illustrates the dynamics of class conflict by examining the struggle over the legal limitation of the working day that took place in England in the mid-19th Century.[23]

Taking their cue from Marx's critique of the commodity fetish, which obscures the capitalist organisation of production and its consequences, generations of Marxists have attacked bourgeois thinkers for developing "categories from the surface of social reality, which veils precisely its 'character,' namely the exploitation taking place in the 'hidden abode of production.' "[24] This charge has also been a staple of the debate around Pashukanis, whose concern with the relationship between law and exchange, and lack of attention to the sphere of production, has been characterised as an "unMarxist deviation."[25] Contemporary scholars have, however, sought to undermine these attempts to "question Pashukanis' Marxist *bona fides*."[26] As Dimick has recently argued, while production does have "a sort of ontological primacy in Marx's work . . . the best readings of Marx make clear" that "the production of value under capitalism can only be co-constituted in and through exchange."[27] On this account, Marx does not prioritise production over

22 ibid 280.

23 See Daniel McLoughlin and Talina Hürzeler, 'Marx on the Factory Acts: Law, Exploitation, and Class Struggle' in *Research Handbook on Law and Marxism* (Edward Elgar Publishing 2021).

24 Sonja Buckel, *Subjectivation and Cohesion—Towards the Reconstruction of a Materialist Theory of Law* (Brill 2020) 95.

25 Koen, 'In Defence of Pashukanism' (n 1) 134. Koen uses this phrase as a neat way of summarising the various critiques of Pashukanis for prioritising exchange over production.

26 Matthew Dimick, 'Pashukanis' Commodity-Form Theory of Law' in Paul O'Connell and Umut Ozsu (eds), *Research Handbook on Law and Marxism* (Edward Elgar 2021) 128.

27 ibid.

exchange, but rather, casts the two as interconnected aspects of the process of social reproduction; and, while Pashukanis' analysis of law only focuses on the realm of exchange, this can be justified by the nature of his theoretical project. As Arthur points out, "one of the interesting features of bourgeois exploitation that it inheres in economic relations that do not achieve formal legal expression."[28] That is, under feudalism, the law forced the serf to work for a particular lord; under capitalism, by contrast, the worker is legally free, but is forced to submit to domination and exploitation by the "dull compulsion of economic relations."[29] While the Marxist critique of law has, for the most part, sought to expose legal equality as an ideological fiction by illustrating the class content of the law, Pashukanis is interested in the origins of the legal form, which characterises the worker as being free and equal *despite* their subordination within the sphere of production. *The General Theory* thus focuses its attention on the sphere of exchange because, as Marx himself points out, there is an intimate relationship between exchange value and the abstract equality of the law. However, it does not succumb to the fetishism of the law, as does bourgeois theory, because it acknowledges the exploitation that underpins the exchange economy.[30]

There are, however, some limits to these defences of the commodity form theory of law. The fact that Marx treats the realms of exchange and production as co-constitutive suggests that a Marxist analysis of the legal form cannot simply acknowledge the material inequality of the sphere of production as a background condition of legal equality. Instead, such an analysis should explicitly theorise the relationship between exchange and the legal form, on the one hand, and the exploitation, domination, and class struggle that emerge from the sphere of production, but which do not take legal form. This is why, I would suggest, even Arthur acknowledges that Pashukanis should have laid greater stress on the need to criticise law not only "on the basis of what it shows (the fetishisation of relationships of commodity exchangers) but on what it does not, and cannot, show, and, indeed, ideologically cloaks: the inner world of capitalism's appropriation of labour-power."[31]

Pashukanis comes closest to analysing the relationship between the legal form and the hidden abode of production in the context of his analysis of the state. He develops this account of the state form in response to two strands

28 Chris Arthur, 'Editor's Introduction' in *The General Theory of Law and Marxism* (Transaction Publishers 2002) 30.

29 Marx, *Capital* (n 19) 899. For a theory of impersonal economic coercion that is read out of Marx's work, see Søren Mau, *Mute Compulsion: A Marxist Theory of the Economic Power of Capital* (Verso 2023). It is also notable that, when Marx turns his attention to law in the context of his analysis of production, he is not interested in the form of law, but rather, the content of a specific field of law that is central to the extraction of surplus value, and the political process to which it gives rise.

30 For a good summary of defences of Pashukanis along these lines, see Buckel (n 24) 96–97.

31 Arthur (n 28) 30.

of Marxist thinking, each of which he regards as problematic. The first is the argument, developed most famously by Engels and Lenin, that the state is a coercive institution which maintains exploitation in the interests of the dominant class and which emerges in class divided societies in order to prevent civil war. But what defines the state, for Pashukanis, is not simply the fact that it wields coercive power—something that it shares with the capitalist and the head of the household—but that this power takes a public and legal form. The second body of thought to which Pashukanis is responding is the Marxist critique of juridical ideology, which argues that the universality of law is an illusion concealing the fact that the state acts in the interests of the ruling class. While this draws attention to the legal form of state action, it "does not explain how such an ideology could arise, nor . . . does it explain why the ruling class has access to it."[32]

Pashukanis' account of the state form thus seeks to remedy the deficiencies of both these analyses by explaining the social basis not simply of the state, but of the separation between the political and the economic that is produced by the legal form. This analysis has two strands, the first and most important of which, for Pashukanis, is the claim that regular market exchange requires an institution that can guarantee the peace it needs to function, and which is therefore distinct from the participants within that market;[33] and that, while such institutions can be found in the classical and feudal worlds, it is only in modernity that the state becomes central to the social order, due to the expansion in the quantity of commodity exchange.[34] The more interesting aspect of Pashukanis' analysis of the state, for our purposes, is an argument that he develops this argument in response to Razumobvsky who, like so many others, criticised the *General Theory* for not giving class domination its "rightful place" in the analysis of law. Pashukanis points out that the class domination exercised in and through the bourgois state is qualitatively different from the domination exercised by the capitalist: while the capitalist wields an immediate and personal form of domination, the state acts in the name of the general will to establish a system of objective and impartial norms. This impersonal form of domination is necessary to capitalism, he claims, because "in the society based on commodity production, subjection to one person, as a concrete individual, implies subjection to an arbitrary force."[35] The owner of a commodity, including the commodity labour power, must be free to dispose of that commodity according to their will if value is to be established through the market mechanism, rather than being "determined

32 Evgeny Pashukanis, *The General Theory of Law and Marxism* (Transaction Publishers 2003) 140.
33 ibid 137.
34 ibid 136.
35 ibid 143.

by an authority situated outside the internal laws of the market."[36] The law does not, then, force the worker to labour for a particular capitalist but rather treats the "relation of exploitation formally as a relationship between two 'autonomous' and 'equal' owners of commodities."[37]

The argument that Pashukanis develops in response to Razumobvsky, highlights the imbrication of capitalist production and exchange, and should, as such, put paid to claims that he simply ignores the exploitation of labour and the role that the wage contract plays under capitalism. Yet this argument is very brief, and it plays a subordinate role with respect to his account of the state as a guarantor of market relations. Moreover, while it acknowledges the domination and exploitation that characterises the realm of production, the analysis does not penetrate its hidden abode. Instead, Pashukanis ultimately grounds the juridical form of capitalist domination in the nature of the market: the owner of a commodity must be thought to be free from coercion for a commercial exchange to take place, and it is the fact that labour becomes a commodity under capitalism which necessitates the split between the economic and the juridico-political. He does not address the relationship between the legal form and the process of production; the class relations that arise from the organisation of production; or the role that the legal form plays in the political struggle that arises from class antagonism.

Poulantzas begins his analysis of the legal and state forms from the problem that Arthur cites in defence of Pashukanis' focus on exchange, namely, the fact that the law does not recognise the material inequality that characterises production. The "fundamental distinctive feature" of the capitalist state is, he writes, that the status of political subjects is not determined by their role in production and that "political class domination" is therefore "absent from its institutions."[38] This is enabled by the legal form, which does not define a worker by their position within a community and the specific form of labour that is performed by a member of that class, but rather, as a formally free and equal individual-citizen. Unlike Pashukanis however, Poulantzas grounds his analysis of the separation between the economic and the political on the relationship between the labourer and the means of production. He develops this argument by citing a passage from *Capital Volume III*, where Marx writes that:

> the specific economic form, in which unpaid surplus-labour is pumped out of direct producers, determines the relationship of rulers and ruled, as it grows directly out of production itself and, in turn, reacts upon it as a determining element. Upon this, however, is founded the entire formation of the economic community which grows up out of the production

36 ibid.
37 ibid 141.
38 Nicos Poulantzas, *Political Power and Social Classes* (New Left Books 1975) 123.

> relations themselves, thereby simultaneously its specific political form. It is always the direct relationship of the owners of the conditions of production to the direct producers—a relation always naturally corresponding to a definite stage in the development of the methods of labour and its social productivity—which reveals the innermost secret, the hidden basis of the entire social structure, and with it the political form of the relation of sovereignty and dependence, in short, the corresponding specific form of the state.[39]

Poulantzas builds on these comments by arguing that the economic level of the mode of production is comprised of two different relations: the relation of real appropriation, which involves the appropriation of nature that occurs through the labour process; and the relation of property, which enables the non-labourer, as owner of the means of production and/or labour power, to appropriate the products of labour and realise surplus value from them. It is the relationship of property that, according to Poulantzas, defines the relations of production as such—however, he also insists that this property relation "belongs strictly to the region of the economic and . . . should be clearly distinguished from the juridical forms with which it is invested, i.e. from juridical property."[40] The specific form taken by the mode of production, which provides the "hidden basis" for the rest of the social structure, is determined by the combination of the relations of property and real appropriation. While property has taken different forms within different modes of production, it is common to all class-based societies, and its basic function is to separate the worker from the product of their labour. The relation of real appropriation, on the other hand, has an "essentially invariant form" in pre-capitalist societies, "namely, the union of the direct producer with the means of production."[41] However, the rise of capitalism radically transforms this relation, with the development of heavy industry separating the worker from the means of production—and it is, Poulantzas argues, this change in the organisation of production which gives rise to the separation of the political and the economic that characterises the capitalist mode of production.

Poulantzas explains this point by citing Marx, who argues that

> in all forms in which the direct labourer remains the 'possessor' of the means of production and labour conditions necessary for the production of his own means of subsistence, the property relationship must simultaneously appear as a direct relation of lordship and servitude, so that the direct producer is not free.[42]

39 Marx, *Capital* (n 19) vol III, p 791, quoted in ibid 27–28.
40 ibid 26. This is an important point, and we will return to it later in the chapter.
41 ibid 30.
42 Marx, *Capital* (n 19) vol III, pp 790–91, quoted in ibid.

The form of law and the state in pre-capitalist social formations was dictated by the fact that the worker had some degree of control over the conditions of their labour, which meant that they could materially support themselves through the production of use values, and the non-labourer could only appropriate surplus value through the application of "extra-economic pressure"[43] backed by law and state coercion. Under capitalism, lack of access to the means of production means that workers must sell their labour in order to survive. Direct domination over the person is thus no longer necessary for the mode of production to reproduce itself; instead, capitalism requires a property relation that treats the worker as a commodity owner who is free to sell their labour power to the capitalist in return for a wage. The separation of the worker and the means of production thus transforms the (economic) property relation; and it also changes the juridical expression of this relation by setting up "agents of production at the juridico-political level, as political and juridical 'individual-subjects,' deprived of their economic determination and, consequently, of their class membership."[44]

Poulantzas' focus on the relationship between the state, the legal form, and the sphere of production allows him to address the problem of class struggle that arises from capitalist exploitation. He argues that, while the bourgeoisie share a fundamental interest in the reproduction of the economic system that guarantees their dominance as a class, the capitalist mode of production gives rise to political conditions that make it difficult for them to achieve hegemony. This is, in part, because capitalism is predicated upon competition between the private interests of the bourgeoisie who, as Marx writes, "at every moment" sacrifice their "political interests, to the narrowest and most sordid private interests."[45] Capital is also split between different "fractions," which means that different sections of the bourgeoisie can have competing interests. At the same time, the bourgeoisie face challenges to their hegemony from the petit bourgeoisie and, more importantly, the organised workers movement. The separation between the political and the economic enables the bourgeoisie to achieve hegemony under such conditions, as the state is able to rule in the common political interests of the bourgeoisie (that is, by pursuing the policies needed for the survival of capitalism) where they could not do so if they ruled directly. The state is thus autonomous from the relations of production and the class relations to which they give rise; however, this autonomy is only ever relative, as the state serves to maintain a capitalist order that is predicated on the exploitation of the working class.

Political Power and Social Classes argues that this (relatively) autonomous state plays two crucial roles with respect to the class struggle, the

43 ibid 32.

44 ibid 128.

45 Karl Marx, 'The Eighteenth Brumaire of Louis Bonaparte' in *Surveys from Exile: Political Writings* (vol 2, Verso 2010) 225.

first of which is that it operates as a "factor of political organization of the dominant classes," as it is only in and through the engagement with the state that the various fractions of the bourgeoisie are able to find unity.[46] While Poulantzas does not say much about the role that law plays with respect to this aspect of the state's political function, he does return to this problem in *State, Power, Socialism*. In this context, he points out that the legal form makes bourgeois hegemony possible by enabling the separation between politics and economics, and by giving order to the relations between the various fractions of capital within the power bloc as they vie for power, such that crises that might develop amongst the power bloc are prevented from becoming a crisis of the state, which is defined as an institution through the impersonal order of the law.[47] The second role that the state plays with respect to the class struggle is that it functions "as the factor of political disorganization; i.e. its function of preventing the working class from organising itself into an 'autonomous' political party."[48] The legal form plays a very direct role in the second of these political functions through what Poulantzas calls the effect of isolation, or what is more colloquially known as competition. Law generates the isolation effect, in part, through its ideological function, as it encourages workers to see themselves as free and equal individuals who find unity in and through a nation-state, rather than as members of a class whose economic interests are opposed to those of the bourgeoisie. However, the juridical also enables the operation of the market economy by fixing "the relations of production in the relations of formal ownership" and "constitutes a framework of cohesion for commercial encounters, including those for the purchase and sale of labour power."[49] The sense of isolation that is produced by the law is not, then, simply an ideological illusion that masks the reality of a class unity that is really constituted at the economic level—it is, as Poulantzas puts it, "terrifyingly real."[50]

According to Koen, critics of Pashukanis' focus on exchange have misconstrued Marx's claim that "that property relations are the legal expression of the relations of production." He points out that capitalism is a system in which use values are produced for sale on the market, which means that the totality of the relations of production encompasses those of exchange; he claims that Marx nowhere argues that the legal form can be derived directly from the process of production; and he asserts that "of the totality of the relations of production" Marx consistently points to the relations of exchange as providing "the material source of the legal form." Poulantzas problematises this assertion by pointing to passages from *Capital Volume*

46 Poulantzas, *Political Power and Social Classes* (n 38) 287.
47 Poulantzas, *State, Power Socialism* (n 11) 91.
48 Poulantzas, *Political Power and Social Classes* (n 38) 287.
49 ibid 56.
50 ibid 130.

III in which Marx is quite explicit that, while the juridico-political is not directly derived from the process of production, they nonetheless arise from the relationships within the sphere of production, which "correspond" to a certain stage in the development of the productive process. The analysis of the legal form that Poulantzas develops on the basis of these passages not only points to the imbrication of the constitution of exchange and production within capitalism but accords the latter an "ontological priority" with respect to the former. From Poulantzas' perspective, Pashukanis is right to argue that the distinction between the economic and the political is necessary to capitalism insofar as the worker needs to be free to alienate their labour on the market. For labour power to become a commodity, however, the worker must first be separated from the means of production—and, as Marx argues in *Capital Volume I*, while this separation occurs historically through the process of primitive accumulation, it becomes structurally entrenched as the basis of a new mode of production with the development of industrial capitalism. According to Poulantzas, the separation between the political and the economic made possible by the legal form is structurally necessary to a mode of production that separates the worker from the means of production because it allows the worker to sell their labour in return for a wage. Poulantzas' analysis of the relationship of the state form and the sphere of production also allows him to develop an analysis of the political function of the legal form. The separation between the economic and the political is structurally necessary for the maintenance of hegemony given the class relations that emerge from the sphere of production under capitalism. The legal form makes possible the relative autonomy of the state which enables it to act in the class interests of the bourgeoisie. The juridical form of state power also helps to maintain its stability and unity in the face of divisions within the bourgeoisie, while law's ideological function helps to disorganise the working class, and thereby ward off challenges to bourgeois rule.

Poulantzas and the Critique of Economism

Poulantzas did not always hold to the production-oriented theory of law that I outlined in the previous section. In his 1964 essay, "Marxist Examination," Poulantzas argues that law derives from exchange in terms that are remarkably similar to Pashukanis.[51] However, he also claims that Pashukanis' work

51 He argues that the extension of commodity exchange gave rise to modern private property; that these laws are accompanied by an abstract juridical subject that has its roots in the ancient world but is generalised by the development of market society; and that the idea of abstract equality and freedom that first emerges in the realm of private law migrates into the political realm, where they structure the fundamental political values of modernity.

is characterised by a "simplistic economism"[52] that treats law as part of the relations of production. This might seem like a strange claim, on the face of it, given that Pashukanis is so often criticised for ignoring the sphere of production. However, as we have just seen, the totality of the relations of production includes the relations of exchange. What is at stake in the claim that Pashukanis ignores production, then, is a debate over the relationship between two different spheres of the economic, and the role that these should play in our analysis of law. What is at stake in the claim that Pashukanis treats law as part of the relations of production is, by contrast, an argument that Pashukanis has "an insufficiently complex and not problematised understanding of the relation of 'base and superstructure.'"[53]

The charge of economism is a common one within the literature around *The General Theory*. However, as Sonja Buckel points out, these critiques rarely acknowledge the fragmentary and ambivalent nature of *The General Theory*—an ambiguity that extends to Pashukanis' treatment of the relationship between the social relations of production and the legal form.[54] Pashukanis claims, for example, that "the legal relation is directly generated by the existing social relations of production;"[55] and that, with the development of systematic commodity circulation,

> the social relations of production assume a doubly mysterious form. On the one hand they appear as relations between things (commodities), and on the other, as relations between the wills of autonomous entities equal to each other—of legal subjects.[56]

These passages seem to support the charge of economism, as they pay little attention to the difference between the juridical and the economic, and the latter explicitly cast law as a form of the social relations of production.[57] On the other hand, Pashukanis does develop his account of the legal form, in substantial part, in response to the instrumental theory of law that dominated Marxism, which treated the legal order as a manifestation of the economic interests of the capitalist class, and he provides a quite detailed account of the way that economic relations generate the legal form through a process of

52 Nicos Poulantzas, 'Marxist Examination of the Contemporary State and Law and the Question of the "Alternative"' in *The Poulantzas Reader: Marxism, Law and the State* (Verso 2008) 28.

53 Buckel, *Subjectivation and Cohesion* (n 24) 102.

54 ibid 96. She draws this point from Antonio Negri, 'Rereading Pashukanis: Discussion Notes' (2017) 5 *Stasis* 8.

55 Pashukanis, *The General Theory* (n 32) 96.

56 ibid 117.

57 While China Miéville is a staunch defender of Pashukanis, he argues that The General Theory does treat law as part of the economic base, pointing to these passages in particular. See Miéville (n 3) 89–90.

institutional creation and mediation.[58] Both these aspects of his work indicate an attentiveness to the specificity of the legal relation and its autonomy with respect to the economic base.

A number of important defences of Pashukanis' treatment of the relationship between the economic and the juridical have emerged in recent years. Many of these have highlighted the central role that Poulantzas has played in developing the critique of economism and argued that such attacks misunderstand the role that form plays in Pashukanis' thought. Buckel, for example, argues Poulantzas fails to seriously engage with Pashukanis' theory of form due to an Althusserian hostility to Hegelian Marxism, which Poulantzas believes he detects in the use of terms like mystification and illusion in *The General Theory*.[59] Koen claims that the theory of relative autonomy cannot provide an analysis of the legal form, and that it misunderstands Pashukanis' approach to the problem of form because it is concerned with the causal relationship between the economic base and the content of law.[60] Dimmick argues that proponents of relative autonomy have failed to grasp the fact that, for Pashukanis, the legal form is structurally necessary to commodity exchange but there is a contingent relationship between the legal form and its content:

> for this reason, one cannot simply 'reduce' the law to its base, nor explain its content as a mechanical cause of the economy. At the same time, there is still a relation . . . between law and economy, one that avoids a sociological structural-functionalism giving rise to vaguely causal notions of 'relative autonomy.'[61]

The belief that the theory of relative autonomy cannot provide us with an account of the legal form is not sustainable in light of the analysis I developed in the previous section. Nonetheless, these thinkers ask important questions about the critique of Pashukanis' economism and that of Poulantzas, in particular. In this section of the chapter, then, I deepen my account of Poulantzas' analysis of the legal form, and his critique of Pashukanis, by tracing the development of the charge of economism in his work.

Poulantzas' first critiques Pashukanis for his economism in "Marxist Examination," where he acknowledges that, of all the elements of the superstructure, it is most tempting to analyse law as part of the economic base. This is because ownership of the means of production is central to the mode of production, and it thus "might appear to be situated directly at the level

58 Pashukanis, *The General Theory* (n 32) 181.
59 Buckel, *Subjectivation and Cohesion* (n 24) 102.
60 Koen, 'In Defence of Pashukanism' (n 1) 111.
61 Dimick (n 26) 132. See also Wilén (n 6).

of the relations of production, of class struggle over property."[62] He argues, nonetheless, that this is a form of economism, that in Pashukanis' work, has its origins in the Soviet jurist's hostility to neo-Kantianism. Neo-Kantian thought had responded to Marx's base-superstructure model by reading it in terms of the Kantian distinction between form and substance:

> the superstructure was envisaged as the transcendental form, the rational, ideal and necessary structuration of a 'material', real base-content, essentially distinct from it, and subject to laws of mechanical causality.[63]

This theory led philosophers like Stammler to valorise the ideal and transcendental form of law and state as the political manifestation of reason. Yet these moves were deeply problematic for thinkers influenced by Marx's excoriating critique of idealism, who responded to the neo-Kantian analysis by inverting it "what ensued in the Marxist science of the state political level was an identification of the superstructure with the *ideal* and of the base with the *real*."[64] Law and state were thus treated as real only when they were reducible "to the materiality of the infrastructural levels."[65] In the work of Reisner and Vyshinksy, this was manifest in an argument that the law was a set of norms decreed by the state for the purposes of exploiting the working class, while in Pashukanis and Stuchka, it appeared in the attempt to argue that relations of property were themselves a part of the economic base.[66]

However, Poulantzas argues that the Marxist inversion of neo-Kantianism ignored the fact that Marx's thought was, in fact, indebted to the Hegelian schema of reality and idea. In response to Kant, Hegel developed a monism which asserted the reality of "every economic and sociological datum" whilst arguing that this reality is a product of the self-development of the idea-concept. Marx adopted Hegel's monism whilst inverting the relationship between reality and idea:

> for Hegel, everything ended up being an idea; for Marx, every social datum is . . . reality. However, within this global reality, he discovered the primacy. . . . Of the real-material (the base) over the real-ideal (superstructure).[67]

62 Nicos Poulantzas, 'Marxist Examination of the Contemporary State and Law' (n 52) 28.
63 ibid 29.
64 ibid.
65 ibid 31.
66 For a contrary take, see Wilen, who argues that Pashukanis overcomes the distinction between form and substance that characterised both formalism and instrumentalism: Wilén (n 6).
67 Nicos Poulantzas, 'Marxist Examination of the Contemporary State and Law' (n 52) 30.

Marx does not critique the "illusions" of the superstructure by contrasting it to the reality of the material economic base: instead, he sees the ideal as an aspect of the real that is ultimately determined by another aspect, namely, the relations of production. According to Poulantzas then, Marxism needs to develop a theory which acknowledges that the normative system of law has an existence and a function that is distinct from the economic base.[68] However, in opposition to bourgeois legal science, which studies the law as an autonomous hierarchy of rules, Marxist legal thought needs to show that it is precisely through its independence that the legal order reproduces exploitation.[69]

Poulantzas' critique of Pashukanis' economism thus precedes his Althusserianism and the hostility to Hegel that comes with it. From the beginning, the core of Poulantzas' critique is Pashukanis' ostensible failure to take the (relative) autonomy of the law sufficiently seriously, and in "Marxist Examination," he suggests that a more nuanced account of the relationship between the juridical and the economic could be developed by examining the way that the "infrastructural realities" of the capitalist order are articulated in the language of the law. In *Political Power and Social Classes*, however, he abandons this approach to the relationship between the juridical and the political, and instead adopts Althusser's account of capitalism as a totality comprised of autonomous levels or regional instances which form a complex whole that is determined, in the last instance, by the economic.[70] This shift in conceptual framework allows Poulantzas to reframe and deepen his critique of *The General Theory* by emphasising the difference between the economic and the juridical forms of property. My claim is that Poulantzas is able to develop his production-oriented theory of the legal form by insisting on this difference; and that, for Poulantzas, the absence of such a distinction in Pashukanis' work renders it ideological, insofar as it is only able to theorise the role that law plays in the economic through concepts that are derived from the juridical sphere.

Political Power and Social Classes returns to the critique of Pashukanis' economism in the context of an analysis of the definition of class. Poulantzas argues against economistic attempts to define class purely on the basis of "the position of agents in the labour process and to their relation to the

68 ibid 37.

69 ibid 39.

70 Poulantzas, *Political Power and Social Classes* (n 38) 13–14. On Althusser and Poulantzas see Spyros Sakellaropoulos, 'The Althusser-Poulantzas Discussion on the State' (2019) 9 *International Critical Thought* 128. According to Poulantzas, Marx's *Capital* provides an analysis of the economic level of the capitalist mode of production, while his own task, in *Political Power and Social Classes*, is to provide a regional theory of the ideological and juridico-political, two levels of the capitalist totality that Marx and Engels did not specifically address.

means of production"[71] because class is, on his account, defined by the effect that this ensemble of structures has on social relations. On his reading, Marx and Engels make it clear that the juridico-political and ideological levels are "immanently present" within capitalist relations of production when they argue that property law and the state are necessary to market exchange and that, through the labour contract, they help to define classes as such.[72] Poulantzas goes on to argue that economism has tried to evade the fact that classes are defined by law "by considering formal juridical relations of property as 'economic relations,'" and cites Pashukanis as his primary example of this phenomenon.[73] The problem with this move, he claims, is that it "renders the cardinal distinction between real appropriation (i.e. real property) and formal juridical property . . . theoretically impossible."[74] This passage appears somewhat confused, as it conflates real appropriation and property, two forms of economic relation that Poulantzas elsewhere spends a great deal of time differentiating. Let us presume, however, that the main thrust of the passage is an attempt to distinguish between the economic and juridical forms of property—and if this is the case, we need to ask why it is so important to differentiate between the two. Yet answering this question is somewhat difficult given Poulantzas does not go to great lengths to clarify the point.[75] Indeed, the closest that he comes to defining these terms is the claim that the development of the forms of private property necessary for capitalism precedes the separation of the worker from the means of production and that this "advance of property on the labour process concerns *both* economic property (the organization of labour in manufacture) *and* its instutionalised juridical expression."[76] This suggests that the economic form of property pertains to the site of production while the legal form of property refers to formal juridical institutions.

However, we can further clarify the difference between the two forms of property by turning to Etienne Balibar's 'On the Basic Concepts of Historical Materialism,' an essay to which Poulantzas is substantially indebted.[77] Balibar notes that it is difficult "to distinguish clearly between the relations of production and their 'legal expression,'" and that the very idea that law expresses the relations of production is difficult within the Althusserian schema since we are not talking about a superstructural duplication of the

71 Poulantzas, *Political Power and Social Classes* (n 38) 62.

72 ibid 71.

73 ibid 72 n20.

74 ibid.

75 ibid 160.

76 ibid.

77 The essay is Balibar's solo contribution to *Reading Capital* and appeared in French four years prior to *Political Power and Social Classes*. The two works make a number of identical claims and cite many of the same passages from Marx in support of them.

economic, but rather, "the articulation of two heterogeneous instances."[78] Nonetheless, he goes on to unpack the idea by "uncovering a series of dislocations" between the relations of production and their legal instantiation. As Balibar points out, the law of property "is characterized as universalistic, introducing no differences between the things possessed and their uses."[79] From the perspective of the relations of production, however, the only form of ownership that matters is that of the means of production, and then only insofar as they are combined with living labour. This form of ownership is "not so much a legal 'right'" to the means of production, but

> the power to consume them productively, depending on their material nature, on their adaptation to the conditions of the labour process, as a means of appropriating surplus labour. This power does not come down to a law, but, as Althusser has already suggested, to a distribution of the means of production.[80]

Balibar points to a similar tension in the other juridical form that is essential to the capitalist economy, that of the labour contract: the contract treats labour power as simply one example of a thing that can be exchanged, and applies equally to all forms of labour; yet the only form of labour that defines the relations of production is productive labour, which is defined by "the material nature of the labour and its objects."[81] The conclusion that Balibar draws from this analysis is that the juridical and the economic structure social relations in very different ways, as the "systematic structure of the law . . . defines its bearers as individuals (persons) confronted by things,"[82] while the economic designates its bearers as members of a class.

Poulantzas' claim is that economism treats law as part of the productive relations and, in the process, ignores the relative autonomy of the economic and juridical levels of the capitalist totality. Yet, as Balibar argues, the two remain distinguishable even in the case of those social relations in which they enter into the greatest proximity. Property, as a legal phenomenon, establishes relations between persons and things that are universalistic and abstract. This is necessary to capitalism insofar as it makes the capitalist control over the means of production enforceable, something that is particularly important given the resistance that exploitation produces. As an economic phenomenon, however, property is defined by the material

78 Etienne Balibar, 'On the Basic Concepts of Historical Materialism' in *Reading Capital: The Complete Edition* (Verso 2015) 392.
79 ibid 394.
80 ibid 394.
81 ibid 395.
82 ibid 396.

organisation of production, the practical control over the productive process, and the relationship of exploitation that these establish.

While this shows that it is possible to distinguish between the economic and juridical dimensions of property, we have not yet explained why the failure to differentiate the two is so deeply problematic for Poulantzas. To establish this point, it is useful to read Poulantzas' attack on Pashukanis' economism in light of a second criticism of the commodity form theory that he makes in *Political Power and Social Classes*, which is that the use of the concept of civil society leads to an ideological account of law. The Marxist tradition has, Poulantzas claims, mostly understood the distinction between politics and economy by "reference to the concept of civil society and to its separation from the state."[83] This includes the commodity exchange theory of law, which he claims has tended to draw its concept of the state from Hegel via the early Marx. Within this schema, the state is conceptualised as the universal, over against the particularity of a civil society structured by private property and exchange relations. While bourgeois political theory valorises the state's capacity to act in the general interest, the early Marx argues that the particularity of civil society—that is, the reign of property—is the real content of the state's supposed universality and that the state can only ever provide an alienated form of community.[84]

However, following Althusser, *Political Power and Social Classes* argue that there is an epistemological break between Marx's early "humanist" work and his "mature" critique of political economy. This Althusserian position on the development of Marx's thought informs a rather biting critique of the role that the concept of civil society has played in Marxist legal and political theory. Marxism has, Poulantzas argues, generally conceptualised the process of freeing worker and owner from feudal ties as one that produces atomised individuals. Civil society is understood as a sphere that brings these atomised individuals together through exchange and competition; this realm forms the economic basis for the political superstructure of the state; and the state acts as the guarantor for the market. The problem with this approach to the legal and state forms, for Poulantzas, is that it constructs its analysis of the state "on the schema of alienation, i.e., on the schema of the relation of the subject (concrete individuals) to its objectified essence (the state)."[85] In doing so, it takes the individual as the basic unit of analysis, rather than treating agents of production, as the later Marx does, as "the personification of economic categories, the *bearers* [Träger] of particular class-relations and interests."[86] According to Poulantzas, this methodological individualism

83 Poulantzas, *Political Power and Social Classes* (n 38) 124.

84 ibid. See also Nicos Poulantzas, 'Preliminaries to the Study of Hegemony in the State' in *The Poulantzas Reader: Marxism, Law and the State* (Verso 2008) 78–79.

85 Poulantzas, *Political Power and Social Classes* (n 38) 124.

86 Marx, *Capital* (n 19) 92.

makes it impossible to define classes as such; and, because the bare individual is the ground of the legal and state forms, rather than the class relations and interests that arise from the mode of production, it becomes difficult to theorise the relationship between the state and class struggle. Further, Poulantzas argues that the concept of civil society masks "a whole series of real problems posed by the capitalist state,"[87] most notably, that of "the specific autonomy in the CMP of the economic and the political" and "the effects of the ideological on these instances."[88] This is because the schema of alienation reduces the separation of politics and economy to an ideological illusion rather than theorising it as a constitutive feature of capitalist social relations.[89]

Drawing on the later Marx, Poulantzas argues that the commodity exchange theory of law has misinterpreted the process by which capitalism has freed both the worker and owner from feudal ties. When Marx writes that the "bare individual" is the historical precondition of the capitalist mode of production he does not mean "that agents, who were previously 'organically' in unities, arise in reality as atomised individuals, to be later inserted into combinations of capitalist relations of production."[90] Instead, Marx uses the term to refer to the dissolution of the legal, political, and economic structures of feudalism as they are replaced by new structures, those of the capitalist mode of production. This process strips producers of the status that they had under feudal law and "*appears* in its effects as a 'bareness,' 'liberation,' and 'individualisation' of the agents."[91] However, it also inserts workers into a system of productive relations that drive a process of collectivisation, with the development of industry leading to the socialisation of the labour process, the growth of the world market, and the concentration of capital in the hands of fewer owners. This generates a conundrum, namely, how and why the collectivisation of production appears to its agents as a process of atomisation—and the legal form is central to Poulantzas' response to this problem. While capitalism gathers workers together in factories in ever greater numbers, and the growth of the world market makes production and consumption dependent on ever larger supply chains, the isolation effect means that economic activity is experienced through relations of antagonism and domination: workers are forced to compete with one another for jobs; capitalists have control over and co-ordinate the work process; and the interdependence produced by the world market is masked by both the commodity fetish and the antagonism between capitalists.

Balibar's analysis shows us that the juridical and the economic structure social relations in different ways. The economic structure designates workers

87 Poulantzas, *Political Power and Social Classes* (n 38) 125.
88 ibid.
89 Poulantzas, *State, Power Socialism* (n 11) 50.
90 Poulantzas, *Political Power and Social Classes* (n 38) 126.
91 ibid.

as agents of production and as members of a class; and it is the capitalist organisation of production that generates the dynamics of exploitation, class antagonism, and the tendencies towards the socialisation of production and crisis, all of which provide the terrain on which revolutionary transformation becomes possible. The law, by contrast, designates the worker as an individual, both by representing them as the bearer of individual rights and by providing the framework of rules that enables exchange and competition, including with respect to the commodity labour power. The juridical is thus "immanently present" within the economic insofar as it works together with the economic to produce the form of exploitation and domination that is specific to capitalism. However, because the critique of civil society is underpinned by juridical concepts it gives us an ideological account of law, as it cannot illuminate the relationship between class, the juridical order, and the state.

Political Power and Social Classes levels this critique of the role that the schema of alienation plays in commodity exchange theory at a range of thinkers, including Lefebvre, Rubel and Marcuse, and the Italian Marxist School of Della Volpe, Cerroni and Rossi; and when Poulantzas repeats these points in *State, Power, Socialism*, Pashukanis is added to his list targets.[92] But while these criticisms might apply to the other thinkers at which Poulantzas takes aim, it is problematic when applied to Pashukanis, not least because the Soviet jurist reads his account of the legal form out of *Capital Volume 1*, and makes many of the same points about the limits of Marxist legal and political theory as Poulantzas. Both thinkers are critical of instrumental theories of the capitalist state, arguing that they elide the problem of the specific form that domination takes under capitalism, with its separation between the political and the economic, and the formal freedom this entails. They also both critique the way that Marxism has tended to treat law as an ideological illusion,[93] and both insist that the legal order does not simply produce false representations about society, but organises those relations in line with the image of legal subjectivity.[94] Finally, while *The General Theory of Law and Marxism* does employ the category of civil society to discuss the realm of exchange, it does not use the term alienation other than to describe the appropriation of the product of proletarian labour that is made possible by property relations; it does, by contrast, frequently describes people as the bearers of economic categories such as value.

The general critique of the commodity exchange theory that first appears in *Political Power and Social Classes*, and which is later extended to Pashukanis, thus reads more like Poulantzas' attempt to distance himself from his

92 Nicos Poulantzas, 'Marxist Examination of the Contemporary State and Law' (n 52) 50.
93 Pashukanis, *The General Theory* (n 32) 39.
94 ibid 40.

earlier account of the legal form, than a serious critical engagement with Pashukanis. Nonetheless, Poulantzas' Althusserian attack on commodity form theory can help us to unpack the stakes of his critique of Pashukanis' economism in *Political Power and Social Classes*. We have seen Poulantzas charge Pashukanis with economism on the basis that he treats the law as part of the relations of production and, as a result, fails to distinguish between the economic and the juridical. However, the core of this critique is not, as it is for many other critics, that Pashukanis indulges "in all the vices of reductionism"[95] by explaining all legal phenomena as an extension of exchange. It is, rather, that by setting out to explain the seeming autonomy of the legal form, whilst also treating law as part of the economic (and thereby ignoring the distinction between the legal and economic forms of property and contract) Pashukanis is only able to theorise those aspects of the economic that most closely resemble the legal form, namely, the relations of exchange. It is only by rigorously distinguishing between the economic and juridical that one can theorise the different roles that property and contract play in the organisation of capitalism and the mediation of class struggle. While Pashukanis does not treat the law as an ideological illusion, his analysis of the legal form is ideological, in Poulantzas' terms, because the lack of such a distinction means that he is unable to theorise the relationship between the legal form, on the one hand, and the class politics that emerge from a sphere of production that is structured by the economic forms of contract and property.

As we have seen, defenders of *The General Theory* have argued that the critique of Pashukanis' economism misses the ambiguities of the text and misconstrues the way that it understands the relationship between the commodity form, the legal form, and legal content. Yet the critique that I have just outlined stands even if one believes that *The General Theory* does not simply treat the law as part of the relations of production. As we saw in the first part of the chapter, while Pashukanis does not ignore the sphere of production, his theory seems uninterested in penetrating its hidden abode. It is, I suggest, the failure to theorise the difference between the economic and juridical forms of property and contract which generates the problem that so many commentators have noted in Pashukanis' work, namely, the absence of an analysis of the relationship between the legal form, the sphere of production, and the class struggle. I have argued that, while *The General Theory* is by no means an "unMarxist deviation," a Marxist analysis of the legal form should also address the relationship between the legal form and the sphere of production. This is precisely what Poulantzas does in *Political Power and Social Classes*, where he provides an account of the structural necessity of the legal form for capitalist production, and in so doing, foregrounds the role that it plays in

95 Collins, *Marxism and Law* (n 3) 109.

the class struggle. The distinction between the economic and the juridical levels of the capitalist totality, particularly with respect to property, is crucial to his capacity to develop this analysis. It is the transformation in the economic property relation that occurs with the rise of industrial capitalism, namely, the separation of the worker from the means of production, which necessitates the change in the legal form. Meanwhile, the juridical form of property disorganises the working class by producing the institutional framework that makes these economic arrangements function and propagates the ideology that masks and legitimises them. It is then, through Poulantzas' emphasis on the relative autonomy of law that he is able to develop his own account of the legal form, which is grounded in the sphere of production, but addresses its relation to exchange, and in so doing, is able to theorise the relationship between the legal form, the state, and the class struggle.

Acknowledgement

Many thanks go to the organisers and participants of the Legal Form Workshop (Krakow, Poland, 14–15 April 2023). Particular thanks are due to Eduardo E Chia, Ben Golder and Premizlaw Tacik for their very insightful comments on drafts of this chapter.

Chapter 8

Impossible Objects of Marxist Legal Theory of Law

The Limits of the Legal Form

Cosmin Cercel

Turning to Pashukanis one hundred years after the publication of his *opus magnum* takes place under the strain of a present marked by a generalisation of class conflict and a resurgence of imperialism, as politics, tactics and warfare. Moreover, our return is placed under the conditions of a capitalism that have moulded into a social form[1] and pervades every aspect of our subjectivity, that has imposed itself as the ultimate horizon of our existence. Last, it happens historically, jurisprudentially and philosophically in a timeframe that is placed *after* the demise of communism,[2] or at least after the demise of one of the historical instantiations that bore this emblem.[3] Such a return therefore cannot be done otherwise than an attempt to grasp some guidance,[4] solace and perhaps some intellectual tools from the debris of the historical legacy of Marxist jurisprudence.

Writing as critical lawyers in the midst of the unfolding catastrophe, in this attempt to recuperate the forms of thought of a by-gone project is not an easy task: recuperating Marxist legal theory is not only a matter of returning to ideas, but requires understanding of each extent they, as frames of thinking and representing the law, partook within the inner politics of knowledge, and were entangled in the broader intellectual history that befell us. Thus, while this might be a celebratory moment in the encounter with our legators, there is a need for clarity, that should mark a reflection on the historical and perhaps political distance with our past.

Searching within the debris of this legacy necessarily begs the question of what resists in this project, and what was part of its pitfalls. It follows that I start with two caveats with regard to my endeavour: first, I believe that Pashukanis' work has relevance beyond its particular historical moment and that it can be useful for present projects that critically challenge the

1 Fredric Jameson, *Postmodernism, or, the Cultural Logic of Late Capitalism* (Duke UP 1991) xix.

2 Alain Badiou, *D'un désastre obscur: Sur la fin de la vérité d'Etat* (Editions de l'Aube 1998).

3 Alain Badiou, *L'hypothèse communiste* (Nouvelles Editions Lignes 2009).

4 Alain Badiou, *Méfiez-vous des blancs, habitants du rivage* (Fayard 2019).

DOI: 10.4324/9781032724522-9

contemporary status quo in its complacency and collusion to the current erasure of liberal legality. Second, I also believe that for a number of reasons that I shall expand on, his work partook within the general theoretical and historical debacle of the really existing socialism.

The main argument I defend here is a simple one: Pashukanis' theory of law is a serious Marxist attempt to find a legal theory of law. As committed as it is to Marxism, it falls within the traps of legal history. While the first limb of the argument is largely uncontroversial,[5] the second part needs some further explanation. I claim that the ways in which Pashukanis builds his concept of legal form are characteristic of a strand of legal theory that I call modernist.[6] In this respect I believe that he is more of a lawyer, and for that matter even less a critical one, than a Marxist. Yet, I believe that this construal of the legal form also has important epistemological and political implications, some of which are entangled with his tragic end at the hands of Stalinist repression, as well as with the further politico-legal developments in the Soviet that ended up in a generalisation of repression, compulsion and emergency turning into a darker legacy of law.[7]

I shall begin with a plea in defence of the general intellectual project defended by Pashukanis. His work *General Theory of Law and Marxism* offers valuable insights into the operation of law in modern societies as well as a sobering reminder that a full-fledged, authentic and successful revolution grounded in Marxist theory and Leninist politics is structurally anti-legal insofar as it aims at deposing the machinery of law. Writing within the historical conditions of the New Economic Policy, following the revolutionary takeover of October 1917, the vagaries of the civil war and war communism, his stand is uncompromising on the future of legality within a radically new socio-economic context. Law will and should disappear:

> during our transition epoch the form of law does not as such conceal within itself the unlimited possibilities revealed therein for bourgeois-capitalist society at the dawn of its birth. For the time being, on the contrary, it closes us within its narrow horizon. *It exists only for the purpose of finally exhausting itself.*[8]

5 Michael Head, *Evgeny Pashukanis: A Critical Reappraisal* (Routledge-Cavendish 2008); China Miéville, 'The Commodity-Form Theory of International Law' (2004) 17 *Leiden Journal of International Law* 271; Bill Bowring, 'Yevgeniy Pashukanis, His Law and Marxism: A General Theory, and the 1922 Treaty of Rapallo Between Soviet Russia and Germany' (2017) 19 *Journal of the History of International Law* 274.

6 David Luban, *Legal Modernism* (U of Michigan P 1994); Peter Goodrich, 'Law and Modernity' (1986) 49 *Modern Law Review* 545; David Trubek, 'Weber's Tragic Modernism and the Study of Law in Society' (1986) 20 *Law & Society Review* 573.

7 Cosmin Cercel, *Towards a Jurisprudence of State Communism: Law and the Failed Revolution* (Routledge 2018).

8 Evgeny Pashukanis, 'The General Theory of Law and Marxism' in Hugh Babb (tr), *Soviet Legal Philosophy* (Harvard UP 1951) 180 [emphasis added].

In following this path, he is a tributary of the original anti-legal stand that pervades the Marxist tradition from the early days of *The Law on the Theft of Wood*[9] to the sober analyses of the *Introduction of the Gotha Programme*,[10] and *Anti-Dühring*[11] to the polemic thought of the *State and Revolution*.[12] The law, as such, is deemed, one day, to wither away. Throughout its existence, law is not only an instrument of class domination to be deposed by revolutionary politics, but once the material conditions of its existence are exhausted, its days are counted, culminating with 'the dying out of the juridic form in general'[13] Otherwise said, legal normativity is fully historically and materially determined being enmeshed within the fabric of society: it is not an ideal form, nor a transcendental presupposition, or a natural a-historical propension of human nature. Rather, the law is a peculiar historical category grounded in 'a real history which unfolds, not as a system of thoughts, but as a special system of relationships into which people enter because they are constrained thereto by the conditions of production, not by conscious choice'.[14]

This being said, Pashukanis' work is both an exercise in a descriptive theory of law as it is an exercise in a form of anti-legal criticism of the law. As many of the scholarships written from within a Marxist perspective are, at the same time, descriptive and normative. Its descriptive dimension consists in its attempts to grasp and conceptualise the legal phenomenon, while the normative rests with the politico-legal conclusions he draws based on advancing such a concept of law as fully historically determined. The future withering away of the law is, on the one hand, a total event, meaning that law *as such* is supposed to disappear, whereas at the same time, its disappearance cannot be supplanted by a new type of legality, be it socialist, proletarian or communist:

> The dying out of the categories—but not of any injunctions—of bourgeois law by no means signifies that they are replaced by new categories of proletarian law—precisely as the dying out of the category of value, capital, gain, and so forth will not . . . mean that new proletarian categories of

9 Karl Marx, 'Proceedings of the Sixth Rhine Province Assembly: Third Article Debates on the Law on Thefts of Wood' in Karl Marx and Friedrich Engels (eds), Clemens Dutt (tr), *Collected Works* (vol 1, Lawrence and Wilshart 1975 [1842]) 224–63.

10 Karl Marx, 'Critique of the Gotha Programme' in Karl Marx and Friedrich Engels (eds), Peter Ross and Betty Ross (trs), *Collected Works* (vol 24, International Publishers 1989 [1875]) 75–99.

11 Friedrich Engels, 'Anti-Dühring: Herr Eugen Dühring's Revolution in Science', in Karl Marx and Friedrich Engels (eds), Emile Burns (tr), *Collected Works* (vol 25, International Publishers 1987 [1878]) 5–298.

12 Vladimir Illich Lenin, *State and Revolution* (Haymarket Books 2014 [1918]).

13 Pashukanis, 'The General Theory of Law and Marxism' (n 8) 122–23.

14 ibid 127.

> worth, capital, rent and so forth appear. The dying out of the categories of bourgeois law will in these conditions signify the dying out of law in general: that is to say the gradual disappearance of the juridic element in human relations.[15]

This theoretical position is consequential upon later developments within legal theory that also influenced further the Soviet—at that time still Marxist-Leninist—political praxis, being at least a temporary part of the official stand on jurisprudential matters.[16] First, the moment of demise of the law as a result of the revolutionary transformation is delayed, in a position that is consistent with Lenin's reading of Engels: it is only within the context of communism that law vanishes.[17] Second, and this is perhaps the point of difficulty, the legality during the interregnum of the dictatorship of the proletariat is in essence bourgeois, insofar as the legal form cannot but be bourgeois. While this is itself consistent with Lenin's argument advanced in the *State of Revolution*,[18] it is a position that by the 1930s will become difficult to follow and defend[19] in many respects insofar as it finds itself at odds with, and to some extent eschews, the question of revolutionary transformation operated by the proletarian takeover.

In what follows I aim to problematise some salient elements grounding the descriptive dimension of the Pashukanis' project. In particular, I take aim at his framing of the concept of legal form in relation to private law, one of the blind spots of his legal theory that I find to of particular importance in understanding the limits of this project. Subsequently, I reflect on how such a reading sheds a new light on the normative core of his theory and problematises his Leninist undertones concerning the withering away of the state and the legal form.

Along the way, I shall operate two displacements of the usual rendering and construal of Pashukanis' legal theory. First, while addressing the descriptive elements of his theory, I shall aim to move beyond jurisprudence by drawing on psychoanalytical theory. This displacement aims to offer a new way of approaching the intellectual legacy of the concept of 'legal form' in relation to material history, politics and economics. As I claim, Pashukanis' legal form is a specific rendition of the concept of legal ideology that places the law at the interface of ideology proper and commodity fetishism. In doing so, it offers a strong, yet peculiar understanding of the operation of the law

15 ibid 122.

16 Henry A Freund, 'Soviet Law Under "Stalinism"' (1939) 19 *Slavonic and East European Review* 175, at 180–81.

17 Lenin (n 12) 132.

18 'The abolition of capitalism does not immediately create the economic prerequisites for such a change': ibid.

19 Freund (n 16) 181.

that can be best understood by recourse to psychoanalysis. The turn to psychoanalysis seems to me necessary as providing a device for mapping the intellectual operation that Pashukanis is deploying in addressing the question of the legal form.

As a subject subjected to the unconscious,[20] and instituting a specific concept of the law, he engages in a specific dialogue not only with a Marxist tradition, or for that matter with a jurisprudential tradition, but also with a way of structuring legal knowledge and intellectual history that is necessarily connected to a problematisation of the symbolic order.[21] His endeavour is traversed both in form and content at any moment by a constant tension between the commitments to Marxist theory, to revolutionary politics and the fact of being a lawyer. As a clinical knowledge and as a form of social semiotics, psychoanalysis, especially as a formalised discourse over the speaking subject as it becomes in the work of Jacques Lacan,[22] is able to trace and render the deeper meaning of these tensions and provide us with the possibility of seeing what escapes the subject in its wrestle with the matter of the law.

Second, when reflecting on the normative side of Pashukanis' project, I intend to add a level of historical grounding, in order to problematise further the politics supporting the possibility of overcoming the legal form. As the legal form is primarily conceptualised in relation to categories of private law, such as personhood, contract and property at the expense of categories of public law, that are positively relegated to the sphere of ideology, or worse, theological inquiry, I argue that repression remains a blind spot of this type of theory. As such, rather than addressing fully that which is 'rotten at the heart of the law',[23] Pashukanis clings to an embellished concept of the law that disregards its collusion to violence, repression and its necessary reliance on 'naked force'. Pivotal to his analysis is a specific forgetting of the figure of the principle of expediency and a problematisation of the concept of dictatorship, that pushes legal repression and legal violence at its margins. In doing so, I intend to inquire into the ethical and political lessons that we can draw from his work, especially within the current context of critical jurisprudence.

20 Sigmund Freud, 'The Unconscious' in Peter Gay (ed), *The Freud Reader* (Norton 1989 [1915]) 573; Sigmund Freud, 'L'instance de la lettre dans l'inconscient ou la raison depuis Freud' in *Ecrits* (Le Seuil 1966) 493–530.

21 Jacques Lacan, 'La science et la vérité' in *Ecrits* (Le Seuil 1966) 868.

22 Jacques Lacan, *Le Séminaire: Livre VII. L'ethique de la psychanalyse* (Jacques-Alain Miller ed, Le Seuil 1986 [1960]) 21.

23 Jacques Derrida, 'Force of Law: The Mystical Foundation of Authority' in Drucilla Cornell, Michel Rosenfeld and David Gray Carlson (eds), *Deconstruction and the Possibility of Justice* (Routledge 1992) 3–67 at 42.

Beyond Ideology: The Locus of Legal Form

Legal form, as we know, is not ideology proper, unless we supplant Pashukanis' reading with Althusserian's reading of ideology as a material category,[24] a notion to which he comes at times surprisingly close, as I shall underline. This being the case, legal form is not superstructure, that is not a mere reflection of the economic basis as such. Building his work on Marx's exchange theory Pashukanis notes in his criticism of Reisner's law-as-ideology theory:

> we have . . . a perfect right to speak of a goods ideology . . . and to include this phenomenon in the category of psychological phenomena. This by no means signifies . . . that the categories of political economy possess an *exclusively* psychological meaning . . . The general concepts of political economy are thus not only an element of ideology; they are also an element of abstraction, from which we can scientifically . . . construct economic objective reality.[25]

Rather, legal form is the product of a complex interplay between economics, that is relations of production and modes of production, ideology in the sense of general ideas supported by the economic structure and the authoritative interpretation of these ideas: 'our problem . . . is: *can law as a social relationship be understood in the same sense as that in which Marx called capital a social relationship*'.[26] In this sense, legal form is nothing short of the ultimate horizon of modern legality, in so far as 'only bourgeois-capitalist society creates all the conditions essential to the attainment of complete definiteness by the juridic element in social relationships'.[27] It is *law properly so-called*[28] seen through the lenses of commodity fetishism,[29] a form that develops and shifts through time within and through economic relations as a special relationship. Thus, law 'portrays the true historical process of development which is nothing but the process of the development of bourgeois society'.[30]

The concept of legal form aims to do justice to legal doctrine[31] and to the peculiar force of law that emerges in modernity that it is able to command, order and organise reality within the capitalist society. As such, from the very beginning, the concept presupposes the existence of a market and market

24 Louis Althusser, 'Idéologie et appareils idéologiques d'Etat', in Louis Althusser (ed), *Positions 1964–1975* (Editions Sociales 1976).

25 Pashukanis, 'The General Theory of Law and Marxism' (n 8) 131. (original emphasis).

26 ibid 131.

27 ibid 120.

28 John Austin, *The Province of Jurisprudence Determined* (John Murray 1861) 1–2.

29 Pashukanis, 'The General Theory of Law and Marxism' (n 8) 140.

30 ibid 120.

31 ibid 125–35.

relations. Legal form cannot be usefully conceived outside the horizon of a society already organised by market, and in which private economic interests[32]—and to some extent modern, capitalist relations—are already articulated, and (at least seemingly) rational: 'the basic conditions of existence of the legal form—a condition rooted in economics itself is the unification of labor exertions upon the principle of an equivalent exchange'.[33] This is an essential prerequisite of the legal form and what differentiates it from mere assertions of 'naked power'.[34] It also does retain important consequences for the ways in which law is conceptualised, as *ab initio* a synonymy between the economic layer and the legal one is presupposed, insofar as 'legal fetishism complements goods fetishism'.[35] This synonymy goes beyond a mere determination (be it in the last instance), rather it is to be understood as a specific way of coding economic structures under the form of social relations that are based on the logic of equivalence specific to the exchange of goods. As such, 'a society which according to the condition of its production forces is constrained to preserve an equivalency between expenditures of labour and compensation . . . *will be constrained* to preserve also the form of law'.[36]

Second, the legal form is conceptually distinguishable from ideology. On one hand, it has little to do with ideas; with a conscious or an unconscious distortion of reality or with the limited, class-determined representation of reality. Legal form is not a false universality as we find in Marxian criticisms of Hegel,[37] nor is it an element of the superstructure,[38] simply put. It is real, insofar as it reconstructs with the sphere of the law, a second-level form of coding reality that parallels, obscures and renders economic relations logical, necessary and efficient. In other words, 'it is not only in the minds and in the theories of learned jurists that law . . . taken its general definitions—law as a form—exists'.[39] The law, as an objective social relationship[40] is socially, materially, and politically effective, that is real:

> At a certain stage of development, the relationships of human beings take on during the process of production a form which is doubly puzzling: they come out on the one hand as the relationship of things which are also

32 ibid 146–47.
33 ibid 127.
34 ibid 166.
35 ibid 123.
36 ibid 124.
37 Karl Marx, *Critique of Hegel's "Philosophy of Right"* (Annette Jolin and Joseph O'Malley trs, CUP 1977 [1843–1844]) 14.
38 Karl Marx, 'Preface to a Contribution to the Critique of Political Economy' in Karl Marx and Friedrich Engels (eds), Victor Schnittke and Yuri Sidobnikov (trs), *Collected Works* (vol 29, International Publishers 1987 [1859]),
39 Pashukanis, 'The General Theory of Law and Marxism' (n 8) 127.
40 ibid 134.

> goods, and on the other as the will relationships of units which are independent and equal *inter se*: juridic subjects . . . there appears something no less puzzling: law[41]

The way in which Pashukanis posits the legal form is revealing, first, in relation to the possible connections with other legal theories of modernity and second in relation to the politics underlying such a jurisprudential stand. It is useful to note that in order to distinguish between legal form and mere ideology, Pashukanis denounces constitutional law and public law as revolute and inferior distortions of social reality, insofar as 'the state is not a juridical superstructure, it can merely be conceived as such'.[42] A simple critique of ideology, and perhaps even less than that will expose them as obsolete and crude, as being parasitical upon the categories furnished by private law: 'the juridic . . . interpretation of authority'[43] emerging only after the development of a market economy. Insofar as this area of the law is operating, based on the principle of expediency and the supremacy of the state,[44] it relies ultimately on naked power. In other words, the legal form is not to be sought there, as 'State law can exist solely as a reflection of the private law form in the sphere of political organization or it ceases in general to be law'.[45] The simple juxtaposition of the promises of public law and the constant interference of political authorities/bodies in its operation is enough to expose it as a lie or a direct theological import:

> As an organization of class dominance and an organization for the conduct of external wars, the state neither requires—nor essentially admits of—legal interpretation. These are domains where the so-called *raison d'état*—that is to say, the principle of bare expediency—holds sway.[46]

Things are different within the sphere of private law: legal doctrine, legal praxis and especially the legal subjects act within this sphere not only *as if* the law exists, but *in accordance* with it, insofar as the law necessarily reproduces economic organisation.[47] This is because concepts such as property, rights over things, contracts, validity, etc. are not only conceptual legal constructs but find themselves at the interstices between the basis and the superstructure: they are active as structuring relations of production and instituting legal reality as a part of the capitalist reality. This is not inconsistent, as

41 ibid 167.
42 ibid 156.
43 ibid 182.
44 ibid 183.
45 ibid 156.
46 ibid 183.
47 ibid 170.

private law is an expression of egotism and individual economic interests, that is, built primarily on the existence 'of private isolated subjects'.[48] The form of law is enmeshed in the fabric of a society always already alienated.[49] The centre of the production of legal relationships, otherwise said the locus of legal form lies within this area where the individual takes possession of goods. It is by its proximity and participation to the sphere of exchange that private law offers the typical construct of the legal form. First, it is by offering the categories of subjecthood and possession that the legal form emerges as a mediator of private interests; 'the thing is a private thing, the individual is a private individual and the law is private law'.[50] Under its operation, 'man is converted into a juridic subject by force of the same necessity as that whereby a natural product is converted into goods with its enigmatic quality of value which goods possess'.[51]

Thinking as a Lawyer: Legal Alienation

I claim that this is a peculiar position. One would be tempted to read Pashukanis' revival of the ages-old public law-private law distinction in an Althusserian vein: public law and constitutional law are, as we know, about repression—they are simply repressive apparati with a veneer of ideology,[52] as they function 'through violence',[53] or in Pashukanis' words, based on the principle of expediency. On the other hand, private law is the true place of *ideology* as the operation of ideological state apparatuses: the only difference is that the state is not there. For Pashukanis, as for many a private law scholar of his time, the state is secondary within this operation, compulsion being only ancillary to the operation of the law which is essentially consensual.[54] We just need to recall that the market is presupposed and the economic interests are already articulated, or at least distinguishable as such.

Private law categories act as some form of magical interface, not only reifying, alienating economic reality but, also, making it possible. It is what law *qua* legal form reveals to be in the last instance, a practice that is almost purely performative: 'the authority of man over man is effectuated as the authority of law itself—that is to say, as the authority of an objective and impartial norm'.[55]

48 ibid 153.
49 ibid 155.
50 ibid 173.
51 ibid 127.
52 Althusser, 'Idéologie et appareils idéologiques d'Etat' (n 24) 83–84.
53 ibid.
54 Pashukanis, 'The General Theory of Law and Marxism' (n 8) 188.
55 ibid.

I think that there are some problems with the ways in which Pashukanis understood, at his time, legal form and the ways in which we could use his understanding today. I believe that beyond all his good anti-legal intentions and his perspicacious prescience, he gives too much credit to both law, as such, as well as to the operation of legal ideology. By focusing on the private law dimension of legal discourse he reproduces one of the mythological assumptions of the doctrinal canon of modernity, that is the fact that there is a private sphere which would be somehow cut off from the assertions of power and their 'theological' representation.

To be sure, Pashukanis is aware of how close he gets to reproducing the object of his criticism, noting clearly that 'for bourgeois thinking the framework of goods production is the eternal and natural framework of every sort of society and it, therefore, declares that abstract state authority is an appurtenance of society of every sort'[56] And indeed, this type of criticism stands on its own as valid and accurate. In an attempt to build a Marxist theory of law, exposing the primacy of the private (as private property, legal personhood and the private circulation of commodities) is not a surprise. It is ultimately what a Marxist criticism is aimed at: doing away with the appearance of equality, common good, general will and freedom professed by the putatively liberal constitutions of the time by revealing the infrastructure of private legality that makes its utterance possible.

Yet this focus comes at a price: legal form is not only a way of reading in and through law together with economics, but also of revealing how alienation professed through and by law operates: the legal form is an insight into what being and *thinking lawyerly* is about since times immemorial. In Bourdieu's words

> Far from being a simple ideological mask, such a rhetoric of autonomy, neutrality, and universality, which may be the basis of a real autonomy of thought and practice, is the expression of the whole operation of the juridical field and, in particular, of the work of rationalization to which the system of juridical norms is continually subordinated.[57]

The apparent a-historicism of the legal form that floats unwittingly over Pashukanis' writings under the ambiguity concerning the relation of legal form to capitalism, and especially the constant references to Roman law—the imaginary original sphere of juridical thinking,[58] are all necessary to this endeavour. Within faculties of law at the end of the 19th century–early 20th century (and in many respects even today) law was about that: a science of

56 ibid.

57 Pierre Bourdieu, 'The Force of Law: Toward a Sociology of the Juridical Field' (1986) 38 *Hastings Law Journal* 805, 820.

58 Pashukanis, 'The General Theory of Law and Marxism' (n 8) 147–49.

law (at least on the continent) or a trade in which distinctions, definitions and a specific way of reasoning was creating a second level reality.[59] Its most pervasive form, is that of 'a universalising attitude',[60] one that draws on a claim of producing a different type of judgment from basic intuitions on fairness, justice or equity simply because it is deduced from a presupposed body of rules.[61]

If there is anything to reproach Pashukanis in this instance, it is that he falls all too much prey to this understanding of the law. It would be perhaps too much to ask him as a matter of historical and intellectual expression and milieu. As a contemporary to Weber, Kafka, Kelsen and Schmitt—the purveyors of the modern legal canon in and beyond the sphere of jurisprudence—his insistence on private law as the place where capitalist alienation colludes with law and produces the legal form is part of the same *episteme*. First, it is part of a modernist drive of locating the law—be it in the sphere of rationalisation of social processes, of 'pure' normativity or in the 'sovereign exception'.[62] Second, it is part of a specific sensitivity of crisis—the law is never 'truly' somewhere, rather it parallels history as a disembodied ancillary to economic processes. The reference to Kafka is not purely ornamental here. In the tortuous way in which Pashukanis addresses the legal form, there is a clear parallelism between the specific jurisprudential void of a fully historicised and hence contingent law, and the uncertainty of a legal centre that traverses Kafka's works. Pashukanis' hesitation between the historicity of the legal form and its a-historical fetishism is nested within this fascination with the already lost *juridical* centre that pervades the modern experience:

> If the legal system has become so rationalized that all reasoning becomes immanent within it, such that the system becomes unfettered from its normative anchors and begins to appear pointless, arbitrary, and alien, while at the same time it also becomes deified because, after all, it is the sole remaining stand-in for the missing religious and traditional sources of value.[63]

Legal form is where we are in modernity when we think as a lawyer, regardless of our political convictions, and allegiance, regardless of our subjective moral stand, regardless of our class or social position—it is simply

59 Cosmin Cercel, 'Discourse of the Master, Discourse of the University: An Archaeology of Modern Legal Education in Romania' in Michał Paździora and Michał Stambulski (eds), *Democracy, Legal Education and the Political* (Peter Lang 2023) 69–92.

60 Bourdieu (n 57) 820.

61 ibid.

62 Carl Schmitt, *Political Theology* (George Schwab tr, MIT Press 1985).

63 Douglas Litowitz, 'Max Weber and Franz Kafka: A Shared Vision of Modern Law' (2011) 7 *Law, Culture and the Humanities* 49, 56.

legal discourse in modernity, parasitical upon commodity exchange. That is to say, once we embrace an internal perspective on the functioning of legal form, it matters little whether we are a Marxist, a fascist or a liberal. And as such, the legal form cannot be changed from within—neither by critical analysis nor by writing articles in legal science, not even by a revolution and by the seizures of the means of production. The legal form ceases only when the mode of production has become radically different, and thinking like a lawyer simply does not make any sense anymore.

Impossible Objects of Marxist Legal Theory

Here is where psychoanalysis comes into play. And this is not because of Pashukanis' own melancholic attachment to the form of law, and its way of paralleling the evolution of (bourgeois) society. It is not because this attachment to the law, and thinking as a lawyer renders one blind and arrests us insofar we are all deep under the mystical spell of commodity exchange. Beyond the personal, historically contingent idiosyncrasies of the speaking subject[64] lies, nevertheless, the concrete universality of an important intuition about the status of law within a modernity shaped by capitalism. The legal form is what makes us blind to any other possibility of thinking from within the law otherwise. The second level translation of economic reality and the subsequent legitimation of the existing relations of production that the legal form produces and preserves is better understood as what creates the symbolic order of the law. As we know from (at least the early) Lacan, the symbolic is a specific way of covering the void of the Real. The symbolic, that is, reality organised through language and law, is what society and the individual *psychè* carve together out through the impossible unknown of the Real. Symbolically structured reality, *just* as legal form, is what orders and seemingly commands the flow of the Real, being the 'the pact which links . . . subjects together in one action. The human action par excellence is originally founded on the existence of the world of the symbol, namely on laws and contracts'.[65] Legal form is what structures the realm of economy and through that very fact creates a separate order that obscures this economic reality. To be operative, it necessarily expunges—or at least pushes to its margins—(that which could reveal) its inconsistency.

The ambiguous position of the symbolic and the Real within Lacanian psychoanalysis should not be an obstacle to examining the legal form *qua* the symbolic. In his early writings, Lacan insisted on the function of the symbolic order as a veil that keeps at bay the all too presence of the Object (or the

64 Mladen Dolar, *A Voice and Nothing More* (MIT Press 2006) 13–21.

65 Jacques Lacan, *Freud's Papers on Technique 1953–1954: The Seminar of Jacques Lacan, Book 1* (Norton 1991) 230.

Real). Through the ever-fragile and ever-incomplete institution of the Symbolic, the Object is reduced, expressed and rendered. The Oedipean complex is less about some spurious unconscious drive to complete jouissance than it is about the imposition of limits structuring the *psyché* and the institution of the symbolic order: 'with Oedipus we enter a different order, a symbolic, legal order, which assures finally its prevalence to the phallus'.[66] From the void of reality, something emerges, and through it the symbolic and the legal are structured.

Things stand quite differently in the so-called later Lacan, insofar the Real can be thought as a distortion produced by the very existence of the Symbolic: the excess is not some remainder of the unworked through, pre-discursive out-there, but a product of the very institution of the symbolic.

I claim that there is a lot we can learn from this parallelism between the legal form and the Lacanian understanding of the three registers/orders of subject's p*syché*. If we consider economy on the side of the Real and the legal form as the symbolic, then the ambiguous position of the symbolic holds true in any of the Lacanian interpretations—even the historism of Pashukanis' reading of the legal form supports it. Either legal form is what creates itself through recoding the real of capitalism, or it actually institutes it through its very emergence in modernity.

Furthermore, the excess of naked power, of 'extra-economic force',[67] operates as the remainder and the excess that disturbs the functioning of the legal form—an important reason for it to be singled out from its conceptual core. On the other hand, these excesses of extra-legality that adorn the trap of the private law as either constitutional promises and criminal law threats, are also the by-product of the legal form: they emerge out of its very institution. The legal form is then just another name for legal reality as such.

Yet the law, unlike the symbolic in Lacanian psychoanalysis, is neither a curse nor a necessity: it is contingent upon a specific mode of production that can be overcome. It is here where the psychoanalytical excursus comes to an end: the alienation of language is different than the alienation of capital.[68] One would hope that doing away with the latter does not require also getting read of the former. What this metaphor offers us, though, is the limits of representation specific to the symbolic order: it is the impossible objects that stay behind the formalisation. In Žižek's words:

> Such is the effect of the symbolic order on the gaze. The emergence of language opens up a hole in reality, and this hole shifts the axis of our gaze.

66 ibid 116.
67 Karl Marx, *Capital* (vol 1, Ben Fowkes tr, Penguin Books 1976 [1867]) 899.
68 Alex Cistelecan, 'Book Review—Cosmin Cercel, Towards a Jurisprudence of State Communism' (2019) 27 Journal of Contemporary Central and Eastern Europe 281.

> Language redoubles 'reality' into itself and the void of the Thing that can be filled out only by an anamorphotic gaze from aside.[69]

The legal form is effective insofar as it keeps away and posits as impossible, an outside of the law. As exact as this might be, the normative political consequences of such a stand are quite pessimistic. There is nothing that legal theory can do that can be politically meaningful either than registering the existence or the dissolution of the legal form. By acknowledging law's contingency, and to some extent its historicity, such a position opens the possibility for a utopian, or perhaps a messianic position: the law is not necessary, rather it is going to disappear once humanity will be freed from the fetters of capitalism. The subsistence of the legal form, on the other hand, is enough proof of the existence of capitalist relations, even under the banner of revolution.[70]

But by the same opening gesture, the legal form closes our possibility of reflecting on the inconsistency of the law as a project that is historically determined, and a product of class struggle that is constantly unstable and a historical category in itself.

Let me explain myself further: I believe that Pashukanis is erring in side-lining constitutional law and public law as 'deification of authority' and 'unbridled fetishism'. His gesture has been the very foundational move of most modern legal theories—carving out of the legal sphere the naked power of excess that goes beyond legal rationality and is intrinsic to it, its extimate. Not unlike Kelsen in form[71] and Weber in substance,[72] by reducing the experience of the legal form to its ability to code and support relations of production, Pashukanis obfuscates the nexus between repression and ideological interpellation that is at the core of the operation of the law. In doing so, that which institutes the law is bound to remain outside its sphere, as an impossible object. Let us note here, that this is first a departure from Lenin's position that associated the state and the law as two sides of the same coin and emphasised the repressive nature of the law within the horizon of bourgeois society. As he wrote in *State and Revolution*, 'law is nothing without an apparatus capable of enforcing the observance of the rules of law'.[73]

Moreover, within the Leninist view, the law is essentially connected to the material forces that support the state machinery. The inherent alienation

69 Slavoj Žižek, *Looking Awry: An Introduction to Jacques Lacan Through Popular Culture* (MIT Press 1992) 13.

70 Pashukanis, 'The General Theory of Law and Marxism' (n 8) 122.

71 Hans Kelsen, *Introduction to the Problems of Legal Theory* (Bonnie Litschewski Paulson and Stanley Paulson trs, OUP 1992 [1934]) 58–60.

72 Max Weber, *Economy and Society* (University of California Press 1978) 212–23.

73 Lenin (n 12) 126.

brought about by legality ensures on one hand a specific formal, politically useful and necessary equality of rights but, at the same time, hides the inner reality of the state machinery, which relies on a special body of armed men. Moreover, the focus on the consensual element of the operation of the law obfuscates the inner nature of the law within the structure of exploitation; the public-private distinction excludes from the ambit of a legal inquiry the dictatorial nature of bourgeois legality. True, Pashukanis' legalism derives from a clear jurisprudential commitment: the law is not about instituting order or about coercion. He cannot be clearer about it when he notes that legal form finds itself at the antipodes of external command and inner organisation: the military barracks and the Jesuit cloister are something very different from the court[74] insofar it is the place of expressing conflicting interests.[75] In other words, 'the idea of unconditional obedience to an external, norm-establishing authority has nothing in common with the legal form'.[76]

This being said, what is expunged from the ambit of legal form is precisely the darker historical legacy of the law as an 'essentially repressive'[77] structure 'that it could not exist in the absence of a corresponding system of sanctions',[78] and whose ultimate horizon is marked by the shadowy figure of the gendarme.[79] Second, moving the focus away from the sphere of constitutional law is a step back from the important contribution that Marx made to understanding the connection between politico-legal structures and historical processes. Marx's so-called 'political writings' dealing mainly with the tumultuous events befalling France since the July days,[80] through Napoleon III's rule[81] and the Commune,[82] are not mere political commentaries or reflections on a collection of events—some sort of appendices and ancillaries to the serious theoretical work undertaken in the *Capital*. They are of particular interest for lawyers, insofar as they abound in reflections on the minute inner politics of public law: constitutional framing, institution of dictatorship and

74 Pashukanis, 'The General Theory of Law and Marxism' (n 8) 154.

75 ibid 147.

76 ibid 154.

77 Louis Althusser, *On the Reproduction of Capitalism: Ideology and Ideological State Apparatuses* (Verso 2014) 65.

78 ibid.

79 'The gendarme is the violence of the state cloaked by an inoffensive (or not so inoffensive) uniform; operettas are composed about him precisely so as to "forget" that he exists only by violence' ibid 69.

80 Karl Marx, 'The Class Struggles in France, 1848 to 1850' in Karl Marx and Frederick Engels (eds), *Collected Works* (vol 10, Lawrence and Wishart 1978 [1850]) 45.

81 Karl Marx, 'The Eighteenth Brumaire of Louis Bonaparte' in Karl Marx and Frederick Engels (eds), *Collected Works* (vol 11, Lawrence and Wishart 1979 [1852]) 99.

82 Karl Marx, 'The Civil War in France' in Karl Marx and Frederick Engels (eds), *Collected Works* (vol 22, Lawrence and Wishart 1986 [1871]) 307.

full powers, civil and military repression, violation of constitutional standards and so forth.[83]

Looking through those lenses, bourgeois legality is essentially connected with a constant tension between its public pledges and outbursts of 'sovereign' power. Rather than being a purely consensual mechanism that operates within the sphere of commodity exchange, law's material life is entangled with and sustained by the 'rule by the sword'. The collusion between the court and the bivouac, between the codes—and for that matter between the Civil Code and the Criminal Code—and the bayonet cannot be conceived just as a marginalia to the mythistory of private law unless we want to turn a blind eye to the material history of law. This is where I think that Pashukanis misses the opportunity to address the legal form as a truly historical category—as the law is a product of the class struggle. By excluding order and repression from the notion of the legal form, the law is turned into an idealised mechanism that simply codes economy while its role in keeping its own efficiency is pushed away. This is what the 'impossible' sphere of extra-economic constraint, is for such a Marxist theory of law: in its own terms, the rule of the bourgeoisie as a dictatorship and through dictatorial means—at a time when dictatorship had a clear technical meaning of an authorisation to move beyond the limits of the formal or material constitution in order to quell down rebellions—has nothing to do with the law. Not only is an important part of the history of law left behind, but the very possibility of integrating it within a meaningful Marxist theory of law is foreclosed.

Now, leaving repression outside of the ambit of the law is perhaps necessary for the consistency of the argument: indeed, thinking as a lawyer within the context of capitalism means precisely turning away your look from outbursts of state-sponsored violence or from theological or political considerations about the nature of statehood. We can also imply that leaving the sphere of political power outside the field of the law also enhanced conceptually at least the freedom of revolutionary action: the decrees of the revolutionary days were not tied by a presupposed notion of legality—they were simply expressions of political statements and binding in a very different way. While this might be a sound way of distinguishing between law and politics, for the purpose of securing the sovereignty of the Bolshevik movement as a revolutionary force, it simply downplays the way in which modern legal systems under the conditions of capitalism have organised legal thought and praxis in relation to repression—most of it needless to recall exercised at times explicitly against the working class.

83 Cosmin Cercel, 'Marx's Concept of Dictatorship' in Paul O'Connel and Umut Oszu (eds), *Research Handbook on Law and Marxism* (Edward Elgar 2021) 75–76.

The sad irony of this position was revealed historically numerous times following the October Revolution and constituted the blind spot of communist politics. The legal regression from the work of Pashukanis to the crude formalism supported by Vyshinsky, the great retreat of Stalinism, and the institution of people's democracies across Central and Eastern Europe in the wake of the cataclysms of World War II do point in this direction. After the revolution the legal form ostensibly survives—giving Pashukanis' theory a critical and politically uncomfortable edge. But it is not only the legal categories of private law, still carrying on its conservative features against the enacted emancipatory politics; it is a whole host of presuppositions, legal norms and concepts that support the representation of political power and sustain the legal infrastructure, and which create the possibility of modern capitalism.

One century later, living in an age of continual crisis, after the failure of the revolution, and traversing from one regime of emergency to another, just after the era of constitutionalism reached its zenith, we are distant from Pashukanis. Understanding legal form only through the lenses of private law categories is at best reductive, and at most politically dangerous for the purposes of a critical analysis of the law.

Appendix

Hegel. State and Law (On the Centenary of his Death)

The significance of Hegel's philosophy is measured by the greatness of those world-historical movements on the verge of which it is situated.

Deeply rooted in the Reformation and the French Revolution, Hegel's philosophy is further developed through Left Hegelianism.

Marx, Engels and Lenin materialistically reworked Hegel's dialectic, creating the philosophy of dialectical materialism as the greatest weapon of the revolutionary communist movement of the proletariat.

Only on this scale can one evaluate the world-historical significance of Hegelian philosophy. It is too great to be measured by the number of dissertations, university courses, or academic societies devoted to Hegel. In order to understand the significance and degree of influence of Hegelian philosophy, one must turn not to "Minerva", the international reference book of the scientific world, but to the very movement of world history, which, in Hegel's idealistic terms, embraces "the reality of the spirit in all its volume and its internal and external manifestation" (Die geistige Wirklichkeit in ihrem ganzen Umfange von Innerlichkeit und Äusserlichkeit).

It is impossible not to note the comical position in which the organizers of the Berlin Congress, dedicated to the centenary of the death of Hegel, placed themselves. They refused in principle to put forward the reports of the Soviet delegation on such topics as "Marx, Lenin, Hegel" or "Hegel and Modernity", and suggested that they confine themselves to "reporting on the scope and organization of the study of Hegelian theories in Russian scientific institutions."

However, there is nothing surprising in the fact that the venerable neo-Hegelians, united in the arch-reactionary Hegelian alliance, are the least interested in the significance of Hegel for world history. For in this arena, the demiurge and the builder are the proletariat. This is why bourgeois science strives to enclose Hegelian philosophy within the walls of academies and universities, to bring to the fore its weakest and most reactionary sides, to make it a monopoly of Protestant priests and rabid nationalists, to place it at the service of international fascism.

"It would be absurd", asserts one of the initiators of the Hegelian Congress G. Lasson, "to look for the Hegelian doctrine of pure spirit in the materialistic soullessness of Marxism".

But, alas, world history, as Hegel himself pointed out, is least of all inclined to follow the recipes of those who are devoted to "the calm, and orderly course of things sanctified by the existing system".

Only by considering Hegelian philosophy as the "algebra of revolution", as a step towards materialistic dialectics, only through the prism of the historical work of Marx, Engels, Lenin, will we be able to single out in Hegel's philosophy that which is in it an eternal creation—"under the semblance of the temporary and transient to understand our own strength and our own significance". For the task that Hegel posed, philosophy must be resolved in relation to his own creations: "in the appearance of the temporal and transient to understand the substance, the immanent and the eternal, which is something contemporary". (In dem Schein des Zeitlichen und Vorübergehenden die Substanz, die Immanent und das Ewige, das Gegenwärtig ist, zu begreifen).

Hegel's philosophy, like all German classical philosophy, bears the imprint of the backwardness of the economic and political relations of Germany at that time. The bold flights of thought of Kant and Hegel, which stand out especially clearly against the background of the insignificance of their modern followers and epigones, were combined with timidity in practical conclusions in relation to the autocratic-feudal-clerical state, and in relation to the Protestant religion, with which both seek reconciliation. Nevertheless, Mehring is profoundly correct in considering one of the most amusing ironies in world history the fact that Hegel's philosophy was proclaimed the Prussian state philosophy. For no matter how painful were the efforts Hegel made in order to open the mind in the actuality of the Prussian absolutism surrounding him, the spirit of Hegelian philosophy, his dialectics, presented themselves as the strongest explosive.

It is known that Hegel in his "Philosophy of Right" defends the monarchy, the estate system and the bureaucratic-police state against the doctrine of liberalism, which, in his opinion, decomposes the state into separate atoms and leads it to impotence. He fights there against parliamentarianism and, in the spirit of Metternich and the Karlsbad Decrees, turns against the press, which, tends to "general decomposition". Hegel reflects in his social philosophy not only the revolutionary but also the reactionary aspirations of the bourgeoisie, its readiness to come to terms with semi-feudal political institutions, with the monarchy, with the police-bureaucratic machine of absolutism, if only to protect "order" from the encroachments of the "mob". Fear of the proletariat is the source of the half-heartedness and reactionaryness that we find in Hegel. Fascists are now grasping at these propositions of Hegel, in which he appears not as a great scientist, not as a philosopher who developed bourgeois ideals to the most daring logical consequences, but as a Spießbürger, a tradesman who cannot rise above the miserable political level of Germany at that time, not as an apostle of bourgeois freedom, but as a loyal subject of His Majesty, the King of Prussia.

The revival of interest in Hegel, which is noticeable in modern bourgeois philosophy, is in general of a pronounced reactionary character. Modern neo-Hegelians look least of all in Hegel for the rational kernel of his dialectics. They fiddle primarily with its mystical husks, they take from Hegel everything that comes closer to clericalism, to reconciliation with reality. In the review of the book of the Bulgarian scholar Yanev "Hegel, his personality and his philosophy", placed in the journal "Logos", we read:

> Now we can speak, with full right, of returning to Hegel. This return marks the turning of modern man to the eternal questions of life; it means the renewal of faith in the cause of the human spirit, which is the strongest thing on earth.[1]

The bourgeoisie needs Hegel so that it can believe in the salvation of bourgeois culture and the entire bourgeois society, which is heading irresistibly towards its collapse. They seek reconciliation from him, overcoming specific contradictions, grasping at the metaphysical and idealistic side of Hegel's philosophy, interpreting Hegel in a priestly spirit, highlighting the weakest thing in Hegel: "God, the absolute, the pure idea".[2] One of the professors writing about the "Hegelian renaissance" saw the essence of this renaissance in the fact that

> Among the restless, this-worldly and striving for transient blessings of civilization, a consciousness of the groundlessness and meaninglessness of all this feverish activity is awakened, and at the same time, the search for something stable, full of meaning and enduring value.[3]

Hegel is interpreted here in a clerical-quietist spirit; his philosophy is portrayed as a kind of haven of blissful reassurance from the contradictions of the sinful world and the "horrors of the class struggle".

The social-fascist theoreticians do not lag behind the bourgeois scientists either. In his report dedicated to the centenary of Hegel, the notorious Siegfried Marck,[4] digging into the essence of dialectics, identifies it from the point of

1 Yanko Yanev, 'Hegel, His Personality and His Philosophy' [1929] Logos, Bd. XVIII, Hf. 2, S. 293.

2 VI Lenin, *Philosophical Notebooks, Collected Works* (vol 38, Clemence Dutt tr, Progress Publishers 1976) 104.

3 Heinrich Levy, *Die Hegel-renaissance in der deutschen philosophie, mit besonderer berücksichtigung des neukantianismus* (Pan-Verlag R Heise 1927).

4 Here Pashukanis mentions the work of the German philosopher Siegfried Marck (1889–1957), without exact referencing. On Marck's reading of Hegel's dialectic and Marxist philosophy see: Siegfried Marck, *Hegelianismus und Marxismus* (Berlin, Reuther & Reichard, 1922); id.*Die Dialektik in der Philosophie der Gegenwart.* 2 Bände. (Halbband, JCB Mohr, Tübingen, 1929).

view of "historical integrity". He sees the significance of dialectics in the fact that "only in the integrity of historical events can it be possible to understand what are in appearance senseless contradictions as driving factors of development". The social-fascist theoretician contrives to eradicate the revolutionary essence of dialectics, to use it as a justification for passivity, as a means of calming oneself from the contradictions of life. The indignation of the masses at the concrete contradictions of capitalism, which doom them to unemployment, want and hunger, Siegfried Marck tries to lead into a safe channel of philistine reasoning about the "higher" meaning of these contradictions, which, supposedly, can be seen from the point of view of "historical integrity". It is difficult to imagine a greater vulgarization of Marxism and dialectics.

The same Siegfried Marck, of course, rejects "the attempt of communist theorists to understand Marxism in a popular-dialectical way, as an empirical science of the real contradictions of life".

Comments, as they say, are superfluous. It might, perhaps, be added that, even according to the reports of the Social-Democratic press, Siegfried Marck's report was to be read in such a dry and heavy language that most of the audience did not understand it. This is how the theory of scientific socialism is "popularized" by the Social Democrats, this is how they distort and vulgarize Marxism and dialectics.

Meanwhile, Hegel's philosophy is more than anything far from passive contemplation.

> In the theoretical idea—Hegel writes—the subjective concept, as a universal that in and for itself lacks determination, stands opposed to the objective world from which it derives determinate content and filling. But in the practical idea it is as actual that it stands over against the actual; but the certainty of itself that the subject possesses in being determined in and for itself is a certainty of its actuality and of the non-actuality of the world; it is the singularity of this world, and the determinateness of its singularity, not just its otherness as abstract universality, which is a nullity for the subject.[5]

This passage from Part III of the *Science of Logic*, contains the most profound thought, which receives its complete and consistent expression in dialectical materialism and which Marx expressed in his famous theses on Feuerbach. Lenin formulates the same idea in his comments on the *Science of Logic* as follows:

> Theoretical cognition ought to give the object in its necessity, in its all-sided relations, in its contradictory movement, an- und für-sich [in and for itself]. But the human notion "definitively" catches this

5 GWF Hegel, *The Science of Logic* (George di Giovanni ed and tr, CUP 2010) 729 [Hegel GWF Wissenschaft der Logik. Hrsg von G Lasson 1923, Bd II, S 477–78].

> objective truth of cognition, seizes and masters it, only when the notion becomes "being for-itself" in time sense of practice. That is, the practice of man and of mankind is the test, the criterion of the objectivity of cognition.[6]

Self-certainty . . . of the subject . . . of its actuality and of the non-actuality of the world'—this formula reveals the revolutionary side of the Hegelian dialectical method. Having written out this passage, Lenin comments on it in his simple and clear language, '*i.e.,* that the world does not satisfy man and man decides to change it by his activity'.[7]

But, if the highest objectivity is achieved in the sphere of the practical idea, that is, human practice, which "by means of sublating the determinations of the external world, giv[es] itself reality in the form of external actuality",[8] then, on the other hand, the practical idea is doomed to remain in "a realm of subjectivity in the pure spaces of transparent thought, [as opposed to] the other realm of objectivity in the element of an externally manifold actuality, an impervious realm of darkness", if only the will "separates itself from cognition and because for it external actuality does not receive the form of a true existence".[9]

To recognize the truly existing as a reality independent of subjective opinions is, according to Lenin, "pure materialism!",

> The non-fulfilment of ends (of human activity) has as its cause (*Grund*) the fact that reality is taken as non-existent (*nichtig*), that its (reality's) objective actuality is not being recognised.[10]

And vice versa,

> The activity of man, who has constructed an objective picture of the world for himself, c h a n g e s external actuality, abolishes its determinateness (= alters some sides or other, qualities, of it), and thus removes from it the features of Semblance, externality and nullity, and makes it as being in and for itself (= objectively true).[11]

Such is Lenin's materialistic commentary on these most important passages in Hegel's *Logic*.

6 Lenin, *Philosophical Notebooks* (n 2) 211.
7 ibid 212–13.
8 Hegel, *The Science of Logic* (n 4) 730.
9 ibid 731–32.
10 Lenin, *Philosophical Notebooks* (n 2) 217.
11 ibid 217–18.

It goes without saying that social fascists first of all try to break the revolutionary edge of dialectics, tear theory from practice, turn the unity of theory and practice into a harmless "postulate which we proclaim again and again, but which, with our limited forces, can only be achieved approximately" (Siegfried Marck).

Pretending that they reject only the Hegelian metaphysics of the world spirit and its absolute development, social fascists in essence oppose the proletarian revolution. The same Siegfried Marck showed this with complete clarity. Because all the reasoning about the limited forces of our "finite mind" was needed by him only in order to declare that there is no "absolute proof of the perishing of capitalism".

This is how the "certified lackeys of the clergy" fulfil the task assigned to them.

Only the proletariat, as the class to which the future belongs, as the class which, by the very objective course of the development of capitalist society, emerges as the gravedigger of the latter, is capable of seeking in the very reality the grounds for its active influence on it. The ideologist of the bourgeoisie, sensing that the historical ground is slipping from under his class, prefers to make a leap into the realm of subjectivity, into the realm of pure will and absolute actualism. Such is the ideologist of Italian fascism, the philosopher Gentile. He takes upon himself the task of ideologically arming the bourgeoisie for the last struggle in the period of decay and collapse of capitalism, instilling in it courage and confidence in its strength. To do this, he creates a mixture of Fichte's subjective idealism and elements of Hegelian philosophy and presents this mixture under the name of actualism as a kind of ideological doping for the bourgeois world. Eternal striving forward, eternal creativity out of nothing, eternal assertion of one's freedom, one's value, one's strength—such are the recipes that Professor Gentile, Mussolini's faithful servant, prescribes to dying capitalism. This philosophy is capable of stirring up the bourgeoisie and serving as an ideological justification for any brutal reprisals against the working class, for any imperialist war. But it does not indicate any way out of the contradictions of reality, because it does not want to know this reality.

This is very little like Hegel's dialectical formulation of the problem of theory and practice, for in him confidence in the limitless powers of the human mind, inspiring to struggle, is combined with a courageous and stern recognition of objective reality. This formulation comes close to materialism and contains the rationale for an effective attitude to the world, active participation in the historical process. Hegel's philosophy is permeated with the desire to embrace and comprehend the social and political tasks of the era in all their historical breadth, in their deepest objective significance. In this respect, Hegel is incomparably superior to other representatives of classical German philosophy.

To see this, it suffices to compare the meagre formalism and vacuity of Kant's doctrine of the categorical imperative with the richness of content that the Hegelian philosophy of objective spirit contains. The same thing is striking when comparing Hegel with Feuerbach. The latter, as you know, despite the break with the idealistic system of Hegel, despite the fact that he rejected the mystical pre-eternal existence of the absolute idea and returned man to the only real world that external senses reveal to him, not only remained an idealist in his ethics and philosophy of religion but also incredibly narrowed the understanding of human relations, reducing them to one side—to morality.

> [H]ere we are again struck by Feuerbach's astonishing poverty when compared to Hegel. The latter's ethics, or doctrine of moral conduct, is the philosophy of right, and embraces: (1) abstract right; (2) morality; (3) social ethics [*Sittlichkeit*], under which are comprised: the family, civil society, and the state. Here the content is as realistic as the form is idealistic. Besides morality, the whole sphere of law, economy, politics is here included. With Feuerbach, it is just the reverse. In the form he is realistic since he takes his start from man; but there is absolutely no mention of the world in which this man lives; hence, this man remains always the same abstract man who occupied the field in the philosophy of religion. For this man is not born of woman; he issues, as from a chrysalis, from the god of monotheistic religions.[12]

Two historical elements are possessed by the philosophical thought of Hegel and raise it to an unattainable height. These are the Reformation and the French Revolution. Hegel's philosophy of history and the philosophy of the state can only be understood in the light of the great class battles of the bourgeoisie, which created a new world under the slogans of political freedom, freedom of thought and freedom of property.

The militant spirit of the bourgeois revolution appears in Hegel in a veiled philosophical form. This is a feature common to him and other representatives of the idealistic German philosophy. "What the French wanted to realize in practice remained with the Germans a calm theory", Hegel himself remarks.

"German philosophy", Marx wrote on the same point, "is the ideal prolongation of German history".[13] However, the abstract form of Hegelian philosophy cannot hide its political purposefulness. Hegel stands among the fighters against feudalism, against the gloomy oppression of the Catholic Church. Hegel, who put forward the thesis: "What is rational is real, and what is real is rational", did not belong to the direction of thought which,

12 Frederick Engels, *Ludwig Feuerbach and the End of Classical German Philosophy* (Foreign Language Press 1976) 31–32 [K Marx, F Engels Soch, vol 21, p 295].

13 Karl Marx, 'Contribution to the Critique of Hegel's Philosophy of Law: Introduction' in MECW vol 3, p 180.

in the words of Marx, "the baseness of today by the baseness of yesterday, a school that declares rebellious every cry of the serf against the knout once that knout is a time-honoured, ancestral, historical one".[14]

Even in the *Elements of the Philosophy of Right*, where reconciliation with the surrounding political reality is most strongly expressed, we have a rather sharp polemical speech against the arch-reactionary Haller, against the historical school, against those who exalted the feudal-serf system and preached a return to the Middle Ages.

Hegel throws a direct accusation at the Catholic Church that it burned Giordano Bruno at the stake and forced Galileo on his knees to beg for mercy, as well as renounced the theory of Copernicus. In his philosophy of history, Hegel says that the Church "severed itself from advancing science, from philosophy and humanistic literature; and an occasion was soon offered [declared] its enmity to the scientific pursuits of the period".[15] In the footnote to § 270 of the *Elements of the Philosophy of Right*, Hegel quotes the passage from Laplace, which tells of the humiliating violence to which the papal inquisition subjected the seventy-year-old man, forcing him to renounce his convictions and declare scientific truth to be heresy.

For modern bourgeois philosophy, which loves to dress up in Hegelian clothes and comes out under the slogans of neo-Hegelianism, there is nothing more alien than this unambiguous position of Hegel in the dispute between science and the church. For Hegel, the fate of Giordano Bruno and Galileo are historical facts, full of significance for today. He cannot ignore them, he acts as a party, as an accuser, for he himself embodies the spirit of protest against the medieval Inquisition, against the obscurantism of the Catholic Church, which sought to impose shackles on the development of the scientific study of nature. How far from this are the modern followers of Hegel, ready for any compromise with church dogma, ready for an alliance with all the forces and remnants of the Middle Ages; how unlike their teacher are those "neo-Hegelians" such as Gentile who proclaim the slogan "More discipline, obedience, less philosophizing!"

Hegel deeply understood the revolutionary significance of the Reformation. The Reformation destroyed the monasteries, rejected the temporal authority of the bishops and the Pope, undermined the external authority of the church in matters of faith, secularized church possessions, freed the bourgeois man with his carnal aspirations, with his enterprise and thirst for the use of capital from the constraints of medieval ascetic morality. In the words of Hegel, it "made trade and industry moral", opened the way for free scientific research and freed the state from the guardianship of the church. Protestantism declares inner conviction to be the basis of religion. That is

14 ibid 177.

15 GWF Hegel, *Vorlesungen über die Philosophie der Geschichte* (Suhrkamp 1986) 499.

why in Protestantism Hegel saw the reconciliation of reason with religion. At the same time, he hoped to ensure the hegemony of reason by deifying the logical process itself. The refined idolatry of the "absolute idea" was supposed to make direct and crude idolatry unnecessary.

Only the dialectical materialism of Marx and Lenin, as the only consistent philosophy of the revolutionary proletariat, only the latter's victory over capitalism brings about the complete liberation of human consciousness from the power of supernatural forces created by itself.

If Hegel saw in the Reformation "the latest banner about which the peoples rally, the flag of free spirit, the with-itself [*der bei sich selbst*], which indeed is in the truth, and only in the truth is with itself",[16] then Marx reveals the half-heartedness of this emancipation:

> Luther, we grant, overcame the bondage of piety by replacing it by the bondage of conviction. He shattered faith in authority because he restored the authority of faith. He turned priests into laymen because he turned laymen into priests. He freed man from outer religiosity because he made religiosity the inner man. He freed the body from chains because he enchained the heart.[17]

Declaring an irreconcilable war against any religious intoxication, revolutionary Marxism-Leninism in particular sharpens it against the most refined, the most "spiritual" and therefore the most dangerous forms of religious ideology, the sources of which are Protestantism in its various varieties. I remind you what Lenin wrote in a letter to Gorky:

> Just because any religious idea, any idea of any god at all, any flirtation even with a god, is the most inexpressible foulness, particularly tolerantly (and often even favourably) accepted by the democratic bourgeoisie—for that very reason it is the most dangerous foulness, the most shameful "infection". A million physical sins, dirty tricks, acts of violence and infections are much more easily discovered by the crowd, and therefore are much less dangerous, than the subtle, spiritual idea of god, dressed up in the most attractive 'ideological' costumes. The Catholic priest corrupting young girls (about whom I have just read by chance in a German newspaper) is much less dangerous, precisely to 'democracy', than a priest without his robes, a priest without crude religion, an ideologically equipped and democratic priest preaching the creation and the invention of a god. For it is easy to expose, condemn and expel the first priest, while the second cannot be expelled so simply; to expose the latter is 1,000 times

16 ibid 496.

17 Marx, 'Contribution to the Critique of Hegel's Philosophy of Law' (n 12) 182.

> more difficult, and not a single "frail and pitifully wavering" philistine will agree to 'condemn' him.[18]

The dialectical materialism of Marx, Engels and Lenin raises the bold atheism of the French materialists of the eighteenth century to a new, higher level.

On the other hand, it is absolutely inevitable that under the guise of the revival of Hegelianism in modern bourgeois philosophy, we see an attempt to kill and immobilize Hegel's philosophical teaching, to perpetuate what is weak, transient in him, his far-fetched schemes, his scholasticism, his vague metaphysics, throwing out the dialectic. Hegel's philosophy has been overcome and "removed", that is, destroyed and preserved in revolutionary Marxism-Leninism. It is mummified, distorted and compromised in the reactionary attempts to connect Hegel with Bergson, with the "philosophy of life", with Eastern mysticism, with all contemporary obscurantism.

Hegelian social philosophy is known in wide circles mainly for its clearly expressed motive of the deification of the state. During the World War, every average inhabitant of the states at war with Germany was informed that Hegel's philosophy required the sacrifice of the individual to the state, that by defining the state as "the reality of the moral idea" and "the embodiment of reason", Hegel justified Prussian militarism and the policy of blood and iron. However, not only in tendentious journalism but also in serious historical and philosophical works, a sharp line is drawn between the ideology of bourgeois individualism and Manchesterism and the Hegelian apotheosis of statehood. Indeed, on the one hand, the state is a night watchman protecting property, and on the other hand, the state as "ultimate end possesses the highest right in relation to individuals [die Einzelnen], whose highest duty is to be members of the state".[19] What greater contrast can you imagine? It is not for nothing that in recent years when the general crisis of the capitalist system is becoming more and more pronounced, we see attempts to create some new, non-bourgeois, anti-individualist, anti-parliamentary conception of the state from the scraps of the restored Hegel. But the fact is that in Hegel we find not only the deification of the state: *Elements of the Philosophy of Right* contains, in addition, the image of bourgeois civil society, and, moreover, done with such depth and content, which is difficult to presume bearing in mind the complete underdevelopment of bourgeois social relations of the then Germany. In understanding the essence of civil society based on the blind play of economic forces, Hegel is two heads taller than the flat epigones of classical

18 VI Lenin, *Lenin Collected Works* (vol 35, Progress Publishers 1976) 122. The letter was written on 13 or 14 November 1913. First published in *Pravda* No 51, 2 March 1924. Sent from Cracow to Capri.

19 GWF Hegel, *Elements of the Philosophy of Right* (Allen W Wood ed, CUP 1991) § 258, p 275.

political economy like Say or the apostles of harmony like Bastiat. In his social philosophy, Hegel stands with both feet on the soil of bourgeois society. At the basis of the so-called abstract law, he puts property, which is nothing but the "external sphere of freedom". He extols bourgeois formal equality:

> it is false to maintain that justice requires everyone's property to be equal; for It requires only that everyone should have property. *What* and *how much* I possess is therefore purely contingent as far as right is concerned.[20]

Hegel appears as a principled supporter of bourgeois individual property, "pure private property", as Marx calls it.

> Since my will, as personal and hence as the will of an individual [*des Einzelnen*], becomes objective in property, the latter takes on the character of private property.[21]

Hegel therefore criticizes Plato, who in his state commits injustice towards the individual, depriving him of private property. The principle of property in Hegel is inextricably linked with the principle of personality. "Be a person and respect others as individuals"—such, according to Hegel, is the highest principle of law. In the doctrine of "abstract right", Hegel depicts in the most idealized form the relations of bourgeois society, portraying them as the embodiment of freedom and reason. Hegel opposes representatives of feudal-Christian romanticism, who argue on the topic that, of course, every person, including a serf, has a free and "immortal" soul, but that this does not at all concern a sinful body:

> It is only because I am alive as a free entity within my body that this living existence [*Dasein*] may not be misused as a beast of burden. In so far as I am alive, my soul (the concept and, on a higher level, the free entity) and my body are not separated; my body is the existence [*Dasein*] of freedom, and I feel through it. It is therefore only a sophistical understanding, devoid of any Idea, which can make a distinction whereby the thing-in-itself [*Ding an sich*], the soul, is neither touched nor affected if the body is abused and the existence [*Existenz*] of the person is subjected to the power of another.[22]

But Hegel's discourses on civil society are most valuable and most significant. Civil society is not only a world of labour and needs in general, but

20 ibid § 49, pp 80–81.
21 ibid § 46, p 77.
22 ibid § 48, p 79.

it is, moreover, a specifically bourgeois society, built on arbitrariness and anarchy, wholly subordinated to spontaneous laws. "The concrete person who, as a particular person, as a totality of needs and a mixture of natural necessity and arbitrariness, is his own end": this is one of the principles of civil society. But along with this, Hegel also points out another principle, that "each asserts itself and gains satisfaction through the others, and thus at the same time through the exclusive mediation of the form of universality".[23]

External necessity manifests itself formally as a contract, "since my will is contained in a thing, it can pass to another only with my consent; this creates the relation of one will to another will, which constitutes the true ground of freedom and the sphere of contract".[24]

These arguments of Hegel must be contrasted with well-known passages from the first volume of *Capital*, where Marx establishes a connection between the fact of the exchange of goods and certain characteristic legal forms of bourgeois private property and contract.

The idealistic theory of Hegel is turned upside down. Legal forms are explained by underlying economic relations.

Hegel not only gives an image of civil society, he tries to substantiate the positive value of the principles embodied in it:

> The right of the subject's particularity to find satisfaction, or—to put it differently—the right of subjective freedom, is the pivotal and focal point in the difference between antiquity and the modern-age.[25]

Hegel, as stated above, criticizes Plato, who, although presenting "substantial morality in its ideal beauty and truth, having expelled private property and the family from his state, came into conflict with the infinite right of the idea to grant freedom especially".[26]

Hegel does not have any illusions about the contradictions that the beginning of singularity and subjective arbitrariness leads to when people are fully dependent on satisfying their needs:

> In these opposites and their complexity, civil society affords a spectacle of extravagance and misery as well as of the physical and ethical corruption common to both.[27]

23 ibid § 182, p 220.
24 ibid § 71, p 102.
25 ibid § 124, p 151.
26 ibid § 185, pp 222–23.
27 ibid § 185, p 222.

Hegel speaks of the inevitable corruption of morals in those societies based on patriarchal and religious principles, where the principle of private property begins to develop.

> In civil society, each individual is his own end, and all else means nothing to him. But he cannot accomplish the full extent of his ends without reference to others; these others are therefore means to the end of the particular [person]. But through its reference to others, the particular end takes on the form of universality, and gains satisfaction by simultaneously satisfying the welfare of others.[28]

This picture of a society, left to spontaneous law which is the result of random arbitrary and self-serving actions of individuals, Hegel, as you know, compares with a planetary system in which only chaotic movements are presented to the eye. In the appendix to § 185 cited previously, Hegel gives a picture of a capitalist society full of gloomy tragedy:

> Particularity in itself is boundless extravagance, and the forms of this extravagance are themselves boundless. Through their representations and reflections, human beings expand their desires, which do not form a closed circle like animal instinct, and extend them to false infinity. But on the other hand, deprivation and want are likewise boundless, and this confused situation can be restored to harmony only through the forcible intervention of the state.[29]

Here the state appears in Hegel in a somewhat different, more real light than elsewhere in his *Elements of the Philosophy of Right*. State power is bound here by the existence of a gulf between the haves and the have-nots. With the help of violence, the state power must establish "harmony" between prodigality and poverty. Every unprejudiced reader reading these lines should have the idea that the class theory of the state is already on the threshold. Even the very expression "entanglement" of the situation directly recalls the well-known definition of Engels, where it is said that the state is the recognition of the fact that society has become entangled in hopeless contradictions, *etc*.

Here again, we come to a point in Hegel's teaching beyond which a further step is only possible in the direction of Marx and Lenin. True, Hegel himself immediately runs away from materialistic conclusions in relation to the state. Turning his back on reality, he begins his frantic idealistic glorification of the State with a capital letter. He reaches his maximum pathos in

28 ibid § 182, p 220.
29 ibid § 185, p 223.

the well-known note to § 258 where we read that "The state consists in the march of God in the world, and its basis is the power of reason actualizing itself as will *etc.*".[30]

In order to make ends meet, Hegel repeatedly in his most diverse works—both in the *Science of Logic*, and in the *Lectures on the Philosophy of History*, and the *Elements of the Philosophy of Right*—starts to prove that it is necessary to distinguish between the reasonableness of the "state in itself and for itself" from the forms in which it arose and was introduced. Thus, in the polemic against the reactionary Haller, Hegel tries in every possible way to prove that it is impossible "to consider the external side of phenomena, the contingency of distress, the need for protection, the power of wealth, not as moments of historical development, but as the substance of the state". But these arguments sound very unconvincing. For civil society is a reality, the features of which are taken directly from life, and exactly the same reality is the "external state" corresponding to civil society, or the "state of need and reason". So, Hegel's philosophy of right, on the one hand, contains the rudiments of the materialist class doctrine of the state, and on the other hand, is the source of the most reactionary ideology of the deification of the exploiting state as a force standing above classes and above all particular special interests, as a principle of the universal, as the realization of moral ideas.

If, in the period preceding the World War, bourgeois philosophy was guided mainly by Kant, now it is making a turn towards Hegel. Kant is too liberal; he preaches universal human ethics and humane internationalism. This is only good for sowing illusions among the working people. Therefore, neo-Kantianism is at the mercy of the Social Democrats, who act as the left wing of the bourgeoisie. The right-wing, represented by the fascists, now prefers to orient itself towards Hegel, from whom they derive justification for extreme nationalism and chauvinism, for the imperialist policy of violence and conquest. Hegel, in his ideology of the nation-state, reflected the first epoch in the development of capitalism, of which Lenin says that

> there is the period of the collapse of feudalism and absolutism, the period of the formation of the bourgeois-democratic society and state, when the national movements for the first time become mass movements and in one way or another draw all classes of the population into politics through the press, participation in representative institutions, etc.[31]

Prussia experienced this upsurge of the national movement during the era of the Napoleonic Wars when its independence was under threat and Hegel

30 ibid § 258, p 279.
31 Lenin, *Lenin Collected Works* (n 17) vol 20, 401.

reflected precisely this period when he wrote that "the substantial goal of every people is to become a state and to survive as such".

In connection with this struggle for national independence, the principle of the absolute sovereignty of the state proclaimed by Hegel should be considered. The state, according to Hegel, does not recognize a judge above itself. Hegel rejects Kant's idea of eternal peace through an alliance of states, because an alliance presupposes a unanimous decision, and it again rests on the sovereign will of individual states. Therefore, Hegel believes that only war can resolve the dispute between states in the absence of an agreement and sees the obligation to sacrifice life and property for the state as the "moral moment of war". These ideas are picked up by the ideologists of fascism and put to use by them to justify the policy of imperialist pillage and violence.

This is all the easier for them to do since bourgeois nationalism even in the first epoch appears in a dual guise. Freedom for "one's own" nation is combined with oppression and violence against a "foreign" nation. In Hegel, the upholding of the principle of national independence is combined with an apology for colonial conquests and violence. Therefore, the ideologists of imperialism can not only directly rely on Hegel, but also use his philosophy to fool the broad masses, to obscure the crudely imperialist essence of their policy.

Thus, in Germany today the fascists are dragging along a part of the petty bourgeoisie and the peasantry, appearing under the guise of fighters for the national liberation of Germany.

Speaking about the exploitation of national ideology, Lenin wrote:

> The national ideology created by that epoch (the collapse of feudalism and absolutism—E.P.) left a deep impression on the masses of the petty bourgeoisie and a section of the proletariat. This is now being utilised in a totally different and imperialist epoch by the sophists of the bourgeoisie, and by the traitors to socialism who are following in their wake, so as to split the workers, and divert them from their class aims and from the revolutionary struggle against the bourgeoisie.[32]

As noted above, Hegel's philosophy of law also includes political economy. We find in Hegel a deep thought about the spontaneous rules of the economy. Characteristic is the calm confidence with which Hegel states the birth of necessity out of the collision of chances, out of apparent arbitrariness. This calmness fully corresponds to the confidence in the future, self-confidence, which bourgeois society possessed in the first third of the 19th century. The bourgeoisie is not yet tormented by fear and anxiety in

32 ibid vol 21, 160.

the face of growing contradictions. Hegel reflected this in his discussion of political economy:

> There are certain universal needs, such as food, drink, clothing, etc., and how these are satisfied depends entirely on contingent circumstances. The soil is more or less fertile in different places, the years are more or less productive, one man is industrious and the other lazy. But this proliferation of arbitrariness generates universal determinations from within itself, and this apparently scattered and thoughtless activity is subject to a necessity which arises of its own accord. To discover the necessity at work here is the object [*Gegenstand*] of political economy, a science which does credit to thought because it finds the laws underlying a mass of contingent occurrences.[33]

However, for Hegel, the main threatening contradiction, which at the same time forms the basis of bourgeois society, is not hidden—the transformation of an increasing number of working people into proletarians. The famous § 243 of his *Elements of the Philosophy of Right* is devoted to this problem. There we read:

> When the activity of civil society is unrestricted, it is occupied internally with expanding its population and industry.—On the one hand, as the association of human beings through their needs is universalized, and with it the ways in which means of satisfying these needs are devised and made available, the accumulation of wealth increases; for the greatest profit is derived from this twofold universality. But on the other hand, the specialization and limitation of particular work also increase, as do likewise the dependence and want of the class which is tied to such work; this, in turn, leads to an inability to feel and enjoy the wider freedoms, and particularly the spiritual advantages, of civil society.[34]

In the next paragraph, Hegel develops the same theme. He points to the presence in civil society of a significant mass of people who are barely provided with the necessary means of subsistence. Hegel calls them contemptuously "rabble". His bourgeois-philistine reactionary spirit manifests itself in this case with particular force. What worries Hegel most of all is the mentality that is generated by poverty, and which manifests itself "in internal indignation against the rich, against society and against the government". Hegel ends this paragraph with an ominous reminder "that the fundamental question of how to cope with poverty is mainly driving and tormenting modern society".

33 GWF Hegel, *Elements of the Philosophy of Right* (n 18) § 189, pp 227–28.
34 ibid § 243, p 266.

At the present moment, when capitalism condemns tens of millions of people to want and hunger, it would not hurt the bourgeois neo-Hegelians to remember this instruction of old man Hegel. Hegel points out that with "an excess of wealth, civil society is not rich enough to prevent poverty". Hegel seeks salvation from contradictions in the estate-corporate system and in the seizure of colonies. These recipes of Hegel, which he gave a hundred years ago, are no less absurd than those put forward today by the luminaries of bourgeois science. Neither colonial plunder, nor the miracles of "organized" capitalism, nor the fascist corporate state, are able to avert the crisis.

Hegel called for studying the contradictions of civil society using the example of England; now he could point to the whole world, except for the only country that took the revolutionary path of resolving the contradictions of capitalism, along the path of Marx and Lenin. They accepted the revolutionary essence of dialectics, discarding its mystical, idealistic husk and took from Hegel that which elevated him above the epoch, discarding that which manifested his historical limitations.

Hegel considered the history of mankind as the movement of the world spirit. In its "absolute universality" he wrote, "individual peoples, appearing on the stage of world history, receive their truth and their definition". Each of the people interprets and realizes one of the moments, one of the steps of the movement of the world spirit. This thoroughly idealistic view of history served as the basis for the ideology of nationalism and for the division of nations into historical, or chosen ones, and non-historical ones, doomed to play a passive role in the development of mankind. But along with this reactionary side, Hegel's philosophy of history is a grandiose attempt to find the general laws of the historical process and to apply the principle of development most widely, fully and comprehensively.

This positive side of the Hegelian philosophy of history was materialistically reworked and developed further by revolutionary Marxism, creating a genuine science of society:

> Inasmuch as this science was built up, first, by the classical economists, who discovered the law of value and the fundamental division of society into classes; inasmuch as important contributions to this science were made, in conjunction with the classical economists, by the Enlightenment of the eighteenth century in its struggle against feudalism and clericalism; inasmuch as this science was promoted by the historians and philosophers of the early nineteenth century who, notwithstanding their reactionary views, still further explained the class struggle, developed the dialectical method and applied it, or began to apply it, in social life—Marxism, which made tremendous advances along precisely this path, marks the highest development of Europe's entire historical, economic and philosophical science.[35]

35 Lenin, *Lenin Collected Works* (n 17) vol 20, p 204.

World history, according to Hegel, is the creation of the new, its creation by action that rejects the established, the old, the ordinary, and rises against it. History is a revolutionary process carried out with iron necessity. But the bearers of this necessity, the actors in this revolutionary struggle, are not the peoples, as Hegel thought, but the classes. They are representatives of a particular era.

Hegel's philosophy of history is the highest limit of a generalized view of world history that the bourgeoisie could achieve. After Hegel, the bourgeois philosophy of history did not rise to such heights. The next step could be and was only the "Communist Manifesto".

Hegel's philosophy is one of the greatest achievements of human thought in the 19th century, for it gave the most complete, comprehensive and profound understanding of development for its time. But only Menshevik idealists like Deborin and his school can think that Hegelian dialectics is the last word in philosophical thought, that it was enough for Marx and Lenin to discard Hegel's idealist system and adopt his method. This fundamentally distorts the relationship of Marxism-Leninism to Hegelian philosophy and paves the way for the restoration of idealism. Not Hegel in itself, but the materialist reworking of Hegel by Marx and Lenin, materialist dialectics as a weapon in the revolutionary struggle for the overthrow of capitalism, for the dictatorship of the proletariat, the inseparable connection of this only consistent materialist philosophy with the tasks of the epoch, with the struggle of our party, with the victorious building of socialism in the United Soviet Socialist Republic and a maturing world proletarian revolution—this is our militant slogan, with which we celebrate the centenary of the greatest representative of German classical philosophy.

Evgeny Bronislavovich Pashukanis
Translated by Anna Lukina and Bill Bowring

Index

Made in the USA
Las Vegas, NV
19 September 2026

754e5302-a571-4d7c-880d-00ffdee94779R01